CATTLE, COWBOYS
AND RANGERS

CATTLE, COWBOYS
AND RANGERS

CALF-BRANDING TIME ON THE ROUND-UP

CATTLE, COWBOYS AND RANGERS

BY WILLIAM MacLEOD RAINE
AND WILL C. BARNES

Originally published under the title

CATTLE

GROSSET & DUNLAP
Publishers   New York

COPYRIGHT, 1930
BY WILLIAM MacLEOD RAINE

Under the title
CATTLE

CONTENTS

CHAPTER   PAGE

   I.   THE CROSS–CURRENT   1

  II.   DAWN IN TEXAS   11

 III.   IN THE BRUSH COUNTRY   27

 IV.   THE DAM BREAKS   59

  V.   THE END OF THE TRAIL   99

 VI.   THE BUFFALO OR THE COW?   113

 VII.   HELL–ROARING DODGE   128

VIII.   THE TIDE SWEEPS THE HIGH PLAINS   144

 IX.   THE BUBBLE BURSTS   226

  X.   MARY'S LITTLE LAMB   249

 XI.   OUTSIDE THE LAW   267

 XII.   THE OLD–TIME COWBOY   282

XIII.   CONCLUSION   304

APPENDIX:

  I.   HOME–MADE TOOLS   309

 II.   ENEMIES OF RANGE CATTLE   316

INDEX   325

ILLUSTRATIONS

Calf-Branding Time on the Round-up   *Frontispiece*

FACING PAGE

The Alamo at San Antonio   12

Day Herd   13

The Round-up Ground   13

Wild Horses on a Western Range   56

A "Trap Corral"   56

A Mustang Hog-tied and Being Branded   57

"I Kin Ride 'Em in the Slick"   57

Whitening Carcasses   92

Indians Hunting the Buffalo   92

Windmill in the Panhandle of Texas   93

Water Piped from an Old Mine Tunnel   93

Superior Cattle   148

Stockyards at Forth Worth, Texas, 1898   148

These Old Corrals and Whitening Sheep Bones Say, "Keep Off the Grass"   149

The Cattleman's Coat of Arms   182

Branding Calves on the Range   236

A Page from the Colorado State Brand Book   237

Sheep Are Great Weed Eaters   252

The Sheep Must All Be Dipped   253

Coming into the Bed Ground at Sunset   253

The Old-time Chuck Wagon   300

FACING PAGE

Some Brands   300

Picking the Hair for a Reata   301

For Roping Animals Such a Reata Was Without
Equal   301

In the Old Days Everybody Carried a Hair Rope on
His Saddle   301

THE cowboy spells romance in American history. The story of cattle is the story of the cowboy. This is his epic, and it tells the tale of the greatest pastoral movement the world has ever known. It is the story of a great industry, of a pioneering effort of stupendous historical consequences, and of countless deeds of valor and villainy. In the wake of the cattle and their guardians came blackguards of every kind. It is a tale of dark deeds, of violence and sudden death. Yet with it were courage, steadfastness, and nobility to make the American heart glow with pride. It is all here: the cattle wars, the desperadoes, the blind devotion to duty in the face of danger—all a part of that endless river of cows sweeping northward over the great plains to establish a trans-Mississippi empire.

We think of the West as having been settled entirely by the emigration from the East. We see pictures of the Argonauts, of covered wagons, of the Oregon trail; later of the Overland Stage, the Pony Express and still later the Union Pacific driving its first train across the Rockies. We usually accept the cowboy and his cattle as just being there. But they were not. The cowboy came later, and he did not come in the endless march from East to West. He came from the South.

The cattle industry in the trans-Mississippi region was born of the economic necessity of the Texas ranchmen after the Civil War. The Spanish brought the first cattle to America. They throve mightily in the soft climate and inexhaustible grazing on the Texas (then Mexican) plains. Texans all had cattle. After the Civil War, when the able-bodied men returned to their homes they found themselves cattle-poor. The South was bankrupt and Texas overrun by cattle with no buyers. Right there was born the industry that created the first wealth of the Western states and the packing industries of Chicago, Kansas City, and Omaha. For the Texans, in their extremity to find buyers for their cattle, began to drive them to Northern markets.

For years, then, Texas cattle and Texas men moved northward in a mighty stream which has for all time put its stamp upon the West. Historically, economically, in customs, in language, this flood of cattle has had a greater effect upon the West than the far better-known emigration from East to West. The main stream of emigration from the Eastern and mid-Western states was composed of two elements—gold seekers and home seekers. The one passed through the high plains country without leaving a trace. The other was the natural enemy of the cattleman, and right there is the seed from which countless dramas of Cattleland have sprung. The home seeker was a farmer. The cattleman, coming north to Oklahoma, Eastern Colorado, Kansas, Nebraska, Wyoming, Utah, Idaho, Montana, and the Dakotas, to sell or graze his herds, needed plenty of land and could not be hampered by a farmer's fields and fences.

The Story of Cattle

Thus the story of the American cattle industry is *per se* the epic of the cowboy. Above all, it is a story of struggle. Into the twenty-five or fifty years (as you care to figure it) of the development of cattle ranching in the territory between the Mississippi and the Rockies, there was more conflict of various kinds, more daredevil heroism, and more villainy than in any other period of American history.

Hence, if we care to look at it that way, we may see that inexorable force, economic determinism, as the father of all the romances and all the thrillers that have been written from the pages of Western history. There is much to be said for the writers of Western stories as students of our pioneering history. They have drunk deep of the well of lurid facts. Often the actual facts were too incredible for fiction, because an empire which fifty years ago was labeled "the great American Desert" could not be settled in half a century without changes, and conflicts so violent as to be beyond belief.

Too rarely, in our opinion, do people separate the various phases and movements of Western history. They overlap, and the interests involved were often antagonistic because of their conflicting aims. First there was the period of exploration in the early 1800's. Then came the fur trappers and the days of the Santa Fe trail. This was in the time of Kit Carson, when Texas and New Mexico were still Mexican territory. Next came the gold rush of '49 and the resultant emigration from the East. The Oregon Trail was a long trail in years as well as miles, and over it passed the wheels of home seekers' wagons until the Overland Stage and the railroad made moving by wagon unnecessary. Then, after the Civil War, came the cowboy and the epoch of cattle, an economic and a social influence opposed in every way to the aims of the gold seekers and the home seekers.

Thereafter the main course of Western History is inextricably mixed with cattle. The exceptions are the great gold strikes such as those in the Black Hills, Cripple Creek, etc. All of this, it must be borne in mind, considers the Pacific Coast as a land apart with a history of its own frequently affected by its own set of conditions more than by those which influenced the section between the Mississippi and the Rockies.

Here then is the story of the cowboy, the bad man, the rustler, the two-gun sheriff, the Indian fighter, the buffalo hunter, in relation to their times and their economic background. We have had many fragments of the story before. Never has it been told in its entirety as a part of the flowing stream of history whose greatest moving force has always been economic pressure.

HARRY E. MAULE.

SENTIMENTALISTS deplore the passing of that old West which in its day was one of the most significantly individual expressions of the American Spirit. The great plains, the snowclad peaks, the rare untempered light of the desert are still here. But with what a difference! They are the setting of a stage from which the actors have vanished. The vast hordes of buffalo are no more. No longer do the antelope flit silently through the shining sage. Great herds of cattle do not pour north in a living stream apparently inexhaustible.

And where, these critics ask mournfully, are the men of heroic stature, the figures in buckskin and chaps who moved so gayly to their appointed destiny in the morning of a glad young world?

They sing a sad refrain for lovers of romance, if one accepts the deductions they make. Gone the long-bearded prospector looking for gold in "them thar" hills. Gone the pioneer's covered wagon. The acrid smoke of the buffalo chip does not rise to the nostril from the prairie waterhole. The historic cattle trails have been plowed up. The Man on Horseback has ridden through the sunset into yesterday's seven thousand years. The mustang he rode is a vanishing species. Dust covers his rotting saddle. In Phoenix the talk is of cotton and not cows; in Denver of oil and the Trans-Mississippi golf championship; in San Antonio of climate and dude ranches.

So they tell us. And nothing could be less true than the inference to be drawn. A boy moving into manhood does not die. He lives in fuller potentiality. The old West is still with us, incorporated in the new. The clothes it used to wear do not fit. Its vocabulary has been enlarged. But what it was once it still is: subject to a swift development that of necessity made social and industrial reactions complex instead of simple. The West to-day in all its up-to-dateness still feels the impress of the influence of cattle. Cotton, oil, industry, golf, yes, but the people, the customs, the very texture of life shows, to him who understands, the result of that mighty current of animals and men which swept northward for a short twenty-five years and profoundly changed the complexion of the westward march of civilization from the "States." Essentially from East to West the emigration was composed of two main elements—home seekers and gold seekers. And yet, what is it that gave the West as a whole its character? Cattle. Those cattle came northward from the plains of Texas in an endless stream which crossed at right angles the much heralded westward march of American civilization. They and their cowboy drivers did more to characterize a period of American history than any other single factor. For, from the economic necessity of impoverished Texas war veterans sprang the grazing industry of the whole region from Texas to Canada and the Mississippi to the Rocky Mountains. Not the least interesting side of that romance is the development of grazing as a *business*. Of that we shall have little to say. Our tale is of the drama of conflict, and of the actors who played large parts in it.

It is true that the conditions which made the old West have been transformed by the flux of life. The prospector no longer scratches the hills. Grass root mining has given place to machinery and scientific methods. The open range has largely vanished. The old-time cowman tilts back in a chair and grows reminiscent, but his son chugs over the salt bumps in a flivver and ropes a cow out of the mire as competently as his dad. Time and circumstance have modified the traditions that were born of early days. Yet those traditions are woven into the very warp and woof of the high plains country.

It is a characteristic of the Anglo-Saxon that he carries with him wherever he goes law and order. From the days of the old witenagemot these have been for him a primal need. As the tide of migration lapped forward and wiped out the frontier it curbed the extreme individualism of the early settlers, tamed it to meet the needs of a more synthetic society. Civilization directed its initiative into channels less primitive and physically not so adventurous. The lawlessness inherent on the range and in the first mining camps has been suppressed. But there is no unbridgeable gulf between the West of yesterday and that of to-day any more than there is between the boy who was and the man who is.

Never in the history of the world has there been a phase of life comparable to that which existed in Cattleland within the memory of those of us not yet old. It was unique. It has had no parallel and can never have one. Because it *was*, the West *is*.

The old-time cowman sitting before an open fire sees in the glow of the piñon knots flitting pictures of that youth which was a part of the winning of the wilderness. He crashes through the mesquite after a four-year-old high-tailing it to escape. He whoops down the dusty street of the trail's end cow town to the drumbeat of clattering hoofs. He puts his bronco into a bankful river with a thousand tossing longhorns breasting the current. In fancy he lives over again the whole tempestuous story of the drama he has seen and helped to make. Youth is in the saddle cantering into a world of sunlit freedom.

Ten thousand thousand such pictures are stamped into the unwritten history of those states which we know to-day as the West. The old-timer played a dramatic and a worthy part, but he was a chip tossed on a great stream of life that flowed up from the South and decided very largely the character of the civilization to be built out of the waste lands. The law of economic determinism made the buffalo country what it is to-day.

It is now a national tradition, fortified by poet and historian and romancer, that the course of empire in this country westward took its way, that it followed parallels of latitude and not degrees of longitude. The stories of the Santa Fe, the Overland, and the Oregon Trails are a part of our patrimony. Pioneer societies perpetuate their memories and preserve by markers the routes they followed. The articles and books about them would fill a library. It has been impressed upon us that the forward lapping tide of civilization flowed due West, reclaiming deserts, stocking farmsteads, running railroads, tunneling mines, and out of the overflow of its energy building cities. San Francisco and Portland and Seattle stand as monuments to its force.

Horace Greeley's epigram, "Go West, young man," hits in a phrase the view of most of us. The gold rushes of '49 and '59, starting at St. Joseph and Westport, on the long dusty bloodmarked trail to the promised lands of gold, epitomize the romance of the winning of the West. We visualize the devotion, the hardships, the dangers of that heartbreaking trek across a desert where death was ready to pounce upon the hardy settler nearly every mile of the journey. We hear the whoop of the redskin and watch the flash of his scalping knife. We follow the lurching ox train from Fort Kearny to Julesburg, where the trail forks, and from there to the banks of Cherry Creek or to Sacramento, and we marvel that out of such a beginning rose in a generation San Francisco, Salt Lake, Denver.

Or we cast back to the Santa Fe Trail, to the Governor's Palace and the plaza and San Miguel Church at Santa Fe, each of them musty with the dim romance of vanished days; to the outpost of old Spain that echoed the tread of her mailed cavaliers and witnessed in turn the dominance of Indian, Spaniard, Mexican, and American civilization.

But in the memory of most of us the trail driver of Texas and the effect of his influx find no place. Historians have almost ignored him, though he abolished the myth of the Great American Desert by pushing his herds into every corner of it and making settlement possible. Statesmen and explorers had decided, though with dissenting minorities, that this wilderness was to be forever the unreclaimed home of the Indian, a great wild game preserve not fitted for the habitation of white settlers. Civilization had taken two hundred years to reach the Missouri, then had jumped in six months to the Pacific Slope. Over the Oregon and the Overland Trails in the '40's the land and the gold seeker had hurried through this waste of plain, mountain, and rolling hill. The explorer had not challenged the priority right of the tribes, nor did the trapper, the soldier, or the miner do so later. It is true that in far-flung mountain gulches towns arose where prospectors found the gold they were seeking. Some of these became great cities; others vanished after the excitement had passed. But it was the Texas longhorn, stretching its neck across a thousand miles of sage and cactus, that consolidated the district around the ore centers and brought it prosperity after the boom had passed its peak.

The Great American Desert had stood for a century a recognized barrier to settlement. The cattleman wiped it out in a decade. As by a magic wand it had vanished. That the cow was the mother of the West is a true apothegm.

Who among the scores of writers about the old historic West has given due stress to the fact that there was this cross-current, slow and irresistible, pouring up from the south in hundreds of clouds of dust, meeting the westbound tide, influencing it, modifying its character so profoundly in a dozen territories as to be the predominant factor in developing the vernacular, the laws, the social customs, the habits of life, the economic conditions, and the individual peculiarities of the citizens? What historian has made it clear that out of the confluence of these tides came Cattleland, the explanation of the peculiar quality that gives the West its solidarity?

Let us examine the westbound flux of settlement. Population followed parallels of latitude, except in the case of New England, where the great lakes intervened and deflected the course of it to the south into the Western Reserve. Kentucky was settled by the overflow from the Virginias, Arkansas by the restless Esaus of Tennessee, Iowa largely from Illinois, and eastern Nebraska from Iowa.

Each of these frontier communities retained the characteristics of the mother state. In so far as they differed, it was because pioneer conditions enforced modification of the customs to which the settlers had been used. The new lands accepted their heritage. Differences were of degree and not of kind. This is true even of Kentucky. The trapper was temporary. He prepared the ground for the farmer. The frontier produced a divergence which gave the flavor of individuality without fundamental change. Though the settler was proud of being a Kentuckian, he was also proud of his heritage as a transplanted Virginian.

Ohio and Kentucky, Arkansas and Iowa, settled by the push of immigration from the East, demand separate classification. They differ from one another as much as Maine does from California. The only bond of solidarity is the common one of membership in the Union.

Note here a singular and significant distinction. The states which we know as the West are tied together by a common bond which makes of them a group entity. Colorado and Wyoming and New Mexico have their local peculiarities, as have Arizona, Montana, Idaho, Nevada, the Dakotas, and Western Nebraska, but deeper than the differences is the common character that unifies them as the West. That character belongs to all of them. It is indigenous. Why? Because the same impulse, profoundly modifying the variant idiosyncrasy of the migration, reached and transformed them, became written in their laws, their customs, their outlook upon the world.

That impulse flowed in upon them from Texas for a score of years, like the waters of a great river impossible to dam. The cattle drives from the Lone Star State unified the West, gave it a solidarity such as the states adjacent to the Mississippi can never have. The swarms of cattle sweeping up from the South determined the peculiar character of the West.

Not more than thirty-five thousand men took part in the Texas cattle drives. Nearly a third of this number were Mexicans and Negroes. The great majority of the trail herders returned to their own homes to live. The amazing fact remains that this relatively small group, swept northward on a current impelled by economic necessity, brought with it the customs and the habits of the cattleman and essentially changed the character of millions of settlers on this new frontier. Yet so scant attention has been given to the cattle trails, so little importance accredited to them by historians, that there has been a mild controversy among old-timers as to who originated the trails and even as to where they ran. This in spite of the fact that hundreds of men are still living who followed the dust of the drag in the long northbound treks.

In that West which had lately been the home only of hordes of bison and of roving Indians the human tides from East and South met and mingled. Here for the first time the men who had fought against one another in the Civil War and those who had inherited the animosities born of slavery and its consequences were brought together on an equal footing. They learned to understand each the viewpoint of the other, and with understanding came respect. The hatreds of the war were forgotten. While Republican politicians in other sections were still waving the bloody shirt and ex-Confederates were fighting the battle of Shiloh over again in groups gathered at small-town post offices, men of the West began to forget that they were Northerners and Southerners and to realize that they were all Americans. The scars left by sectional strife healed in Cattleland long before they did in other parts of the country. The Texas cattle drives did more to cement North and South than any other factor until the Spanish-American War.

The story of the Texas cattle drives is one filled with drama and tragedy. They were epic in proportion. They had in them all the glamour of great adventure, and they did more toward the making of the West than all the other factors combined. After due credit has been given to the explorer, the trapper, the miner, the old army, the railroad builder, and the Mormon, it was cattle that stamped the West with its individual flavor, that welded it to a solidarity unique in this country.

The character of the West was determined by the old-time range men who replaced the herds of buffalo with longhorn cattle. The trapper and the gold seeker left little behind them but streams depleted of their furred inhabitants and abandoned mining camps. The gambler and the boomer were parasites. The army posts protected settlement without influencing it. The Mormon, making his own civilization, one deliberately cut off from the life about him, was a most useful but by no means colorful pioneer. His effect upon the West was local. The railroad builder was primarily interested in traffic. As the end of the line was pushed farther into the wilderness the construction gangs moved with it. But from the very nature of his occupation the range stockman was compelled to maintain a headquarters from which livestock operations could be conducted. After Texas had supplied him with cattle he was tied to the district where they ranged. His personality and his occupation colored the land in which he lived, shot it through and through with the romance of cattle.

What our geographies used to call the Great American Desert was his habitat. None but the Indian disputed this. The antelope flitted through the sage for him. Rich grasses grew to feed his herds, and rivers flowed to water them. The West was his world then. For one brief score of summers he was king, lord and master of all his eyes could see to the far horizon.

Then, with tragic suddenness, the scepter was snatched from him. A great human tide, eager for land, swept over the open range and blotted it out as though it had never been. The plains no longer had room for cattle kings. The grassland states had burgeoned into a prosperity in which the cowman had to take a large but not always dominant place. Barbed wire and Babbittry and country clubs came into being, and the stockman accepted the change.

The range man did not build cities. Cow towns grew up of necessity to supply his needs, but even these were brought into being by those who expected to exploit his prosperity rather than by the cattleman himself. His habitat was the open range. He lived and worked outdoors, often ate and slept beneath the stars. For months he never saw towns. Newspapers were old long before they reached him. He talked and thought cows, was guided by the habits, customs, and traditions of his occupation. In his isolation he had to be a law to himself. This molded his character, made of him a forceful individual. He had to be strong to survive. That strength, embodied in himself and in his cowboys, profoundly affected the country in which they lived. Even to-day no observing man can take a trip through the West without realizing that he is among a people not yet standardized to type, a people simpler than those of the East, less sophisticated, more careless and casual, more spontaneous in quick friendships, gayer in temperament, more prodigal of hospitality to strangers, still of the old-fashioned American type. The cow and its herder have differentiated him from his neighbors on the east and on the Pacific Slope.

For the North Pacific Slope is nearer of kin to New England and Ohio and Iowa than it is to the Rocky Mountain West. Beyond the Cascades both Oregon and Washington were settled by immigration direct from the East and from the Mississippi Valley, unaffected by the Texas current. The same is largely true of California, in spite of the cattle drives to the ranch lands there. The romance of San Francisco takes its genesis from the Argonauts. In southern California the Spanish civilization of a feudal pastoral life, flavored by the simple piety of the padre, is now only a tradition. The echoes of the old mission days are merely propaganda for tourist consumption. The flood of immigration from the corn country, too rapid to permit of assimilation by the old régime, has wiped out almost completely the hacienda and the rancheria. To stir real enthusiasm in southern California one must mention real estate or Hollywood.

When we speak of the West, except geographically, we do not include the Pacific Slope any more than we do Illinois and Iowa and Wisconsin. We mean definitely Cattleland, the country into which poured millions of Texas "mossyhorns" to stock the range raken from the Indian and the buffalo.

To UNDERSTAND the Texas cowboy of the great trail-driving days and his effect upon the West it is necessary to study his genesis, to know the stark conditions that begot him. He was a hard-bitten son of the early frontier. Danger he accepted as a matter of course. It stalked him in the piney woods and in the shinnery. It walked with him by day. It lay down with him at night beside his camp-fire and in his cabin. Hardship and rough living were his chosen lot.

It had been so when Stephen F. Austin, "the father of Texas," led his colony into the rich grasslands beyond the Red River, into what was then a far-flung province of old Mexico. It continued to be so when the settlers pushed to the new frontiers of Palo Pinto and Tom Green counties, and along the Canadian into the Panhandle.

In the early Texan were wrapped up a dozen paradoxes. He was the Esau of his tribe, but a deep lover of home; an individualist, yet intensely patriotic; he had the spirit and the urbanity of a cavalier and the harsh brusquerie of a savage. The circumstances of his life, as well as his training and heritage, made him stand on his own firmly

11

planted feet. Because he was a social nonconformist, the restless urge in him drove this wanderer past the boundaries of civilization to the plains where the Comanches roamed. His self-reliance made him a leader, rebellious of restraint, and nearly wrecked Texas in its heroic struggle for freedom. For each man, because of the force in him, would go his own way subordinate to none.

The constant drama of his life gave him color. Indeed, no stage in our national history has been so abundantly, so insolently, splashed with vivid hues as the one across which Bowie, Crockett, Travis, Fannin, Deaf Smith, Burnet, Austin, and Houston strode to play their appointed parts.

The life and character of Sam Houston epitomized the exaggerated virtues and vices of early Texas. So rough and uncouth was the giant Tennessean that the lovely girl he married could not live with him; so sensitive was he because of her desertion that he gave up a great career with the presidency as a possibility to dwell among the Cherokees in drunken squalor; so chivalrous that he swore to go back to the settlements and cut out the heart of any man who spoke ill of the wife who had left him. Later, when once more he had won leadership, he surrendered the governorship of Texas and became anathema to his friends because of loyalty to the flag.

The pioneer Texan had iron in his blood. He was of heroic stature, a man in buckskin striding to his end with grim intensity. Despite his awkwardness, his lack of nice refinements, he was neither ignorant nor stupid. Bowie and Crockett had elements of greatness, though they slaughtered the English language, as well as Indians. As for the Austins and scores of others, they could chop logic with a Harvard professor when they desired.

When Stephen Austin, the son of a Connecticut Yankee, in 1820 led his colony into Mexico, he could not guess that he was lighting a fire that would be blown all over the Southwest until it drove the Spaniard out of not only

THE ALAMO AT SAN ANTONIO
To the old-time cattleman San Antonio was the haven of refuge and romance and the Alamo was at the heart of it.

DAY HERD

THE ROUND-UP GROUND

Texas but Colorado, New Mexico, Arizona, and California. The result was inevitable. The force within the men he led and those who came after was explosive. It contained too much energy to submit to Mexican domination.

They were of a mixed strain, those first Texans, a majority from the South, a sprinkling from above Mason and Dixon's line. Louisiana sent James Bowie, Connecticut and Virginia the Austins, New Jersey David G. Burnet. From South Carolina came William Barrett Travis, from Tennessee David Crockett and Sam Houston, from Kentucky the renowned Confederate general who died at the battle of Shiloh, Albert Sidney Johnston. Georgia supplied Ward and Fannin. Tom Green and Deaf Smith were mavericks ranging the whole wild frontier. The names of these pioneers you may find to-day written all over the map of Texas. Each of them was singularly forceful, tough as hickory, enduring as steel, a man of character expressing itself in original energy.

From the beginning the revolt of the *Tejanos* was foreordained. Stephen Austin tried to keep his pledges to the Mexican government, even to the extent of seeking to get Catholic emigrants. He held the colonists with him at first, though very soon there came a division between those who were for peace and those who were ready to fight. Gradually the faction in favor of rebellion grew stronger.

As early as 1825 the British diplomatic representative in Mexico sounded a note of warning to his government.

They [the Mexican authorities, he meant] are suffering . . . by an absurd mixture of negligence and weakness, the whole disputed territory . . . to be quietly taken possession of by the very men whose claim to it they are resisting here. . . . The lands between the rivers Sabine and Brazos have been granted away to American settlers and . . . the tide of emigration is setting very fast in the direction of the Rio Bravo. . . . Their numbers are increasing daily, and though they nominally recognize the authority of the Mexican government, a very little time will enable them to set at defiance any attempt to enforce it. . . . [They are] Americans—Backwoodsmen, a bold and hardy race, but likely to prove bad subjects and most inconvenient neighbors.

This prediction was soon verified. There were probably twenty thousand Americans in Texas by 1830, the year when a law was passed prohibiting further colonization. It was a law without teeth. There was no means to enforce it. From all over the American frontier settlers continued to pour across the Red River.

The story of the Texas revolution is both shocking and inspiring. The cavalier strain, the passion for adventure, had full play, as did too the wilful individualism bred by border life. Together they led to the glory and the terrible waste of Goliad and the Alamo. It was this combination of high-hearted courage and insubordination that was responsible for the loss of Crockett and Bowie and Travis and Fannin with many hundred other stalwarts, and for the unparalleled tradition of devotion handed down to us. We can forget the disaster these men brought upon themselves. We can never forget that when Colonel Travis drew with his sword the line which meant on one side a fighting finish, on the other a creditable excuse for desertion and probable safety, every man made the same choice instantly. He took his fortune in his hand and stepped across the division line between life and death. Nor can we forget that a score of riders broke through the investing lines to share the fate of the doomed garrison, and that the whole of the night that followed the Mexicans listened with amaze to the sound of the fiddle, of dancing, and of laughter from the lips of those who knew they were about to die. It may be now a trite epigram that Thermopylæ had its messenger, the Alamo none, but it will always be significantly inspiring.

Even after the revolution the restless son of Texas was not content to be anything but a pioneer. The Esau strain was in his blood. Kipling has voiced in verse something of his feeling:

His neighbours' smoke shall vex his eyes, their voices break his
   rest.
He shall go forth till south is north sullen and dispossessed;
He shall desire loneliness and his desire shall bring,
Hard on his heels, a thousand wheels, a People and a King.
He shall come back on his own track, and by his scarce-cooled
   camp
There he shall meet the roaring street, the derrick and the
   stamp:
There he shall blaze a nation's ways with hatchet and with
   brand,
Till on his last-won wilderness an Empire's outposts stand!

The Texan, with his family, his covered wagon, his rifle, and his cows, pushed westward into the Indian country, and as settlement pressed upon him he took to the wilderness that led to the Canadian and the Panhandle and the Pecos.

Gradually the pioneer won his footing. The Indians were driven back and confined to reservations, which at first many of them used as a base of supplies from which to go raiding. The settlers felt that the policy of the government was to coddle the Indian, to bribe him to be good. When the hard winter was on the Indian was a good Indian; when spring began to blossom over the land he grew restless and went swooping out on a raid. The complaints of settlers were frequently ignored. The agents would report that no Indians were off the reservation and the damage must have been done by rustlers. A telegram was once received by the Indian Department. It ran something like this:

"We have often informed you of depredations committed by Indians from the Comanche reservation at Fort Sill, only to be confronted by the statement of the agent that no Indians had been off the reservation. If you will order your agent to go to the lower crossing at Bear

Creek he will find twenty-five Indians off the reservation."
The agent found and buried them.

2

Pioneer life on the Brazos was simple. Houses were
built of unhewn logs snaked out of the woods by a bull
team. The floor was either naked earth or puncheon, the
door of clapboards chinked with mud. A stick and dirt
chimney, with rock back, served for both heating and
cooking. Furniture was primitive. A one-legged bedstead
mortised into the wall, with a rawhide rope upon which to
put the mattress, filled one corner of the cabin. A home-
made table, the boards shaved by a drawknife, occupied
the place of honor in the center. Stools and benches, the
lumber from a split tree and faced by a broadax, served
for chairs. An iron pot, a Dutch oven, a three-legged
skillet, and a teakettle were the cooking implements.
There was no stove, but in the fireplace were pothooks
from which could be hung the kettles. Matches were
scarcely ever used. The fire was either banked or started
by flint on punk. Sometimes a "chunk" of fire was carried
from the house of the nearest neighbor.

The cabin was lit by candles, made either by dipping
string into warm tallow or by pouring the tallow into
molds. For candlestick was used a square block hollowed
in the center. Each family made its own soap, dripping the
lye from an ash hopper. Ashes filled the hopper, and water
was poured over them until the lye began to drip into a
trough.

Farming was elementary. Horse collars sometimes were
fashioned from corn shucks, plow lines from rawhide.
Wagon wheels could be sawed from sweet-gum logs. Both
the turn and the bull plow were made by the settler himself,
as was the hoe that covered the corn dropped by hand.
Oxen were used for cultivating the land, two or three yoke
to a plow.

The frontiersman usually went to his work armed against the chance of an Indian attack. Even in the meeting house, though rifles were stacked against the walls, pistols were never taken off. The men carried powder horn and pouch, in which would be a bit of lead, a bullet mold, and either a box of caps or some flints.

Hospitality was the order of the day. The hostess scraped the bottom of the meal barrel to feed a guest. No stranger was ever charged for a night's lodging, nor would he insult his host by offering pay. When someone killed a bear or an antelope he divided the meat with his neighbors, and they in turn rode with gay good-will to help him raise a barn or cut his corn if he was short-handed. All were on an equality, and friendliness went far. If a man needed money it was loaned him without note or security. One man bought two farms on partial payments, but no mortgage or even note was required of him for the balance.

With rare exceptions the settlers went garbed in home-made clothing, including hats, shoes, shirts, dresses, trousers, and coats. Buckskin was frequently worn by the men, as were caps of coonskin or deerskin. Women did their own quilting and spinning. Boys dressed squirrel hides for shoestrings. Each settler tanned his own leather, using for that purpose sumac leaves and blackjack bark.

It was an age of barter. There was little money in the community, and debt was not quite good form. One borrowed what one could not make, or one did without. Not to have divided with a neighbor would have been a disgrace. The settlers were very ingenious in supplying their own necessities. Very few articles of food, furnishing, or wear could not be devised. Water and wood were hauled on a crude sled which consisted of the fork of a tree supported by standards. This was called a lizard.

A green cowskin had all the raw material for a blacksmith shop, a cobbler's, a saddler's, a tailor's, and a carpenter's. From it evolved rope hobbles, clothes lines, and bedsprings, seats of chairs, overcoats, trousers, brogans, and shirts. It patched saddles and shoes. Strips of it bound a loose tire or lashed together the pieces of a broken wagon tongue.

This life, close to nature, developed self-reliance among women as well as men. A girl would pick up a log chain, pass between a yoke of steers, and hook the chain in the staple of the yoke. Many a mother, when her husband was at the war or away from home, defended her children with a rifle from marauding Indians.

John A. Hart, an old-timer, in *Pioneer Days in the Southwest*, tells of one woman named Williams. Her husband was in the Confederate army and had left her and the four children few resources. She had a little peghorn yoke of half-broken oxen, two cows, an old run-down wagon, four or five knotty hogs, and some chickens. News came one day that the Federals were coming. She decided to hide in the brakes, though wild animals infested the woods. The old wagon was almost gone to staves. She took some soap and greased it, drove wedges under the tires, poured water over the wheels to swell them, and then loaded the wagon. There was no time to cook supper. The children went hungry. When she found the oxen she drove them home and hitched up.

She built a scaffold upon which to put the cornmeal and sowbelly. Before daybreak she returned to the house and brought a load of corn from the crib. She roped the calf and dragged it to the camp. The cows followed.

For weeks she remained in the swamp. After the Yankees had gone she returned home, to find the fence burned for fuel, all the hogs eaten but one, and the chickens gone into the pot for the soldiers. Lightning had killed one cow.

One of the children fell ill and died. She made a coffin and with the help of a neighbor woman buried the child. When one day a bearded stranger appeared and said, "Sally, the war's over," she did not recognize her husband.

Of such stuff were the pioneer women. To live under

these conditions developed hardihood. The weak became strong or died. One woman writes that she was married and had three children before she ever saw a cookstove. "You think," she adds, "that we had a hard time, and so I reckon we did, but we enjoyed it, and it was happiness to us all, for we loved each other, and were always glad to see and help each other, and when one got sick we would go eight or ten miles to sit up with them if we were needed."

Gourds were used to hold water, to milk in, and as containers for food. The children learned to card and spin, to parch corn for coffee, to make soda out of weak lye. A tumbler could be cut from a bottle by seesawing a buckskin thong around the middle until the glass was hot and then dipping it into cold water.

With a graining knife a woman would take the hair from a deer hide, put the skin in strong suds of lye soap and lard, and let it stay warm by the fire all night. In the morning she would wring it out, then pull, stretch, and rub the hide until it was soft and pliable. The skin was then ready to be made into trousers or gloves. If a young woman was anxious to look well she could color a fawnskin shirt with chaparral root and wear it over her other clothes while she was running cattle through the brush.

Mrs. Mary A. Nuney, living in the Panhandle, writes that her father built a log cabin on a knoll for a schoolhouse. The floor was the ground. The benches were made of split logs with poles put in for legs. A plank along one wall served for a desk. The light came from cracks in the wall.

It is impossible to have known these early settlers without realizing what a profound impulse religion was in their lives. A personal God, close to them as breathing, directed and watched over them. They were untroubled by doubts. Salvation came through a definite act of conversion. Prior to this conviction of sin many of the young men were wild and dissipated. In the hour of conversion God pardoned their sins and they turned a new page in their lives. It was as simple as that.

The camp meetings were great social occasions. Guns and pistols were usually laid aside at the edge of the arbor, though on occasion a preacher would pray with a revolver belted around his waist. The horses were tied and guarded if there was danger of an Indian attack. It was old-time religion. Sometimes there would be two ministers, perhaps one a Methodist and the other a Cumberland Presbyterian. They preached no namby-pamby religion but old-fashioned hell fire. The hymns were joined in by all. Men, women, and children rang the bells of heaven and held the fort, lustily admitting they were the vilest of worms but for the grace of God who had sent His Son that they might be washed in the blood of the Lamb.

Into Texas poured later hundreds of hard and desperate characters. Many of the young men became contaminated by these outlaws and murderers. A good many of the punchers on the trail were hard, tough youngsters. But it is worth noting that many of these returned to the religious fold of their fathers in later life and became pillars of the Church.

In certain localities both agriculture and stock raising had already reached a condition far more advanced than that described. On the Brazos, just after the Civil War, there were fine farms where a large acreage of cotton and corn was raised. This was also a region of excellent pasturage, and fed many thousand cattle and horses.

The extent of the live-stock industry of Texas and the development of the trail trade was as early as 1870 challenging the attention of the nation. The Department of Agriculture report of that year is authority for the statement that along the coast could be found cattle lords with herds surpassing in number and value "even the flocks and herds of the great man of Uz." One of these was Captain Richard King, who had settled at Kingsville, Texas, before the Mexican War. Captain King, owner of the Santa Gertrudis ranch, which embraced nearly 85,000 acres, ran in his brand ᴡ, the Running W, 65,000 cattle,

10,000 horses, 7,000 sheep, and 8,000 goats. He had 300 Mexican herdsmen and 1,000 saddle horses ready for instant service. Each year he branded 12,000 calves and sold 10,000 fat bullocks. The widow of Captain King died in 1925, leaving an estate which included a ranch of 1,000,-000 acres, the largest in the world, one which has more game on it than any known private preserve.

Below Goliad, on the San Antonio River, O'Connor's ranch had 40,000 cattle as early as 1862 and realized $80,000 in one sale of stock. O'Connor had begun business ten years earlier with 1,500 cows. The Rolideaux ranch, between the Nueces and the Rio Grande, was a fertile peninsula of 142,840 acres which jutted into the Gulf of Mexico and fed 30,000 beef cattle, as well as great numbers of other stock.

Scarcely one in ten of the cattlemen, McCoy says, lived on their ranges, but in towns or neighboring villages. Life was a very different thing here than it was on the frontier, though even there were large outfits. Barrett and Nicholl had three big ranches in Llano, San Saba, and Lampasas counties respectively. All over the cattle country shrewder men were gathering together large herds and holdings. By the time the trail drives began there was already established, especially in the south of the state, an easygoing pastoral life built somewhat on the feudal principle.

The cattle baron had his retainers who lived on the estate and were essentially a part of it. Legally they were free to move, but practically they expected to live and die on it, they and their sons and their sons' sons. The relationship carried on both sides a responsibility that could not be measured in dollars and cents. The lord of the estate looked after his dependents, their physical and to a certain extent their moral welfare. He was the source from whom bounties flowed, the authority to consult when purely family difficulties arose, the judge who passed upon quarrels. The vaqueros and their families on their side gave unstinted loyalty and a service not checked by a time clock. It was an easy-going existence akin to that of the nomadic tribes in the time of Abraham, in one sense quite idyllic. Under the pressure of economic determinism it vanished just as the kindlier aspects of slavery did.

In their palmy days the cattle barons lived like princes. Their wealth, pouring down to them from the North in exchange for the great herds which went up the trail, increased faster than it was possible for them to spend it. Wild extravagance and display characterized their manner of life. Their wives wore diamonds and rode in carriages imported from London. They traveled far, and were the first Americans to create the impression in Europe that this was a country of boundless wealth. During the late '70's and early '80's the cattle kings dominated the Lone Star State, its politics, its business, and its social life.

Yet Texas was and continued to be rural. Men alive to-day remember when a section of land in what is now the business heart of Dallas was offered for a pair of boots, with no taker.

And always, from the time of Stephen Austin's first colony till long after Charles Goodnight settled in the Panhandle, the settlers were harried by marauding Indians. The Kickapoos, the Comanches, and the Kiowas timed their raids to reach the Texas settlements during the light of the moon in order to have clear nights to steal the horses. Coming in from the plains to western Texas, they took short cuts to the headwaters of the Concho, Colorado, San Saba, Llanos, Guadalupe, and Nueces rivers.

The western Texas frontier was a bloody hunting ground. Through three generations it continued to be so. A hundred stories could be told to justify this statement. The tales of the pioneers are full of such incidents as these, taken from *Pioneer Days in the Southwest:*

We came to where they had killed and scalped old man Long.

The tongue of the lead ox wagon had been propped up with an ox yoke, and across it in spread-eagle fashion lay the naked body of one of my men. He had been tortured to death. There was a burnt place on his breast where the Indians had driven splinters under the skin and set fire to them.

In June of 1868 W. H. (Tip) See, he went by the name of Tip, lived on Buck Creek in Palo Pinto County and was out hunting stock. The Indians killed him. He was a good man, and we were in the same company in the army. He was one of God's noblemen, and all the company loved Tip See.

In January, 1870, the Indians killed Mr. Ripley and his wife about seven miles north of us on Rock Creek. His dogs barked at something about a hundred yards from the house. He went to see what it was across a small field. When he got there the Indians shot and wounded him. His wife, seeing the trouble, went to his relief, and the Indians killed them both.

On and on the record goes. One man, James D. Newberry, writing of his own early life, gives the names of twenty-nine settlers killed by Indians and mentions others whom he does not name.

John A. Hart tells the story of a still hunter's rescue of two girls. The Indians had raided Bell County, killed several people, and carried off the two girls. A party pursued the Comanches and lost the trail. The still hunter, so called because he hunted Indians alone and without a horse, did not give up. He knew that it was the custom of the Indians to rest for several days when they thought they were entirely out of danger. On the fourth day he saw the smoke of the camp fires. The raiders had killed a buffalo and were having a feast.

In the darkness the hunter crept close. Entirely stripped of clothes, the girls were tied to a tree a little distance from the feasting circle. The trailer cut the girls loose, was discovered, killed two redskins, and drove the rest away. He dragged the girls into the night and managed to get them several miles before dawn, although they were very weak and exhausted.

During the day he hid them in brush and stood guard. Their bodies were raw and blistered from exposure. To one he gave his shirt, to the other his trousers. Reaching a creek, he made them bathe. Here he caught frogs and crawfish to feed them. The second night they moved a few miles. It was a rough country of cactus and sharp stones. He killed an antelope, fed his charges, and made moccasins for their feet. Enough of the skin was left to serve as a jacket for one of the girls. Later he killed a deer and out of the hide tailored a dress for the other. After three weeks, watching them faithfully as a mother, he brought the girls to a ranch. None of the settlers gave great applause to this man. What he had accomplished had been all in the day's work. Any of them would have done it if he had had the skill and finesse. Life was cheap in those days when the call came to risk it for those in need.

Monroe Littlefield was wounded in a battle with the Comanches. He was carried to the house of Fuller Millsap. For many months he lay there helpless. The neighbors worked and harvested his crop. The Millsaps charged nothing for his board and care while he was with them.

A year or two later the Indians jumped the Millsap place, killed a hired man, and penned Millsap and his son-in-law Loving in the barn. The two men killed three or four Indians before they ran out of ammunition. Donie Millsap filled her apron with cartridges, flew like a deer across the line of fire, and reached her father in time.

The fear of savages was drawn in by the children with their mothers' milk. If their dogs barked they thought of Comanches. When they went to the spring for a bucket of water they watched to make sure no Indians were waiting behind trees to scalp them. They lived in constant dread of being killed.

Reduced to its lowest terms, the war was one between the longhorn and the buffalo. The settler wanted a range for his cows. The Indian fought to hold it for the buffalo, upon the existence of which his free life depended. If the buffalo lost the range the Indian's tribal life was doomed.

No frontier in the Southwest suffered as much from Indian raids as this. All the territory between the Red River and the Rio Grande beyond the western border of the Cross Timbers was Comanche land. It had belonged to them from prehistoric days and they, together with their allies, the Kiowas, fought for it against the encroaching whites. The borderline extended for nearly six hundred miles and a force of Rangers was maintained to guard it. The frontier battalion had orders to bring in no Comanche prisoners. All Texans agreed in those days that a good Indian was a dead Indian. On this subject there was no divergence of opinion. They all hated the Comanche, the Kiowa, and the Apache cordially and without equivocation. To them the Indian was the sweepings of the earth, "a lazy lousy dirty deceitful race," to quote one of them. They had seen too many of their friends and relatives killed and tortured to have any doubts. They felt that the attitude of the government in coddling the tribes was criminally dangerous. This feeling was largely shared by the army in the West.

When sentimentalists deplored the destruction of the buffalo and introduced a bill in the Texas legislature to protect the herds against the hunters, General Phil Sheridan went before that body and bluntly spoke his conviction.

Instead of stopping the hunters [he said] you ought to give them a hearty, unanimous vote of thanks, and give each hunter a medal of bronze with a dead buffalo on one side and a discouraged Indian on the other. These men have done more in the last two years, and will do more in the next year, to settle the vexed Indian question than the regular army has done in the last thirty. They are destroying the Indians' commissary, and it is a well known fact that an army losing its base of supplies is at a great disadvantage. Send the hunters powder and lead if you will, but for the sake of peace let them kill, skin, and sell until the buffalo are exterminated. Then your prairies can be covered with cattle and the cowboy, who follows the hunter as a second forerunner of an advanced civilization.

The evidence of the bitterness always existing between the Indians and the Texans stands out in one significant fact. The only border state which never had any squaw man was Texas. The feeling was too deep, memories too harrowing, to permit of any intermarriage. For fifty years it was war and nothing but war.

Texas was feeling growing pains. The Civil War lay behind her. The Lost Cause was a memory. For twoscore years her herds had multiplied exceedingly. The leading industry was ranching, and she was the greatest producer of live stock in the country. Her grazing lands were wide and of the best, especially in the western part. Cows thrived on the excellent range grasses, many of which had a rich nutritive value retained as hay dried on the stem, long after the summer had passed. Nor should the feeding value of the mesquite leaves and especially the mesquite beans be overlooked. In times of drought, to quote an old Texan, "the old cows clim' the trees or wore the hide offen their knees from wallerin' round under the low branches to git the long yellow beans coverin' the ground." When the soldiers drifted home after Appomattox the state had within her borders 3,500,000 cattle, 500,000 horses, and 750,000 sheep.

Rich with an abundance of potential wealth such as nature had given no other state, Texas was none the less poor as a church mouse. In this she was not unique. The defeated South was financially bankrupt. Of the seceding

states Texas had the best chance for a rapid recovery if
she could capitalize her quick assets. These were land,
cotton, and cattle.

But the market for cotton had for the time been entirely
destroyed. For cows there was no available outlet. The
faster they increased the greater the embarrassment of the
owner as to what to do with them. It had reached a point
where a man's poverty could be measured by the number
of his longhorns and the amount of land he held by scrip.
If he was a cattle baron with vast herds ranging for scores
of miles it could be said of him that he was fifty thousand
cows poor. As the excess grew, naturally stock became
less valuable, according to the universal law of supply and
demand. The surplus tended to regulate and depress
prices.

As for land, prior to and just after the war the pioneer of
west Texas gave it little consideration. Very likely he took
up a claim on a creek and raised some corn on it. But
why get in a sweat about land? Millions of acres rolled
before him from Mexico to Manitoba, all unoccupied, all
open range. He could buy it in state scrip, by the ten-
thousand-acre parcel, for a few cents an acre. But what
would he do with it when he had title? How could he own
it more completely than he did now? It was his to use, with
none to object, except for the occasional incursions of the
Comanche and the Kiowa. He could range his cattle on
it and not be troubled by the tax collector. Would it belong
to him more in any practical sense if he got a paper from
the state saying it was his? It is worth noting that the cattleman of Texas then counted his property in cows and in
the improvements he had made upon his holdings. In-
trinsically the land did not count.

The reasons for the glut of cattle may be found chiefly
in conditions produced by the Civil War. Prior to that
time there had been a market, though the matured supply
had long exceeded the outlet. Herds could be driven to
points on the Mississippi from the eastern part of the

state or they could be shipped by water from Gulf ports. Mexico too had been a buyer.

During the war practically all the self-respecting lusty Texans were in the Confederate army. Only women, children, shirkers, and those feeble of body stayed at home. Of necessity the herds ran wild. Calves were unbranded, except those stolen by Indians, Mexicans, and the stove warmers who had dodged enlistment. The increase was nearly 25 per cent a year. If Texas had been a battlefield for the contending armies the soldiers would have taken care of the surplus. The Lone Star State, however, was definitely cut off from the armies of the South by Union gunboats which controlled the lower Mississippi. The troops of Bragg and Johnson and Beauregard needed meat. There came a time when they wanted it desperately. But the Union leaders recognized that Texas was the great storehouse of the seceding states and locked the larder from the rest of the Confederacy by an effective blockade. There was no chance to get the longhorns to the Southern armies. A few herds swam the river and made contact at great risk. The herds that reached the troops helped the state little financially, since the pay was in Confederate money, which soon ceased to have a value.

That some of the stock got through, we know. Branch Isbell, in *The Trail Drivers of Texas*, mentions meeting a company of Confederate soldiers driving a herd of Texas steers the while they sang a bit of doggerel of many stanzas. Two of them ran as follows:

> Driving cattle's our promotion,
> Which just exactly suits my notion,
> And we perform with great devotion;
> There's work enough for all.

> I'd like to be a Virginia picket,
> But I'd rather be in a cattle thicket
> Where the hooting owl and screaming cricket
> Make noise enough for all.

For a few years after peace was declared New Orleans and Mexico absorbed a limited number of cattle, but the outlet took care of a very small proportion of the maturing stock. Insufficient though it was, the market pinched out. Landowners in Mexico deserted their holdings on account of the unsettled political conditions which made ranching unsafe.

The outlook was blue. Texas bulged with fat sleek cattle, many of them unbranded and ownerless, but the stockman faced gaunt poverty, for the best cows on the range were quoted at from three to five dollars a head with no takers.

So low was the price that thousands of cattle were killed for hide and tallow alone. The "skinning war" resulted, in the course of which rustlers killed and skinned quantities of cattle, leaving the carcasses to the buzzards. The skins were sold to factories which specialized in hides and tallow. Sometimes these packeries salted down the best part of the beef. There were nearly a score of them, and they did a large export business. Since the big Texas ranches were then near the coast, transportation by ship was easy. Some of the ranches had factories of their own. They fed the meat from the slaughter houses to hogs or let it rot. Captain Richard King, "Shanghai" Pierce, and Miflin Kenedy all owned packing plants. Hundreds of thousands of cattle were skinned, but the diminution of the total number was relatively inconsiderable.

The effect of the war in the North upon cattle prices had been the reverse of that in the South. The Union armies offered a large and steady outlet. Indeed the demand had been so great that the supply on the farms of the East and the Middle West was cut to a close margin, with the result that in 1865 a select matured animal was worth ten times as much in Illinois or Ohio or Connecticut as in Texas. No workingman could afford steak at forty cents a pound. Inevitably the stockman of the Southwest looked to the North for his market. The difficulties in

reaching the buyer were great. Hundreds of miles of unknown Indian country had to be traversed, with no assurance of arriving at the journey's end. But the ranch owners were determined to invade the North with their herds
regardless of the danger.

At this opportune hour there was offered an unexpected
solution of the problem. From Kansas City, along the valley of the Kaw, the Kansas Pacific Railroad was pushing
due westward across the plains. If the Texas trail driver
could reach the end of the line he could ship by rail to a
market.

Texas buzzed like a beehive with the prospect. In spite
of demoralized conditions there was a feeling that better
times were at hand. Men began to bestir themselves to
prepare for a revival of trade.

2

Thousands of unbranded cattle ran the range. Legally
they had no owner, though undoubtedly the cattlemen
whose cows grazed that territory had the best claim.

Prior to the war there had been very little stealing of
stock in Texas except by the Indians. The settlers were
pioneers, hard as granite, but honest, neighborly, and religious. There was land enough for all. There were cattle
enough for all. Free grass, often knee high, covered the
prairies. Cows fed wherever they would, on a range that
extended unbroken from the Gulf to the Red River. Any
industrious man could start a herd and watch it grow,
welcomed as an asset by the other settlers. They branded
calves for one another and divided those of doubtful
ownership.

The stockmen had their spring and fall cow hunts.
These were the genesis of the more modern round-up.
They were simple affairs with no captain of the rodeo, no
chuckwagon and cook, no horse wrangler to look after a
big remuda. A day was set to meet at an assigned place.

Half a dozen or a dozen cowmen arrived, each with a pair of horses, a hard-woven Mexican blanket, and supplies enough to last during the hunt. The bread was already made. The only cooking done was the broiling of a steak on hot coals and the making of a pot of coffee. In case the bread gave out, one of the men rode to the nearest ranch house with a sack of flour and asked the woman there to bake it into bread. This request was never refused. The custom of the country was that the housekeeper must drop whatever she was doing and spend a day cooking the bread for the cow hunters. No money was offered. Perhaps half a sack of flour was left with her as evidence of thanks.

On these cow hunts and on the trail at first there was no standardized costume for a cowboy. The riders were merely sons of neighboring ranchmen. When they went into the prickly pear country they wore chaparajos and brush jackets such as the vaqueros of Mexico used. Ordinarily homespun linsey-woolsey shirts were worn, and checkerboard or striped trousers, black and white, thrust into boot tops.

The method of the cow hunt varied with the nature of the country. If it was a district with a heavy growth of mesquite and cactus the rounding up of the stock was hard and dangerous work. This was true also in the timbered country where the scrub oak and the jack pine flourished.

It must be kept in mind that no cattle in the North, even these same transplanted longhorns, were as wild and untamed as the Texas ones. In the Lone Star State they were rarely worked in winter and very little in summer. They grazed in the dense mesquite and were wary as wolves. They sniffed approaching danger and at once were off like bullets from a rifle, crashing through the cactus or leaping over it like deer. "Horned jack rabbits" a disgusted cowman dubbed them, and the appellation was so apt that it stuck. After they had been driven a thousand miles, had become used to the trail, to the sight of men on horseback, to being guided in one direction and another, the cattle were never the same as at home. Even physically they became different animals. In Texas the longhorn, of Spanish ancestry, was a light, wiry, long-legged, angular creature, active and wild as a coyote. Except when fat there was little meat on him, and what there was ran to muscle. He might be almost any color, but he would always be tough. Prominent of hip and often pot-bellied, he would never have won a prize for shapeliness. One or two years on the feeding grounds of the North added a couple of hundred pounds to the weight of even a full-grown animal and tended to trim down his eccentricities of appearance.

Sometimes a decoy herd was used, tame cattle taken along to make the wild ones more easy to handle. Tame is a comparative word. Even the gentled ones, used to the sight of men on horseback, were savage enough according to present-day standards. One of them, cornered and frightened, might be as dangerous as a bear with a sore paw. During the hunt they were likely to stampede and go charging into the shinnery. In which case the stockmen might go home without any cows at all.

When a bunch of cattle was sighted in the brush the decoys were headed toward them. Slowly the riders followed. After the decoys had become thoroughly mixed with the others the stockmen circled the herd, singing softly a lullaby. Gradually the herd was pushed, very gently, in the direction of the corral where it was to be inclosed. The riders kept well back from the longhorns and moved quietly, for any unexpected sound might start a stampede.

The corrals were very strongly built. Posts were sunk several feet into the ground and placed side by side. Strips of green cowhide lashed these together firmly. Flaring wings ran several hundred feet from the corral, and into these the herd was moved. Once within the corral the heavy gate was shut and the cattle were left to mill.

It might be that the timber or the prickly-pear thickets were so dense that the riders lost their sense of direction and did not work together. A "run" was likely to follow, in which case each rider roped or tailed one of the racing long-horns, flung it to the ground, hogtied it, and left it there while he chased another. Later these animals were released among some tame ones. Any still too wild to drive was again thrown, then attached to a decoy by a short rope fastened around the necks of both. This was known as "necking," and was a less friendly process than the term implies to-day. After the two animals had worn themselves out trying to go in different directions at the same time the wilder one was enough subdued to move along in the company of its fellows rather than to yield to an imperative impulse to "hightail it" into the chaparral.

Another method of rounding up was to wait until the cattle moved out from the chaparral to an open plain to feed. Each rider than selected one and pursued it. If he made a catch he felt the jar of several hundred pounds of live bone and muscle on the rope tied to the saddlehorn. Rider and horse had both to be expert, or the furious animal might regain its feet and charge the waddy who was annoying it.

The cow hunters rounded up the stock and branded the calves. The rights of all the stockmen in the vicinity were regarded, whether the cowman was present in person or not. Each man helped his neighbor and knew he would be helped in turn. That was the first unwritten commandment of the frontier. One for all and all for one. Only by holding to it could the settlers survive against the stark conditions which confronted them. Comanches and Kiowas were a constant threat, so that every man was dependent upon his neighbor. At heart the settlers were to a certain extent communists. What a man's neighbor needed he could have. Ranches were many miles apart, counties not organized, and courts far away. Each man was a law unto himself. But each recognized the necessity of standing well with his neighbors.

When the ownership of calves could not be determined they were apportioned to the ranchmen in turn, though often with a sly preference for some woman in the settlement who had been widowed by the Comanches. The best of feeling prevailed, as did also absolute democracy. They were knit together in a close bond of fellowship produced by the isolation and dangers of their common existence. All were poor as far as actual money went. All were rich in health and hope.

These unkempt brown men, lank and bearded and ragged, did not ask for much in the way of comfort. Corn bread and "sowbelly," with chicory coffee, did well enough for food except when they killed a dogie or shot wild game. It was a country where black bear, whitetailed deer, antelope, and jaguars were common. Peccaries roamed the chaparral in droves. Wild turkeys could be found on every creek, sometimes in flocks of hundreds. Rattlesnakes, centipedes, and tarantulas infested the mesquite.

All the animal life in the jungle was wild. It protected itself by flight or fight. Many an earmarked hog, come upon suddenly in the brush, has turned and charged the intruder. A sow with a litter of young squealers might be as dangerous as a wolf brought to bay. These hogs fed on mast and grew fat on acorns, nuts, and mesquite beans. Occasionally they could be "toled" home by an ear of corn, but it was often necessary to shoot them when hog-killing time came in the fall. The settlers went hog hunting, as now people go out to shoot deer, and would bring home a wagonload of fat hogs to be cured for winter use.

Through west Texas in those days the law of the survival of the fittest was operative. It applied to the character of the vegetation, to the furtive animal life in the brush, and to the lean brown bearded men in wide hats, checkerboard trousers, and run-down-at-the-heel boots.

It held true too for the gaunt fearless women who made homes for their hard-riding husbands, and for the children begotten of the union. One and all lived by a combination of courage and caution not called for in more civilized communities.

The riders were almost as wild as the scurrying animal life. They had none of the refinements of a nice civilization, these brush combers. Nearly all of them chewed tobacco or smoked corncob pipes. A considerable number swore and drank and told ribald stories. They were hot-tempered and ready to fight at the drop of the hat. But, in the phrase of the day, they would do to ride the river with. No higher compliment could be paid one of them. It meant that when the herd was milling in a bank-full stream, the swift current sweeping the longhorns down, he could be depended on to fight for the safety of the herd and forget his own. It meant that he would set his tired bronco to breast the powerful tide in the hope of rescuing an unhorsed comrade even though the waters might close over him and his weary steed. No old-time trail driver ever hears that crisp summary of a man, "He'll do to ride the river with," and fails to get the full poignant meaning of it. Many a gay cowpuncher kissed his girl good-bye and rode north to lose his life in the Red, the Canadian, or the Cimarron.

One old pioneer of the Panhandle, writing of the others, says: "You may go where you will and never again find such a people, fearless, brave to a fault, hospitable and sociable, ready at any and all times to extend a helping hand in case of need. Round them all up, and you will find fewer cutbacks in the herd than among any class of people on earth."

The character of the early Texan has been hammered out on the anvil of the frontier, which in those days included all the western half of the state. His environment made him what he was. J. G. McCoy, the man who stabilized the first Northern market for Southern trail herds, in his *Historic Sketches of the Cattle Trade of the West and*

Southwest, has left a picture of the trail driver. The Texans (he sets down) had a strong natural sense of justice, were close observers, well skilled in judging human nature, suspicious but easily gulled, and so clannish that they would trust a Texan much more readily than a Northerner. They were all tipplers but few of them drunkards. If a woman was modest, they were chivalrously courteous to her; if she was bold, they accepted her at her own valuation. They had a strong innate sense of right and wrong, loved horses and were good riders, spent their money freely, especially to help a comrade in trouble, quickly resented an insult, and did not easily brook restraint. Their word was usually as good as a bond.

3

The war made a change in the spirit of the country. Army life had taken its toll of moral fiber, as it always does. Those who came home were poverty-stricken. Many a rider had nothing but the horse he rode and a smooth-bore Enfield musket. Some of them were wild young fellows, toughened by years of warfare, who had pushed out from their earlier home to the edge of the frontier. They saw great numbers of cattle running the range wild and unbranded. It was all very well for the ranchers of the neighborhood to claim them, but the stockmen could not legally prove ownership, since most of the unmarked stock were not calves following branded cows, nor had they means to employ vaqueros to do the branding for them. No law covered the case adequately, or if so it did not reach the mesquite. At any rate, it was a nice enough question for the young man on the make to give himself the benefit of the doubt. He rode the chaparral with a rope and a running iron. Many a cattle baron of later days got his start from branding mavericks.

The term maverick arose from the name of Samuel A. Maverick of San Antonio. In 1845 he received in payment

of a debt four hundred longhorns. Colonel Maverick was
not interested in cattle, and he left his herd in the care of
an indolent colored family on a ranch forty miles below
his home town. The guardians of the cattle paid little attention to them, branding only a small per cent of the
increase. The rest ran wild and unmarked until they were
almost mature. Enterprising neighbors decided that if
Colonel Maverick did not want his dogies they would do
some branding on their own account. It became a custom
in the neighborhood, which spread all over Cattleland in
time, to call any unbranded animal a maverick.

It is only fair to add that the branding of a maverick
was at first something less than theft. Even the state,
after it took cognizance of a growing evil, regarded mis-
takes of ownership as mere misdemeanors punishable by a
fine. Immediately following the war there was a kind of
tacit general license to brand wild unmarked cattle, and
the brushpoppers engaged in it were not regarded as outlaws. But after conditions became stabilized the laws were
changed to make promiscuous branding a more serious
offense. It may be mentioned parenthetically that some of
those most active in advocating the change were those who
had swung wide ropes in the mesquite a few years earlier.
Having acquired brands of their own, they were now
naturally in favor of drastic punishment for those who
branded and earmarked calves not belonging to them.
Whatever the rights or wrongs of hunting mavericks may
be, the result was an unfortunate one. It bred a state of
mind that in later days produced hundreds of rustlers who
were cow thieves pure and simple.

W. S. James, an old cowboy who wrote nearly fifty
years ago an interesting book called *Cow-Boy Life in
Texas*, with a subtitle *27 Years a Mavrick*, speaks out
very plainly on this subject.

A great many of the more active and better equipped among
the scramblers [for unmarked cattle] began to accumulate large

herds, and as there were no pasture fences then, they were compelled to turn loose their cattle on the range. The less thrifty and more extravagant classes refused to recognize the rights of the growing nabobs to have their unbranded calves left alone, while they were still keeping up their old game of branding "mavricks" indiscriminately, and the little fellows thus antagonized their former associates. The consequence was the wholesale thieves, now grown powerful, had the legislature pass laws making it an offense against the peace and dignity of the state to brand and mark a calf that didn't belong to him.

Then began the battle that for years waged unceasingly until the big fish swallowed up the little ones. We had as a result the cattle king and the common cowpuncher. The real difference being that the king no longer had to do his own stealing, for he was able to hire the cowpuncher to do it for him, and if the poor cowpuncher presumed to steal a little scrub for himself once in a while, the king wouldn't kick unless someone tried to raise a fuss about it. If he could settle it without too much noise he would do it, and thus add one more link to the poor boy's chain with which to hold him in line. If there was too much noise about it, the king turned honest and sent him down east to work for Texas.

James says that those who refused to maverick went broke. They could not stand out against the wholesale thieving on the range.

As a rule [he adds], the men who grew rich in the cattle business were the ones who were the best rustlers and who stuck closest to business, let that be in branding mavricks or looking after the ones already branded.

James overstates the case. Not all, or nearly all, of the men who a few years later became the cattle kings of Texas obtained their start by mavericking or increased their herds that way, though it is undoubtedly true that many an honest cattleman went to the wall because the rustlers in the chaparral drove away his stock and robbed him of his increase. It is also true that the ethics of the cattle business has been variable, dependent somewhat on time, place, and circumstance. This was inevitable as to property which moved about at will and as to which there was sometimes doubt of ownership.

Moreover, there was a certain generosity in the matter of cows, of which there were an unlimited number. Since no fences existed, all cattle were scrubs. It did not matter if some were killed for food by those who were not their owners. J. Frank Dobie, in *A Vaquero of the Brush Country*, quotes an advertisement of a cowman on the Nueces River in 1877, to the effect that all honest poor men were welcome to kill calves occasionally for food and to skin and sell the hides of any of his dead animals, provided it was not done in secret. This taking of the hide of an animal found dead was then a custom of the country.

The young man not well grounded in moral principle was influenced by the evil example of those about him. Hundreds of tough characters, released to civil occupations by the disbanding of the armies, scores of guerrillas and jayhawkers, many criminals and murderers flying from justice, headed for the Texas frontier. The Lone Star State was a sink into which the riffraff of the country drifted because law and order did not yet prevail there. During the next few years the number of these evil adventurers increased. Toughs pushed south from the railroads building across Kansas. In 1877 an official list was published of those in Texas "wanted" by the law. It had upon it five thousand names, few of these outlaws native Texans.

Never before had there been such an opportunity for the adventurous Esau of easy morals. All he needed was a horse, a rope, and a running iron to get the nucleus of a herd. This was the beginning of cattle rustling. The mavericker sometimes went in groups of three, four, or five, sometimes he played a lone hand. At first he ran brands only on unmarked cattle. Later the brush runner enlarged his operations to brand blotting, running of cattle out of the district, and other methods of thievery.

Men had become used to firearms and to taking life. Gradually, as the more settled states cleaned house, their bad men moved to Texas, a new country, beyond the law. Killers and outlaws, thieves and bandits, turned toward the frontier of the Lone Star State. Here they went on the dodge. Many of them became cowboys, for the wild free life of the open appealed to them.

A little later the buffalo hunters, having exterminated the vast hordes, looked around for another vent for their energies. They were a bold, rough class, frontiersmen who had taken their lives in their hands and pushed beyond the Arkansas into the Indian country. Many of them were estimable citizens, though none of them had hesitated to shoot down Indians if necessary. But some were hard characters. They had killed the buffalo without cost. They moved down into the cattle country and began to take cows and calves on the same terms.

The good citizens, the old settlers, and many new ones, continued to live as they had, honest and upright neighbors one to another. Many were church members. They constituted by far the greater number of inhabitants. But in the chaparral, on ranches, in the towns, was another class, lawless and uncontrolled. They were "bad men." This class was recruited from the ranks of honest lads falling into bad company and stepping over the borderline to join them.

One finds, all over Cattleland, from the time of the war until the end of the open range, this curious phenomenon. Lads lived decent lives, were brought up by God-fearing parents, then slipped across the line into outlawry. Some impulse within them, some outward circumstance, the pressure of evil companions, was too strong for them. They "went bad." This is the story of the Daltons, of the Sam Bass gang, of John Wesley Hardin and his many cousins, of the Horrells, of scores of men who took part in

the Lincoln County and the Johnson County wars. They
made a wrong step, and from that hour their faces were
set against the law, against the good citizens who were
building up the country. Not many of them were wholly
bad as youths. Many had good qualities of a high order
which never were extinguished. In the deplorable histories
of the Bass, the Younger, and the Dalton gangs there were
flashes of loyalty and gallantry worthy of a far better
cause.

4

San Antonio was then, and continued for many years to
be, the Mecca of the Texas cattlemen. It was a gay little
town, bubbling with irrepressible spirits of youth. One
might observe a difference between it and the trail's end
towns of Kansas which came into existence later. It was no
more decorous than they, but it was less raw. The town
had sat in the sunshine for two hundred casual and indolent
years while the river wound its way murmurously through
it toward the Gulf. There was a touch of insouciance about
the atmosphere, a good deal of romance. In the moonlight
one could almost see shadowy figures flitting about the
Alamo—the ghosts of Travis and his immortal band.
Slow-moving Mexicans in tight-fitting trousers flared at
the bottom, girt with gay sash and embroidered sombrero, twanged guitars beneath the windows of soft-eyed,
demure, mantilla-clad señoritas. It was a town in which to
play, a town where dollars were valuable only to spend.

No spirit of Puritanism dominated San Antonio, not in
the days when the cattle kings of Texas reigned there. It
was wild, but it was not woolly. For some reason the outlaw and the cowboy were more soft-spoken than at Dodge
and Newton. The gayety was a little less obstreperous.
Enjoyment did not depend upon noise. It was not necessary that everyone in the town should know how good a
time one was having.

There were the Buckhorn and the Green Front and the

Jack Harris Variety Theater, where one could start excitement of almost any kind. There was the Black Elephant, where stalwart buffalo hunters and, later, trail drivers gathered.

John Fitzhenry, a retired police officer of San Antonio, writes in *The Trail Drivers of Texas* that when he went there in '64 it was a jumping-off place for all the desperadoes in the country, a rendezvous for Mexican bad men as well as frontier outlaws. Bandits would hold up a train and come to San Antonio to spend the money. At one time or another might have been seen there the Yeager boys, Pitts, of the James gang, the feudist Suttons and Taylors, Sam Bass and Joel Collins, John Wesley Hardin and his group of relatives, the Dixons, the Clements, the Bowens, the Cunninghams, the Barrickmans, and the Milligans, fighting men all.

Those were desperate days. Marshal Gosling started with Pitts and one of the Yeagers to the penitentiary. Some women relatives of the prisoners boarded the train and gave them a basket of fruit. Yeager reached into the basket, drew forth a revolver, and shot down Gosling. During the battle one of the women and a guard on the train were also killed.

They were hard and lawless men, but they had the saving virtue of gameness. While Billy Taylor was in jail at Indianola, awaiting trial, there came up a great storm, and hundreds of lives were endangered. Taylor was released from prison and saved many from drowning. The jury that tried his case later brought in a verdict, "Not guilty." That was Texas.

The country around San Antonio was full of outlaws. According to C. W. Ackermann there were about forty of them in Bexar County, mostly in gangs of five and six. They continued to get worse, and by 1874 the cattle and horse thieves were so bad that cattlemen organized an association to get rid of them.

It was in the Jack Harris Theater that Ben Thompson

and King Fisher were killed by Billy Simms and various other gentlemen who decided that Mr. Thompson should be taken off in the interest of their own health.

King Fisher was a desperado of sorts himself with a good many notches on his gun. He had a taste for humor of rather a grim kind. Travelers up in his country were astonished to read at a crossroad a suggestive sign:

THIS IS KING FISHER'S ROAD.
TAKE THE OTHER.

They were fighting men, these travelers, just released from armies where they had become familiar with battle. But when they read that sign most of them accepted the mandate and took the other road. King Fisher was not a safe man to annoy. His fame was assured, but it has been somewhat dimmed by the greater glory of Ben Thompson as a killer.

Bat Masterson knew all the gunmen of his time, Wild Bill Hickok, Wyatt Earp, Billy Tilghman, Charley Bassett, Luke Short, Doc Holliday, Clay Allison, and Mysterious Dave Mather. None of these would have declined combat with Thompson if he had tried to "run on" them, but the San Antonio man was at once so swift and so deliberate with a gun, so cool and so deadly, that given an even break he would have been returned the victor against any of them. That was the opinion of Bat Masterson, himself a killer not unknown to fame.

Ben Thompson came to this country from England when a boy and settled at Austin. Here he learned the printer's trade, but when the Civil War broke out he enlisted in a Texas regiment under General Kirby Smith's command. His gallantry earned him a commission. Thompson was absolutely without fear, and his nerves were like chilled steel.

One story will serve to illustrate the quality of his audacity. The cattlemen of Texas had gathered at Austin for a big convention. Before the convention adjourned forty of the chief cattlemen sat down to a formal banquet. For some reason Thompson chose to get offended at them. One reason given is that they had not invited a congressman who was a friend of his. Ben appeared, a six-shooter in each hand. (This was contrary to his usual custom, for Ben was not a two-gun man. He claimed that with two six-shooters a man could not concentrate on the important business of the moment.) Beginning at one end of the table, he smashed every bottle of wine in sight. The cattlemen were tough old-timers, but they did not wait to argue the question with Ben. They took the nearest exit, whether it happened to be a door or a window. Major Seth Mabry, a whimsical old trail driver known by thousands in the cattle country, one who could lose a herd on the turn of a card and never bat an eye, when asked what he thought about it, complained of Ben's exploit.

"By jacks!" he said with a drawl, "I thought until last night Ben Thompson was a game man, but I notice he didn't attack us in the convention hall when we were a thousand strong. He waited till he could cut out a little bunch of only about forty of us and jumped on us then."

Thompson had killed Jack Harris in his own theater, and it was only just that he should get retribution in the same place. Both he and King Fisher were shot very dead. One of them was hit eight times and the other five. There was something feline about these gentlemen, and those engaged in their taking off did not want any chance of a return engagement on account of having one of the deceased come back to life.

5

A Texas difference of opinion called for a quiet and studied restraint or the blaze of six-shooters. There was no middle course. Law had not reached the chaparral. It would have been about as effective to bind a man over to keep the peace, if one had time to ride a hundred miles to find a justice, as it would be to get an injunction against mice in the house. Even when Law, in the person of the Texas Rangers or such cool, fearless sheriffs as Rome Shields of Tom Green County or Smith Lipscomb of Fannin County and his deputies Tom and Jim Ragsdale, came riding into the mesquite, it did not make the mistake of assuming that any innate respect for its authority would have weight. Judge Colt was the arbitrator between the officer and the criminal, and the manhunter had just as much respect as his personal prowess could win him.

It was the day of the six-shooter. There was no fist fighting, though there was among boys some friendly "knocking," as boxing was called in the Southwest. A quarrel had to be settled by mutual concessions or by guns. As a result quarrels were reduced to a minimum. When a man drew his "cutter" it was for business. Bluffs did not go, and a bully who habitually made them discovered this too late one day when called by some quiet gray-eyed citizen.

Because Texas had become a sink of refuge for so many wild and reckless characters the sound of the six-gun was heard often in the land. It would be a mistake not to realize that more than ninety-nine men out of every hundred in the state were peaceable and law-abiding, even though they carried pistols as a protection. But that other fraction of one per cent was obstreperous and insistent. It swaggered jauntily across the stage until the forward sweep of enforced public opinion wiped it out. In this process of elimination the Texas Rangers played a large and important part. Nearly a hundred murderers were brought to justice by them in less than a year and either buried or dragged out of the chaparral along a frontier six hundred miles in length. Such men as Jones, Reynolds, Roberts, Coldwell, Baylor, and Gillett did more to civilize the Lone Star State than all the legislators assembled at Austin. They demonstrated to the bad man that the bullets of law and order traveled straighter than those of the outlaw.

No other such police force has ever existed as that of the Texas Rangers. Its personnel was of the best, and the esprit de corps back of it in the days of its prime made for efficiency. Hard characters crept into the force and had to be discharged, but by and large this was the finest body of fighting police ever brought together.

Its reputation was a large asset when trouble loomed in the offing. All desperadoes knew that when necessary they could and would shoot straight and fast. Sam Dunn, one-time bartender at Tascosa and later for many years cattle inspector (peace to his ashes!), used to tell the story of the lone Ranger who arrived on the stage in response to an excited hurry-up call of the mayor for troops to quell a riot.

"Where are the Rangers?" demanded his honor.

"I'm here," replied the solitary representative.

He was a smooth-faced lad not yet of age, but the blue eyes in the tanned face were very steady and frosty.

"I asked for a company and one kid shows up. What in Mexico can you do alone—just one of you?" sputtered the local man.

"Only one mob, isn't there?" the young man countered lightly.

The Rangers date back to the days when Sam Houston organized a troop of sixteen hundred mounted riflemen to defend the border. At the battle of San Jacinto, where Texas captured Santa Ana and won its independence, the Rangers were the flower of the offense. During the Civil War Terry's Texas Rangers were greatly distinguished and lost three fourths of those enlisted. After Reconstruction days the Rangers were again organized, chiefly as a border defense against the Comanches and Apaches, and six companies of them, known as the Frontier Battalion, held the line from the Brazos to the Nueces. They fought eighty-four battles with the raiding Indians and recovered six thousand cattle stolen by them. It would not be possible to put into figures the services they rendered against outlaws and killers.

But the Frontier Battalion did not come into existence until 1874, and for a time its energies were devoted to the raiding redskin. The outlaws in the chaparral branded calves, stole cows, held up stages and village stores, and when the neighborhood in which they operated got too hot for them, went up the trail as honest cowpunchers. In time the law would reach them, but during the late '60's and the early '70's they were in the heyday of their insolence. The sheriff who took his job seriously was heavily handicapped, for the small ranchman protected the man on the dodge, not from preference but because it would be dangerous to incur his enmity. A two-gun man, well mounted and dressed with a touch of flamboyant color, was denied food and shelter at no cowcamp. The stranger might be a suspect, but the doubt about him was tinctured with wholesome respect for his six-shooters and those of his friends. Moreover, at every camp fire the exploits of Hardin and Sam Bass and Clay Allison were discussed admiringly. These men had a cool and resolute nerve— and the primal virtue on the frontier is gameness.

Prior to the reëstablishment of the Rangers the United States army coöperated with the cattlemen both against the Indian and the white thieves, but generally troops were ordered out only after the depredators were well on their way to escape. A general orders from the headquarters of the Fifth Military District of Texas, July 8, 1872, shows how serious was the condition.

Information received from all parts of the state shows that cattle stealing prevails to an unprecedented extent, and that in many cases the persons in charge of droves refuse to permit them to be inspected. It is therefore ordered that post commanders furnish military aid to effect inspection of drove cattle on request of responsible parties interested. . . .

There were no banks in those days in western Texas. When a buyer bought cows he often paid for them spot cash. James B. Gillett, the famous Indian fighter and law officer, in his book *Six Years with the Texas Rangers*, mentions that in 1873 he saw a buyer lift a pair of saddle-bags from his horse and pay three thousand dollars in gold pieces for a bunch of fat cattle. This was not at all unusual, and the outlaws in the brush sometimes lay in wait for men traveling with large sums of money.

For almost forty years, almost into the '80's intermittent private warfare lasted between the Texans and their neighbors to the south. An enormous amount of rustling was carried on, often in the most wholesale fashion. The Mexican bandit Cortina, who operated during and for many years after the Civil War, was a thorn in the side of the ranchers north of the Rio Grande. He had made himself a power in the land, and he invited fellow bandits to prey upon the Americans provided they paid him a commission on their steals. He himself was the boldest raider of them all. Often he lifted herds numbering thousands. One of his favorite expressions, according to W. D. Thomas as quoted by J. Frank Dobie in *A Vaquero of the Brush Country*, was that the gringos were raising cows for him.

A conservative estimate, based upon testimony before a United States commission and upon other evidence, is that more than a quarter of a million cattle were rustled from Texas by Mexicans and bandits in league with them during the decade of the seventies.

The most intense feeling prevailed on both sides. Scores of Mexican raiders were shot down. Innocent settlers of Spanish blood suffered because of the depredations of their countrymen. The Mexicans retaliated and killed many Texans. This guerrilla warfare was bitter and often without quarter.

Any Mexican living in Texas who gave information to local authorities against the raiders was likely to be murdered. Captain McNelly of the Rangers said that he knew of a dozen shot down for this reason. Even Americans who were active in running down the rustlers were in great danger, and were often killed or forced to move out of the country.

McNelly himself in 1875 caught a band of Mexicans driving stolen stock, shot down thirteen of them, and took the bodies to Brownsville, where they were laid out as a warning to other outlaws.

Feuds among Texas cattlemen were not uncommon. These had their origin usually in quarrels connected with cattle. The Taylor-Sutton war was the best known and deadliest of these. Scores of men were enlisted on each side, and either the Taylors or the Suttons generally controlled or were influential in the government of Gonzales and DeWitt counties during the height of the trouble. Feudists always had a strong penchant for getting on the weather side of the law, regardless of the ruthlessness of their actions. They preferred some pale color of authority for their cold-blooded killings. John Wesley Hardin and his relatives joined the Taylor forces. So did that wholesale killer Bill Longley, who had the distinction of being hanged twice, the second time after he had slaughtered more than a score of men. It seems rather a pity that Hardin and Longley did not quarrel at this time, as very nearly occurred, and exterminate each other before the notches on their respective guns had become as numerous as they later did.

The Horrell-Higgins feud in Lampasas County was another of the local wars that reverberated through Texas. The Horrells were cattlemen, well thought of in the communities where they lived. There were six brothers, Sam, Mart, John, Tom, Merritt, and Ben. Unfortunately they were hard drinkers, and like many Texans when they went to town were given to exuberant horseplay that annoyed quieter neighbors. This was in the days of the carpetbagger. A body of state police under the command of Captain

Williams went to Lampasas to settle the difficulty. This body of police had no connection with the Texas Rangers, which had not yet been reorganized since the war. They were Republicans, some of them Negroes, and exceedingly unpopular in the state. Williams and his men walked into the Jerry Scott saloon, attempted to arrest the Horrells, and were exterminated in thirty seconds, with the exception of one colored trooper left outside to hold the horses.

The Horrells gathered their effects, quite publicly, and migrated to the Hondo River in Lincoln County, New Mexico, where they very soon had another feud going with the Mexicans on account of trouble at a *baile*, in the course of which some natives were killed. Sheriff Gillam, his deputy Martinez, and other citizens attempted to arrest the Texans as they were leaving Lincoln. There was a pitched battle, during which the sheriff, his deputy, one citizen, and Ben Horrell were slain.

A lot of bushwhacking followed this battle. Some Mexicans were shot down. Ben Turner, an ally of the Horrells, was dry-gulched. Several score were murdered before the Horrells decided to return to Texas.

This was an unfortunate move for them. Texas was again in the Democratic column, and they surrendered to the authorities, were tried for killing the state troopers, and were acquitted. But they seem to have been born for trouble. A charge was made by Merritt that one Pink Higgins was rustling Horrell stock. Higgins shot young Merritt in the Jerry Scott saloon, while the youngster was unarmed. The Horrells came clattering to town as fast as horses could bring them. They were waylaid, and Mart was wounded desperately. Later a pitched battle was fought between the factions in the streets of Lampasas and several combatants killed.

Lieutenant Reynolds of the Rangers at great risk to himself trapped the Horrells asleep and arrested them. They were released, were later rearrested, and were lynched by a mob while prisoners in the Bosque County jail.

It is difficult now to understand the character of such men as the Horrells. They were intensely loyal one to another, brave, generous, full of lusty energy. Their virtues were exaggerated until they became destroying vices. Brought up on the frontier in constant danger, they had little regard for their own lives or those of other people. Like thousands of others who "went bad," they had in them fine qualities that could not save them from their own lack of discipline and self-restraint.

Nearly all of the men named, Sam Bass and Joel Collins, Hardin and his relatives, Bill Longley, the Taylors, the Horrells, the Suttons, the Higgins family and their friends, went up the trail at one time or another on the long drives with the longhorns to Northern markets. In spite of which fact, it cannot be stressed too strongly that the great majority of the men who followed the dust of the herds on the long trek from Texas were quiet and peaceful citizens who drew the line at lawlessness even though the fire of youth ran in their veins.

6

Neither the longhorn nor the mustang was an original product of Texas. When Columbus rediscovered America there were in this continent no horses and no cattle. The nearest approach to the latter was the bison, the "humpbacked ox," as the Spaniard called it.

The Cavalier of Spain clanks picturesquely across the pages of the history of our Southwest with magnificent but futile gesture. The desert was no country for him. It calls for a never-ending patience, and this virtue was not his. It is an ironic commentary on the lack of human foresight that Coronado's vision of a recrudescent Spain was of far less importance to posterity than the fact that he was a negligent herdsman.

Sailing from Cuba, Cortez landed near Vera Cruz in 1515. He brought with him horses, sixteen of them, and in his report we find the name, color, sex, and character of each animal. Whether he had cattle with him is not sure. There is no record of any in that region until 1521, when Gregorio Villalobos, sent to New Spain as governor general, landed troops and supplies near Vera Cruz. The written history of the expedition shows that he brought a number of calves [oviese ganado] from San Domingo, "he being the first to bring them to New Spain." Undoubtedly these calves were the descendants of cattle left on that island by earlier explorers.

The live stock landed in Mexico prospered amazingly, since the grassy plains adjacent to the coast furnished an almost unlimited range in a mild, even climate.

In 1555, Robert Tomson, an Englishman who had been trading with the Spaniards for many years, in his letters home tells of the live stock in New Spain. This was only thirty-four years after the importation of cattle into the country.

There is in New Spain [he writes] a marvelous increase of cattell which dayly do increase and they are of greater growth than ours. You may have a great steer that hath a hundred weight of tallow for 16 shillings and some one man hath 20,000 head of cattell of his own. They have great increase of sheep in like manner. They have much woole and as goode as the woole in Spain. They have many horses, mares, and mules which the Spaniards brought thither. They have as goode jennets as any are in Spain, better and cheaper than they be in Spain.

On February 23, 1540, when Coronado, the Spanish captain general, left the little town of Compostello, on the west coast of Mexico, on his celebrated expedition to the northeast, he took with him large numbers of live stock. All the historians of this expedition agree closely as to the numbers of horses and mules taken along. Coronado had with him "about 300 horses for his soldiers, more than 1000 horses and mules for pack animals," and according to Winship's translation of Castenada's *Narrative*—"large droves of *ganado mayor* [big stock—cattle] and *y ganado menor* [little stock—sheep and hogs]."

The Spaniards rode mares, stallions, and geldings, for they were colonizers as well as explorers, and breeding stock was a prime necessity for their purpose. They brought their animals from Spain, of course, and it is doubtful if their horses were other than the somewhat common stock with which the Spaniards were satisfied.

They were constantly losing horses. When turned out at night to graze on the prairies the animals either became merged with the immense herds of buffalo and were lost, or because of hard use were worn out and had to be abandoned and left behind. From these "escapes" came the vast numbers of wild horses, mustangs, that were found on the Northern plains by Lewis and Clarke in 1804 and by Captain Pike's party while crossing Kansas in 1806–1807.

The earliest Texas pioneer found wild horses, mustangs, running from eastern Texas to the Staked Plains and as far north as Colorado. From these herds of mustangs the pioneers not only got their cow ponies, but captured enough to ship droves into Arkansas and Louisiana.

From Mexico the line of Spanish settlements swept forward fan-shaped north along the Pacific coast, where were founded many Franciscan missions, northeast up along the Rio Grande into what is now New Mexico and Arizona, and east along the Gulf coast into the rich coastal plains of Texas. From these various colonies of the Spanish the live-stock industry of the Southwest spread gradually until it merged with that moving westward from the eastern coast of this country. The mating of the herds of the East and of the South marked the conquest by the adventurous pioneer stockman of the Great American Desert.

The first authentic statement as to live stock brought by the English is found in a letter written from Virginia by M. G. Aucher, dated August 31, 1609, describing his voyage to the colony:

On May 15, 1609, seven sail left [England]. Arrived Plymouth 20th day. We took into the *Blessing*, being the ship wherein I went, 6 mares and 2 horses.

Under date of July 1, 1630, Winthrop in his Journal makes the following statement:

The *Mayflower* and the *Whale* arrived safe in Charleston harbor. Their passengers were all in health, but most of their cattle were dead; whereof a mare and a horse of mine. Some "stone" horses [stallions] came over in good plight.

Owing to the nature of the grasses and herbage, as well as the character of the country itself, the business of grazing live stock under open range conditions was much less extensive east of the Mississippi River than in the West. Climatic conditions in the Eastern part of the continent made it nearly impossible to utilize the forage and grasses all the year round. As a rule they had to be harvested, cured, and stored for winter use.

As the lower and more open lands along the Atlantic seaboard came under the plow the cattle herds were forced farther and farther back until, following the line of least resistance, they took the Western course, crossed the Alleghanies, and followed closely the fringe of frontier settlements to the Missouri where they met the stock from the South.

There is no question, however, but that the wild horses of our Western plains, so plentiful when the first explorers from the East entered that region, were escapes from the mounts of the early Spanish *conquistadores* under Coronado. Captain Zebulon Pike, who in 1806 marched up the Arkansas River, across what is now portions of Oklahoma, Kansas, and Colorado, seeking a water route due west from

St. Louis to the base of the Rocky Mountains, mentions in his diary the great herds of wild horses he found everywhere on the open prairies.

From some point on the Arkansas River in the vicinity of Dodge City, Kansas, he writes:

Sunday, November 1st, 1806—Encamped in the evening on an island. Upon using my glass to view the adjacent country, I observed on the prairie a herd of horses. Dr. Robinson and Baroney accompanied me to go and examine them; when within about quarter of a mile, they discovered us, and immediately approached, making the earth tremble under them; they brought to my recollection a charge of cavalry. They stopped and gave us an opportunity to view them. Amongst them were some very beautiful bays, blacks, and greys, and indeed all colors. We fired at a black horse with an idea of creasing him, but did not succeed; they flourished around and returned to view us.

Describing these horses later in his military report, Pike says:

Wild horses . . . go in such large gangs that it is requisite to keep an advanced guard of horsemen in order to frighten them away; for should they be suffered to come near your horses and mules which you drive with you, by their snorting and neighing, etc., they alarm them and are frequently joined by them and taken off notwithstanding all the exertions of the dragoons to prevent them.

It was from these wild bands, of course, that the Western Indians obtained their first horses, an accession which turned them from footmen to horsemen. The horse undoubtedly caused as tremendous a change in their whole mode of life as did the invention of the steam locomotive in that of the present civilization.

In the early '70's, when the pioneer stockmen began to push out into the prairies of western Kansas and the plains region, many of them began the raising of well bred horses

WILD HORSES ON A WESTERN RANGE

The author spent several hours in hiding waiting for this band to come within camera range. Note the effect of the camera "click" on their ears.

A "TRAP CORRAL"

for capturing wild horses or cattle. Inside looking out. The gate opened easily inward and closed behind so the animal could not escape.

A MUSTANG HOG-TIED AND BEING BRANDED

"I KIN RIDE 'EM IN THE SLICK—I TOLD THAT
DAD-BLAMED BOSS"

along with their herds of cattle. They shared the ranges with the mustangs, and naturally some of the tame horses joined wild bands and were lost. Horse raising was profitable, for the West of those days was wholly dependent on horseflesh for carrying on business of nearly every kind.

"Mustanging," like buffalo hunting, was a pursuit fascinating to the sportsman. In Texas it became a business about the time the cattle trails opened up, as it did later in the plains to the north. There was, however, a distinction. The masterless horses ranging in Texas were mustangs, those caught later in Colorado, Nevada, and various other states were not true mustangs but descendants of escapes from wagon trains, from ranches, and from army posts in the Indian country.

The mustang was a hardy little animal, compact, wiry, and graceful. He adapted himself surprisingly to the country and had a remarkable knack of roughing through a hard winter and coming out fit and in fair flesh. The color varied. Some bands would be almost entirely brown, others black, buckskin, laybank, or even cream. A dark stripe down the back from shoulder to tail was not unusual.

The Texan horse hunters captured the mustangs exactly as the Spaniards did in the time of Zebulon Pike, by driving them into inclosures. The corral had to be very strong and high, for the frightened animals milled furiously striking one another down in their terror and dashing blindly against the fence. Many broke their necks or wore themselves out and died. After the fear and panic had subsided, the animals judged good enough were roped, thrown, hobbled, and broken to the saddle.

There were two ways of getting the mustangs into the corral. One was by rounding up a bunch and driving the animals into projecting wings built from the pen for some distance out upon the prairie. But the professional hunter usually employed a method he called "walking 'em down." This required three or four men who placed themselves at intervals eight or ten miles apart, each having camp supplies and an extra mount. Started by the first rider, the mustangs fled in a burst of speed. The rider cantered easily after them until they reached the second man, who then took up the chase while the first rested. The third hunter relieved the second in turn. For days this procedure was followed. The mustangs were never permitted to stop for food or drink. At last fatigue conquered them. They were unable to spurt into a gallop when the riders approached. It became easier to handle them. Exhausted and dispirited, the mustangs were forced into the chute and from it into the corral.

Sometimes the hunter watched the watering places on bright moonlight nights. And when the horses had drunk their fill it was great sport to follow the band and try to rope one or two selected animals as they made their way up the trail, fairly waterlogged. With this handicap a good lively saddle horse had rather the best of the chase, and occasionally the pursuer was able to lie alongside of a horse after a five- or six-mile run and rope him. If the rider succeeded in hogtying the captive, he sometimes waited until morning and returned at daybreak with a burro. By means of a leather strap, he tied the two animals together, neck to neck. Twelve hours later the horse had given up, defeated by the stubborn donkey.

Thousands of these wild horses were captured, tamed, and either sold by the hunters into the adjoining states of Louisiana and Arkansas or to neighboring ranchmen who used them for cowponies. The number of them ranging the plains cannot be estimated. As late as the early '80's many bands ran in west Texas, the Indian Territory, and Kansas.

JANUARY, 1866. Moving day for Texas. She was "busting" north, breaking barriers that isolated her from the Union she had joined, left, and into which she had now been coerced. Cut off by hundreds of miles inhabited only by buffalo, and by Choctaws, Chickasaws, Kiowas, and Comanches, western Texas was a wilderness surrounded by other wildernesses. She had no railroads, few roads of any kind. She was still in effect a Lone Star State.

But now she was on her travels. It was go north or go broke. There was no question of choice. The trail herds had to point northward as inevitably as the overflowing waters of a great lake have to find a channel of escape. They were driven by irresistible pressure along the roads of empire that led to a vast stretch of country out of which a dozen states have been carved.

The Texan was not starting on the long trek north with any assurance of success, but because of the pressure of economic conditions. He had to find an outlet for his increasing herds. South of him lay the Gulf and poverty-stricken Mexico. To the east stretched prostrate Louisiana. Westward lay the Indian plains, untenanted by whites. Remained only the country north of 36. It was known that there was a scarcity of cattle in that section and plenty of money to pay. Between Texas and the promised land waited danger and hardship in plenty, possibly complete disaster, but at the trail's end, if it could be reached, there must be buyers.

So Cattleland buzzed with activity. By the middle of February hundreds of "brushpoppers" were combing the thickets for longhorns. Out of the chaparral were being hounded and dragged all the cow "critters" that could be found, mossy-horned steers old enough to vote and untamed as antelope, spring calves trotting at the heels of their wild-eyed mothers, bulls savage with the insensate fury of fear. Into the chutes of corrals they were forced, and as the red-hot iron of the road brand sizzled on their flesh the bawling of cattle and the smell of burnt hair filled the air.

Dust, noise, the shouts of men, the clatter of horns and hocks, rose incessantly as the work of making up the trail herd moved forward. The bulls were cut out, but everything else went: dogies, yearlings, cows heavy with calf, steers hoary with the frost of years. It was the habit of the drivers in the earliest days of the trail herds to take all stock turned in by the cow hunters. What the market demanded at this time, it was soon to develop, was choice four-year-old beef and up, but even after he discovered this the trail boss for years continued to take whatever was brought in. The Texan was easy-going, and it was felt to be unneighborly to cut the bunches rounded up. Since the cowman wanted to get rid of all his surplus odds and ends, the first trail herds were generally made up of nondescript stuff.

In some cases three or four owners threw their cattle together to make a trail herd, in others drivers bought from the local stockmen, often taking the longhorns without cash but with promises to pay after the herd had been disposed of at whatever point a market was found.

Property rights in stock were rather casual, since cows,

as all cattle were called regardless of age or sex, were an investment which traveled on the hoof unwatched and unguarded, subject to loss by disease, drought, flood, Indian raids, and the cupidity of the rustler. By the simple process of rebranding, one's drifting capital or the dividend therefrom might any day change ownership. A waddy ran his brand on a cow, and it became his. It did not at first matter much, from a monetary point of view. The price of a calf was a plug of tobacco.

The early ethics of the range had peculiar angles. A good many cattlemen did not like the taste of their own beef but much preferred that of another brand. Only the choice parts of the butchered animal were eaten. The heat and the flies spoiled the rest so quickly that it was thrown away. This custom of killing in the camp for food stock belonging to another outfit was considered a good joke by the cowboys. When Shanghai Pierce, a well known driver, rode into an alien camp one day and found the cook skinning a calf with the D brand, which chanced to be his, he looked reproachfully at the *caporal* and mentioned that a day was coming when each outfit would have to eat its own beef. All the satisfaction he got was an assurance that it was good meat and a warm invitation to sit down at the tail of the chuck wagon and eat. Shanghai made no undue point of his prophecy and sat down to share his own steak so generously offered.

The first trail herds were likely to include a good many cows not paid for. Without permission of the owners the drivers put the road brand on these, checked them in a notebook, and after the herd had been marketed turned over the proceeds to the owners, less a fair price for the drive. But shortly after the drives began, in 1866, the Texas legislature passed a law making it a misdemeanor punishable by fine or imprisonment to take up the trail cattle in the brand of another man without a bill of sale for them. Too many drivers had bad memories and forgot to account for the strays. By this law a driver had to prove ownership. It was not sufficient for him to make a memorandum and settle later, if and when convenient. A few years after this the driver was required to burn a road brand back of the left shoulder. At the 1866 session of the legislature it was also written on the statute books that one could not without penalty either blot a brand or put on a maverick a brand not legally recorded. These enactments were intended to buttress the property rights of a cattleman in the unmarked stock running on his accustomed range. Already the big cowman was trying to protect himself against the nester and the rustler, though that is not the way the small man usually put it.

Later an association of cattlemen was formed and inspectors employed to check up northbound herds at the Red River crossing and other strategic points on the drive. Associations of this nature and the inspectors are in operation to-day.

Early in March, 1866, the first herds were moving up the trail from southern Texas. These might be put up near Corpus Christi or Lockhart or even as far north as Lampasas. Nearly all of them headed northward. It is estimated that in the summer of 1866 herds totaling 270,000 cattle took the road for a market and crossed the Red River. Since many of these were sold to feeders in various states it is difficult to check accurately the figures.

2

According to Colonel Charles Goodnight, who ought to have known, the first cattleman to drive a trail herd north from Texas was Oliver Loving, Sr. More than ninety-three years old at the time of his death, December 13, 1929, Colonel Goodnight was the most famous cattleman produced by the Panhandle. He went into the stock business as early as 1856 in Palo Pinto County with a herd he bought on the Brazos.

One year after that time Oliver Loving trailed a herd

through "the Nation," eastern Kansas, and northwestern Missouri, to Quincy, Illinois, selling it to local farmers there. The next season he took another to Pueblo, Colorado, wintering the herd in the Arkansas Valley. Later he joined forces with Goodnight. Taking an outfit of sixteen men, the two trailed by way of Fort Belknap to Fort Sumner, New Mexico. This was soon known as the Goodnight Trail and was eventually lengthened to extend by way of Raton Pass to Trinidad, Pueblo, Denver, and Cheyenne. It is worth noting that the first chuck wagon ever used was taken on this trip by Goodnight. He had had it built of *bois d'arc*, and it took ten yoke of oxen to haul it over the rough plains. The Osage orange tree was employed by the Indians to make bows and war clubs. Therefore the early French explorers called it *bois d'arc* [bow wood]. The wood is hard, strong, and flexible, though of small dimension. The settlers used it for wagon wheels and gears and other purposes.

The beef of this herd was sold at eight cents a pound to the government to feed the Apaches on the reservation. The culls Loving took to Colorado, through Raton Pass, where he was forced to pay the old scout Dick Wootten ten cents a head to use the trail across the mountains.

Meanwhile Goodnight hurried back to Texas in order to rush another herd through the same season. The gold paid them was loaded on pack mules, and six thousand dollars of it was almost lost in a stampede of the cavvy. The second herd was taken up the Pecos by Goodnight in a little over a month. This time he brought the money back in a wagon. He had been paid in silver, a good deal of the coin in dimes and quarters. The wagon announced its coming like a brass band.

In the spring of '67 Loving and Goodnight again took the trail with two herds. With them went W. J. (Bill) Wilson, who had brought a bunch of cows up from the Clear Fork of the Brazos. From the first the fates had marked the expedition for disaster. The partners went with the lead herd. On the Clear Fork, near Camp Cooper, the Indians attacked the outfit. Goodnight barely escaped with his life. One of the herders, Long Joe Loving, had an arrow driven through his neck. Goodnight pulled it out with a pair of nippers. Three hundred cattle were lost in the stampede which followed. The second herd reached the Pecos minus a thousand cattle taken by the Comanches and driven away by them.

On the Pecos, a hundred miles above Horsehead Crossing, the partners separated late in June. It was necessary for one of them to reach Fort Sumner before the beef contracts for feeding the Indians were awarded in July. Loving rode ahead, accompanied by Bill Wilson, a one-armed man, cool and of the most determined courage. It was a dangerous trip for two men to take alone through the Comanche country, but the risks could be minimized by traveling only at night. Repeatedly Goodnight impressed this upon his friends.

But Loving was rash, a man not given to caution or fear. He did not like night travel and at the end of two days, having seen no Indians, decided to get on as rapidly as possible in the daytime. The travelers were sighted by a big bunch of Comanches on a plain between the Pecos and the Blue rivers. The cowmen raced for the Pecos and reached it. There was a high bluff, below which were sand dunes and brakes covered by high Spanish cane. Still mounted, the hunted men clambered down to the shelter of the bank below. The horses were shot almost at once, but the Indians could not easily get at the men, though they crept forward through a bunch of polecat brush. Wilson estimated that there must have been five or six hundred of the enemy.

Loving was wounded twice, once desperately. He was persuaded that he could not live. The Comanches charged and were driven back. Wilson got his friend down to the river and concealed him in a clump of smartweeds. The Indians did not know exactly where they were. One brave crept very close to them and was driven back by a big rattlesnake that coiled in front of him.

Night fell. Wilson brought water in his boot to his fevered companion. The moon rose, went down again. The trapped men could hear the Indians all around them.

In whispers they decided that the only chance was for Wilson to go for help. The one-armed man exchanged weapons with Loving because the Henry rifle of the latter had metallic cartridges that were waterproof and it was necessary for Wilson to swim the river. All the pistols and the other rifle were left with the wounded man.

The stories of the ensuing experiences of these two men are almost without parallel in Indian warfare. Wilson crept to the river, which was so sandy that swimming was difficult. He had to discard his shoes and his coat. It was impossible to keep afloat while hampered by the rifle. He buried it. A hundred yards down the river, on a sand bar, an Indian sentinel was posted. The intrepid Wilson pulled some smartweed and floated down the river underneath it, so close to the Comanche that discovery seemed almost inevitable. He drifted past the guard and crawled out of the river. Barefooted, unarmed, half-clad, the frontiersman traveled three days through the cactus country toward the herd. He had nearly a hundred miles to go. He trudged on, feet swollen, starved, exhausted. All through the last night the wolves followed him howling and snarling. More dead than alive, at last he caught sight of his brother and Goodnight pointing the herd.

Goodnight started at once to the rescue of Loving, though none of the party believed he was still alive. They reached the scene of the battle, but the wounded man was not to be found. Nearly two weeks later the driver learned from Jim Burleson, a Texas cowman, that Loving was at Fort Sumner. He had reached the trail, lived for seven days without food, and been picked up by Mexicans. Loving was out of bed and on his feet when Wilson and Goodnight reached him. Unfortunately blood poisoning from his wounds set in, and he died in a few days. His body was taken back to Weatherford, Texas, by his friend and buried there. Goodnight turned over to the Loving family $40,000, the amount due them from the partnership which had been dissolved by death.

Goodnight changed his route and drove through to Trinidad, Colorado. He sold the herd to John W. Iliff, one of the most energetic cattlemen the West has ever known. Even before the Civil War Iliff, ranging up and down the South Platte for a hundred miles with Julesburg as a center, had large herds that supplied the Denver mining district with beef. These steadily increased until he became known as the cattle king of Colorado. The herd of longhorns bought from Goodnight was driven by him next spring to Cheyenne.

Colonel Goodnight continued to drive for several years. When he had accumulated more than seventy thousand dollars he quit driving and went to ranging stock on his own account, as did many shrewd Texans who realized that the opening of immense ranges of free grass would give great opportunities to those who understood the stock business. Near the town of Pueblo, Colorado, he bought a large piece of land and another ranch near Trinidad. On these properties he prospered until caught short in the panic of 1873. He had increased his holdings on credit, and the depreciation in prices, taken in conjunction with the necessity for the banks holding his paper to liquidate in self-protection, swept away almost his entire assets. With a herd of 1,800 cattle he located in Paloduro Cañon: the first settler in the Panhandle of Texas. Within three years a quarter of a million cattle ranged over the country where only the buffalo had been.

3

While Loving and his partner were breaking out of Texas by way of the Goodnight Trail hundreds of columns of moving dust in the clear air signified that herds were doing the same thing farther east. The push for a market was experimental, and it was encumbered by difficulties which in some cases were disastrous.

Already it was being told that there was buffalo grass to the north that would supply feed all the way. There were rumors to the effect that these territories, for a thousand miles in each direction, were natural cow country. Oxen had been left to die by freight outfits at the end of summer, thin and worn out from poor feed and overwork, and had been found in the spring sleek and fat. These millions of untrodden, unknown acres could never be farmed, but cows could run on the rich grasses as on a paradise. So the story began to circulate in Texas.

Later it must have seemed to the harassed driver that these were fairy tales, as elusive as mirages beckoning the parched traveler to destruction. Apparently every man's hand, as well as that of the Lord, was against him. The drive north was hazardous beyond expectation.

Many outfits crossed the Red at the Rocks Bluff ford, others at Colbert's Ferry. Most of the Texans moved up the Kiamichi Valley into the Choctaw Nation. Here their troubles began. The Choctaws were a civilized tribe and had herds of their own. They objected to this swarm of longhorns which invaded their country like locusts, ate up the feed, and, mingling with their strays, enticed them to join the army moving northward. They demanded a toll fee of ten cents a head and were legally entitled to it. They insisted that the Texas cattle keep to a specific well defined trail and not wander all over the country because the feed was better. They claimed the right to cut the herd in search of any of their own cattle that might have joined the trail herd.

The drivers met this annoyance in various ways. Some paid the tax, some compromised by giving the Indians a few cattle, some slipped past unnoticed, a few bluffed through by a show of armed resistance. To escape another tax certain to be imposed by the Cherokee Nation the herds turned east to Fort Smith into Arkansas and moved along its western line through the Ozarks. There were a good many white outlaws in the Nations, and some herds lost cattle through stampedes instigated by them.

From Arkansas the herds either pushed west to Baxter Springs, Kansas, or north into southwestern Missouri. In either case the driver was faced with more trouble. Bands of marauders composed largely of ex-guerrillas and jay-hawkers of war days, infested the country. The Texas cattlemen were apparently sent by a kind providence for them to devour. They levied unconscionable tribute upon the driver. If the trail boss objected he was bullied, his hair pulled, his face slapped, and his cattle stampeded. Some were tied to trees and whipped. Others were killed.

J. M. Daugherty was one of the drivers who in '66 took a herd from Denton County, crossed the Red, and headed for Sedalia, Missouri. He was then a lad of about twenty, fearless and resourceful in emergency. Several herds were being held at Baxter Springs on account of outrages committed by Kansas ruffians. A driver had been killed, his cattle stolen, and his cowboys run off. There is no doubt that the Kansas grangers, both now and later, were really afraid of the Spanish fever imported by Texas cattle, but the men who used this fear as a pretext to rob the drivers were generally ruffians who owned no cattle themselves. In some cases, after stampeding the herd, they would round up the cows and with their tongues in their cheeks return them to the owners, charging a big fee for their services.

Daugherty rode up the trail to spy out the land. At Fort Scott he met a buyer named Ben Keyes and made a bargain to deliver the herd there. He returned to his outfit and moved north. It was a short drive of about a week, but before he reached his journey's end a bunch of fifteen or twenty outlaws jumped him. John Dobbins was on the point. He tried to draw his six-shooter and was killed by the jayhawkers. One of the ruffians rode into the herd waving a blanket. Instantly there was a stampede. The cowboys followed the cattle to check the run. Daugherty was captured and tried by the raiders for driving cattle into the country. The excuse as usual was that the ticks would infect the local cattle with Spanish fever. The lad was found guilty. An argument started as to whether he should be hanged. One of the big Kansans said flatly that there would be no hanging. He was a man dangerous with a gun, and he had his way. McCoy says that Daugherty was tied to a tree and whipped with hickory saplings till his back was ridged with wheals. In his own story, recorded in *The Trail Drivers of Texas*, Daugherty does not mention this. He was freed and rejoined his outfit. The dead cowpuncher was buried and such part of the herd as had been retrieved taken back to the line. But Daugherty was too game to quit. He got a guide and managed to slip the herd through to Fort Scott, driving by night and "holing up" by day.

Meanwhile, at Baxter Springs new herds were continually arriving. From a hill they could be seen approaching, serpentine lines strung out for a mile or more and led by gaunt longhorns sniffing the breeze as they set the pace. Drove after drove came in and found a bedground around which they grazed, held by the vaqueros while the bosses consulted as to what was best to do. For months the cattle jammed here.

Baxter Springs was the first of the trail towns. Each one, as it rose to its short day of prosperity, put in a bid for notoriety as "the worst town on earth." Baxter Springs was as wild as any of them, especially after the railroad reached there. The Indian Territory was the habitat of as desperate a class of men as one was likely to meet, and many of them hung up their hats at the Springs to exploit the cowboys. Whisky, gambling, loose women, and gunmen could be found in plenty. It was here that a few years earlier the guerrilla Quantrell had ambushed and massacred General Blunt's supply train.

Some of the trail bosses decided to push east into Arkansas, head for the Ozarks, and strike the line of the Missouri Pacific at Sedalia. This route was a rough and rocky one to travel. In the wooded hills of the Ozarks the cattle were very hard to handle. Feed was so scarce that many animals were lost. Those that survived reached the St. Louis market thin, gaunt, and half-starved. They were in no condition to sell, and they brought a low price.

Other drivers turned west from Baxter Springs, drove the herds along the Kansas line for two hundred miles, headed northwest through that state, and then east toward St. Joseph. From here they were shipped to Chicago. Unfortunately there was a prejudice against the meat of Texas longhorns, and the first arrivals at the stock-yards scarcely paid freight expenses. The drivers who sold their stock as feeders to farmers in Kansas, Missouri, and Iowa did better. They received in some cases more than thirty dollars a head. This amazing price was the one bright spot in the year's record. It proved to the Texan that if he could surmount the difficulties of transportation he could find a good market. He knew too that the feasible road lay somewhere west of Baxter Springs, where there was buffalo grass for feed and the Five Civilized Tribes could not impose a tax.

Some of the herds were tied up at Baxter Springs during the winter, but even this early others traveled an amazing distance. It is on record that Nels Story, with a bunch of six hundred Texas longhorns, crossed Wyoming by the old Bozeman Trail in 1866, but it is not likely that any other herd did so for some time. Possibly this one was composed of animals bought by Iliff at an earlier date and moved at this time from Colorado.

4

The winter of '66–'67 was not a cheerful one for the Lone Star State stockmen. The North had not welcomed

the inroad of Southern cattle. For the time at least it
had turned thumbs down on the longhorn as a beef proposition. "Texas was still lousy with cows," as one de-
spondent owner put it. The glut had not been relieved, nor
had the attempt to reach a profitable market been success-
ful except in isolated cases. Unexpected trail difficulties
had developed, and none of them had been satisfactorily
solved. Moreover, there were rumors of Osage Indian
troubles. There was a general disposition among the
Texas cowmen to sit back and let the other fellow do the
pioneer work. As a result only thirty-five thousand cattle
went up from Texas in 1867, by far the lowest number
driven in any of the twenty years of open trail.

What was needed to facilitate the trade was a point
where buyer and seller could get together, one that could
be reached by the drover without the harassing attentions
of disturbed Indians and greedy outlaws, and one from
which the purchaser could ship to the market where he
expected to dispose of the longhorns. Joseph G. McCoy,
an Illinois stock dealer, saw the need and took action to
meet it.

He scouted over the ground and selected Abilene,
Kansas, a desolate village on the Kansas Pacific (then
building into the prairie country), one hundred sixty miles
west of Kansas City, as the best site available. Abilene
was then only "a wide place in the road." It had a general
store of sorts, a saloon, some dugouts, and a frame shack
or two. But the country around it was richly grassed.
There was plenty of water. As yet the advancing tide of
land seekers had not reached so far, though the covered
wagons of the first grangers were beginning to appear.
Only a few fences, east of the town, interrupted the vast
expanse of open range.

McCoy made arrangements with the railroad for shipping any cattle that might reach Abilene, though the officials of the Kansas Pacific showed considerable incredu-
lity. They had no vision of the tremendous volume of trade

that would come to the transcontinental railroads from the drives of Texas cattle. From Hannibal, Missouri, McCoy brought in pine lumber to build a chute and shipping yards that would hold three thousand cattle. He began the construction of a hotel that later became known as the Drovers' Cottage and, under the management of Mrs. Lou Gore, was famous all over the Southwest.

In the spring a reliable man was sent out to meet the herds and let the trail bosses know that Abilene was on the map and that buyers would be waiting there ready to do business with the Texans. The latter were suspicious, but even a promise was better than nothing. They listened, consulted together, and deflected the herd toward Abilene.

The year 1867 was one of great hardship for those who went up the trail. Cholera was sweeping the West. A good many of the cowboys on the drives caught it and some died. The Osage tribe was unruly and ran off a great many cattle, as it continued to do for several years. (As late as 1872 the Redus herd lost more than a hundred killed by these Indians.) The rivers were swollen bank full. There were heavy rains, accompanied by electric storms, a condition which always induced stampedes. Because of the rains the grass was rank and spoony, making poor feed. The cattle reached the trail's end in bad condition, carrying very little tallow.

The first herd that reached Abilene was driven by a man named Thompson as far as the Indian Nation and there sold to a firm of buyers, Smith, McCord & Chandler, but a herd owned by Californians, Wheeler, Wilson & Hicks, crossed the Arkansas at an earlier date. This had been held at a point thirty miles from Abilene to take on flesh.

The grangers had been pushing westward, and a good many of them had taken up land to the east of the town. Some opposition to the trail herds developed among these settlers, principally on account of the Spanish fever. They were afraid their oxen and the few cows they owned might catch it from the longhorns. A meeting was called by them to discuss the matter. The Texans used finesse. All of them in town were present. They moved to and fro among the farmers, buying eggs, chickens, and vegetables. The entire surplus of the neighborhood was contracted for on the spot at high prices. This took the wind out of the sails of the protestors. McCoy quotes the leader of them as saying, "If I can make any money out of the Texas trade I'm not afraid of Texas fever, but if I can't I'm damned afraid of it."

Generally speaking, the interests of the farmers were in conflict with those of the trail men. In these early days the grangers were poverty stricken. Few of them could build fences. They defined the limit of their land by a furrow turned with a plow. Within this they raised patches of corn and vegetables. Though opposed to the march of the great hordes of cattle sweeping north, they could at first offer little effective resistance. Sometimes they emerged from their dugouts, shotgun in hand, and warned the boss to deflect his longhorns. In this the settlers were within their rights. In Nebraska, for example, the legislature had passed a herd law, but the cowboys often ignored it and let the stock drift upon the small acreage of corn planted by the farmer. More than one sturdy pioneer was shot down for defending his property against the invader.

On September 5, 1867, the first shipment of twenty cars of cattle rolled out of Abilene on the Kansas Pacific for Chicago. The wheels of almost one thousand cars loaded with longhorns clicked out of the little trail town that year. The Texas dogie was beginning to come into its own.

Not all of the herds went to Chicago. As has been already mentioned Goodnight was driving into New Mexico and Colorado. H. D. Hunter took twelve hundred steers to Omaha on a government contract.

Those who had contracts to deliver were lucky. There had been a short corn crop in the Middle West, so that cattle were not in demand as feeders. With the slump in the market prices fell off.

Other causes tended to make the results of 1867 unsatisfactory. The Kansas and the Missouri legislatures passed quarantine regulations which prohibited the bringing of Texas cattle into those states during the summer and fall. The danger of Spanish fever was a very real one, especially during the summer months. The longhorns were immune, but they carried with them a tick that dropped off and infected local cattle which used the same feed and bed ground.

Abilene circularized the state of Texas during the winter. The railroad began to see the opportunity for building up a good business and arranged with McCoy and other live wires to go down into Texas early in 1868 and boost for Abilene and its market. Men were also sent to mark the trail and to post the stream crossings and watering places as a help to the drivers. David M. Sutherland says that in 1868 he was employed by the Kansas Pacific to go down the trail to meet herds coming north and steer them to the town. He says that one short-cut was laid out which saved the herds several days' travel. This cut-off he caused to be marked with plow furrows so that it could be followed easily. The railroad also took pains to have plenty of buyers on hand to purchase and ship the cattle as they arrived.

In the spring drovers were down in Texas arranging to have herds put up for the trail. The lessons of the past two years had been severe. Only seventy-five thousand cattle went up the trail in 1868, and most of these appeared to be carriers of disaster. The Spanish fever had gained momentum. It swept through the shorthorns of Illinois, Iowa, and other states, with the result that the market for longhorns was knocked galley west. There was a great deal of excitement, and many regulations were made to protect local stock against the incursions of the rangy brute from the South. One could not give away a

Texas steer to the feeders, far less sell one. The year 1868 closed in more gloom to the longhorn grower than either of the previous ones.

But neither cholera nor Spanish fever, no trail difficulties, no Indian attacks, no loss of riders or cattle, no prohibitory laws, could stop the northern march of the longhorn. They were trudging up one of the great roads of empire, though the drivers themselves did not know it. The territories were beginning to fill up with land seekers, and they had to have cattle, millions of them, to stock their ranges. The American workingman demanded cheap meat. Virginia City and Deadwood and other booming mining camps needed it at any price. The Indians herded on the reservations by the government, debarred from living on the vanishing buffalo, had to be fed with a supply that could be obtained only from the Lone Star State.

The Texas cattle trade, with its thousands of ramifications destined to affect every hamlet in the West, to create out of the wilderness a dozen great states, was born of economic necessity and not chance.

5

In the putting up of a trail herd Cattleland was at its busiest. If the gather began about the middle of February it was likely to be the end of the first week in March before the stock was out of the thicket, cut, road branded, and inspected. The last days before the drive started were, if possible, more hectic than those when the four-year-olds were being harried out of the prickly pear.

Heat and dust. . . . Dust and heat. . . . Perspiration pouring down the grimy faces of vaqueros, sweat dried on the roan flanks of mustangs. . . . Bawling of uneasy cows, blatting of frightened calves dragged out of the herd to the fire. . . . A flanker in striped trousers "going down the rope," and throwing the flitter-ear by an upward and outward fling combined with a pressure of the knees against the side. . . . The sizzle of the red-hot iron on the hide of a maverick, stretched taut. . . . Shouts of lank brown youths on the swing after bolting dogies. . . . Raucous curse and gay banter. . . . Hi-yi-yippi-yi. . . . Rattle of horns in a milling herd. . . . Rounding up of the remuda, breaking of outlaw mustangs, choosing of mounts, all geldings, solid colors preferred, combing of burrs out of tangled manes and forelocks. . . . Overhauling of saddle and bridle, mending of broken wagons. . . . Molding of bullets, cleaning of guns. . . . Checking up of supplies—cheap coffee, salt sidemeat, meal, flour, saleratus, sorghum.

From long before daylight until deep into the night all hands on the jump. . . . Through the starlit hours of darkness riders circling the sleeping herd and singing lullabies, gospel hymns, or ribald range songs. . . . "Hold the fort, for I am coming," the apologia of one herder lifting into the velvety night, and

> I'm wild and woolly and full of fleas,
> Never been curried above the knees,
> I'm an ole she-wolf from Bitter Creek,
> An' it's my main night to h-o-w-l—

the careless response of the other.

Youth in the saddle. . . . A world in the making. . . . The first gray dawn of a new West the summons of which was to ring out like a bugle call to the imagination of millions who longed to ride away from humdrum reality into a sunlit world of romance. . . . The challenge of the Anglo-Saxon to the untrodden wilderness.

No better rider than the cowboy ever lived. He rode close to the saddle, as Westerners do to this day, and his seat was easy, lithe, and graceful. He disdained the "postage-stamp" saddles of the East, and would have none but the kind experience had developed as the best for the plains. It was as much a part of his equipment as the flannel shirt, leather chaps, and bandanna kerchief tied around his neck. These articles of dress fitted loosely, but not his high-heeled boots. The boots must be tight and so high of heel that the owner toddled when he walked.

The cowboy was usually soft spoken and reserved of manner when with a stranger. He was polite and courteous but did not encourage familiarity.

In their book *On a Mexican Mustang through Texas,* Sweet and Knox give a humorous impression of the rough-rider of the plains.

The cowboy is a man attached to a gigantic pair of spurs. He inhabits the plains of Texas, and is successfully raised as far north as the thirtieth degree of latitude. He is in season the year round, and is generally found on the back of a small mustang pony. . . . This fact has given rise to a widely diffused belief that the cowboy cannot walk. . . . Some scientists, however, dispute this, as several specimens have been seen—under the influence of excitement and while suffering from intense thirst— to detach themselves from their mustangs and disappear into business houses where their wants were attended to by a man wearing a diamond breastpin and a white apron.

There was this much of truth to the report that the cowpuncher was a modern centaur. He lived in the saddle. He detested walking, even for a very short distance, partly because his boots were not made for that purpose.

Even if he had to go two or three hundred yards, he preferred to catch and saddle a bronco rather than to furnish the motive power himself.

At last the herd moved. The vaqueros made a point, shook the packed mass to a loose formation, strung it out to a long snaky line stretching for miles. The moss-head longhorns that were self-appointed leaders moved to the front and stayed there till the trail's end was reached. Riders at the point guided the advance. Behind them came the men on the swing. At intervals of every two or three hundred yards others guarded the flanks. Youngsters followed the drag or took charge of the remuda. The cook's long whip snaked out, and the bull team with the chuck wagon lurched forward. The Lazy S (⌒) or the L F D or the Pitchfork (Ψ) was on its way. It was headed north, exact destination unknown, but nothing could keep it from that distant cow town, whether it might be Abilene or Ellsworth or Sydney or Denver or Cheyenne—not fire, nor flood, nor Indian attack, nor rifles in the hands of angry grangers. It would sweep forward carelessly, with laughter and fool boyish horseplay, but as inevitably as a swarm of grasshoppers. Those daredevil riders would somehow get the longhorns through. They were tough and supple as hickory withes, and they raced forward to face danger as eagerly as to meet the women waiting for them in the trail-end towns.

A good many of the herds in the early years ran to three and even four thousand in numbers. The largest herd known to have been driven any considerable distance was the one John Chisum took from the Concho River to the Bosque Grande when he migrated. It included six thousand head of cattle. In later years the size of the trail outfits diminished. Smaller bunches were easier to handle. An outfit of average size in later years drove about fifteen hundred or two thousand cattle. To manage these a dozen riders were necessary, together with a trail boss and a cook. Each cowboy took a pair of blankets and a sack of his "plunder," which was carried on the chuck wagon. Tents were considered superfluous.

The boss pushed the herd for the first few days. He wanted the animals tired by night so that they would be less likely to stampede or to break away and wander back to their accustomed range in the mesquite thickets and the cottonwood bosquets along the streams. It was the old-timers, the moss backs, that gave the most trouble. They were individualists, set in their way, and full of fight. The buffalo grass of the Northern plains held no lure. Home for them was in the watershed of the Brazos or of the Colorado, where they could range wild as deer with only the pestering heel fly to interfere with their unalloyed content. Some were so persistent at crashing the line of riders or at starting stampedes that the boss had them shot for food. The drive was a tough enough proposition at best, without continuing a never-ending feud with outlaw steers. During those early days as much as twenty or twenty-five miles might be covered. Later, ten miles made an average drive.

The cattle were not pushed hard, but merely kept grazing slowly in the right direction. During the day they would be spread out like a great arrowhead, the point forward, the base perhaps a mile or so wide. Toward evening the men under the direction of the wagon boss "rode 'em down" by gradually urging point and drag closer together.

As the leaders were held up they relaxed. Soon the whole bunch would be either standing or lying down comfortably chewing their cuds and preparing for a good night's rest.

This "bedding down the herd" was a scientific job. They must not be crowded too closely, nor yet allowed to be scattered over too much ground. Well grazed and watered, a herd of two thousand cattle will lie quietly about half the night. Then, as if moved by some common impulse, every animal gets on its feet, stretches, yawns, moves a step or two, then lies down again, generally on the other side. The same herd instinct brings everybody in a grandstand to his feet at the seventh inning of a baseball game.

The cattle were allowed to drift from the bed ground at break of day, the last of the three relays of night guards moving them in the right direction before being relieved by the day herders after the latter had finished breakfast. To save time, since the boss was often a mile away from some of his men, signals were made to break camp, to let the herd graze, to hit the trail again, to round up and bed.

These were usually given by the waving of a hat in one or another direction.

Most of the longhorns broke to the trail quickly. For the first few days, in the brush of southern Texas, extra men were needed. These dropped off as soon as the open rolling prairie country was reached. Here grass was knee high. The riders had only to loll on their saddles and think of the girls they had left behind them. What could be more of a picnic? It was singing weather, and during the day, around the camp fire after dark, riding night herd, a dozen old favorites found the air.

> I'd rather eat a pan of dope,
> I'd rather ride without a rope,
> I'd rather from the country lope
> Than . . .
> Than . . .
> Than to fight . . .
> Than to fight the bloody In-ji-ans.

Or it might be:

> There's hard times on old Bitter Creek
>   That never can be beat;
> It was root hog or die
>   Under every wagon sheet.
> We cleared up all the Indians,
>   Drank all the alkali;
> And it's whack the cattle on, boys,
>   Root hog or die.

> Oh, I'm going home
>   Bullwhacking for to spurn.
> I ain't got a nickel,
>   An' I don't give a dern,
> 'Tis when I meet a pretty girl,
>   You bet I will or try,
> I'll make her my little wife,
>   Root hog or die.

Possibly the cowboy sang in semi-humorous strain such a ballad as "The Cowgirl's Lament":

> My mother she's dead in a lonely grave,
> My father he ran away,
> My sister she married a gambling man,
> An' I've been led astray.

Chorus:
> If I'd a-listened to my mammy,
> I wouldn't be here to-day,
> But I quit my home an' family
> An' throwed myself away.

> I married the cook of the S-U bunch,
> A bow-legged galoot was he.
> His head was as bald as a Chihuahua pup,
> But he couldn't keep up with me.

Around the camp fire, the day's sixteen or seventeen hours of work done, except for a shift of a few more at night herding, the cowboys having finished with their horseplay and their practical jokes on one another, some tanned young Texan would raise his voice in alleged music. The song was likely to take the turn of bawling out the life they had chosen or the boss they served so loyally. None of these bow-legged bipeds would have cared to engage in any occupation but the one they followed. To the outfit most of them were faithful unto death. Not a few would lie, steal, kill, or be killed for the brand which employed them. Unmarked graves all the way from San Antonio to Miles City testify to this. But it was part of the game to pretend that they were long-suffering idiots abused by fate. One of these songs was "The Dad-Blamed Boss."

> Oh, the boss he says, "Dick,
> Kin ye ride a pitchin' hoss?"
> "I kin ride him in the slick,"
> I tells the dad-blamed boss.

Chorus:
> *Come-a-tie-wy-waddy,*
> *Inkie-eye-eye-a-a-a,*
> *Come-a-tie-wy-waddy-inkie-eye.*

Now there's old Mose Tate,
The old Spur boss.
He'd rather ride a navvy
Than a hundred-dollar hoss.

A navvy, be it said, meant a Navajo Indian pony, which was held to be about the poorest specimen of horse-flesh on earth. They could be had for ten dollars, and occasionally an outfit, short of mounts for the remuda, filled up its quota with some of these.

We rounded up the cattle
And cut out all the steers;
We branded all the calves
An' put the Spur mark in their ears.

I'll get me a new slicker
An' some Coffeyville boots,
Buy a quart of good red licker
An' quit this crazy old galoot.

Oh, I'll shake this job to-morrow,
Pack my soogins on a hoss,
An' pull my freight for Texas
Where there ain't no dad-blamed boss.

But it was not always days of sunshine and starlit nights for the trail herds. Bill Greathouse was the first man to drive a herd to Kansas from Gonzales County. Many of the men of his outfit caught the cholera. He and one of the vaqueros died. The others were nursed back to health by friendly Indians. At the Horsehead Crossing, Charles Goodnight says, there were a dozen graves of cowboys who had died to the sound of cracking revolvers.

The swift answer to an insult or a suspected one was the flash of a Colt's .45. If it was a fair fight the Texas code found the killer blameless. Every man carried the law in his holster.

Near Ellsworth James H. Cook saw by a flash of forked lightning his bunkie go down to certain death in a stampede. Otis Ivey, his horse, and twenty head of cattle were killed by lightning. Crossing the Red River in boiling flood, with the far shore hundreds of swimming yards away, Billy Brown's head went under the white-capped waves and did not reappear. A cottonwood floating down the bank-full river had swept him from his horse. Eugene Manlove Rhodes, an old-time cowman himself, has put such a situation into stirring verse:

> A brown hand lifted in the splashing spray;
> Sun upon a golden head that never will be gray;
> A low mound bare until new grass is grown—
> But the Palo Pinto trail herd has crossed the Cimarron!

The trail was no place for a "goosy" man, to use an expression of the time. It took one with guts and with nerves not jumpy. He had to ride out months of hard work, exposure, discomfort, and peril. He slept in a "Tucson bed," with his back for a mattress and the hard ground for springs. He ate sowbelly and cornbread. He weathered blizzards, following the drifting herd, beard and mustache and eyebrows frozen stiff by the pelting sleet. He woke in the night to hear the blood-chilling Comanche yell and raced to the remuda to save the horses from the raiders, not knowing when an arrow would come whistling into his body. Always he did a man's work. The hardships and the dangers of the early drives frayed the nerves of the riders. A standing rule was to awaken a man by speech and not by touching him, to avoid the chance of his coming to consciousness with .44 in hand. A man in the employ of one of the authors was always awakened by a cow chip or a small stone thrown from a safe distance.

Romance has been so busy with the cowpuncher that it is worth setting down the opinion of a contemporary, a Northerner who came into very intimate contact with hundreds of these Texans. Joseph G. McCoy gives in his rambling but interesting book, published in 1874, an appraisal that is probably very accurate, for he was a careful observer:

The life of the cowboy is one of considerable daily danger and excitement. It is hard and full of exposure, but is wild and free, and the young man who has long been a cowboy has but little taste for any other occupation. He lives hard, works hard, has but few comforts. He has but little, if any, taste for reading. He enjoys a coarse practical joke or a smutty story; loves danger but abhors labor of the common kind; never tires riding, never wants to walk, no matter how short the distance he desires to go. He would rather fight with pistols than pray; loves tobacco, liquor, and women better than any other trinity. . . . His clothes are coarse and substantial, few in number and often of the gaudy pattern. The "sombrero" hat and large spurs are inevitable accompaniments. Every house has the appearance of a lack of convenience and comfort, but the most rude and primitive modes of life seem to be satisfactory to the cowboy. His wages range from fifteen to twenty dollars a month.

What the cowboy was he continued to be, except as he was modified by circumstances. Living conditions became easier. The common schools gave him a taste for reading. Travel increased his worldly wisdom. The Spanish-American War brought him into larger contacts and disciplined somewhat his individual idiosyncrasies. But until the range closed on him and made of him a farm hand or a garage man or a Hollywood bench warmer he remained essentially what cattle and the outdoors had made him.

Thirty years after McCoy had written of the cowboy John C. Van Dyke in one of his books makes an estimate of the cowpuncher. Van Dyke was too professorial to care much for him, but he illustrates by one example the outstanding characteristics of the type.

I had one summer for a partner a boy who had killed two men, been a gambler, served a term for stealing, and had a decidedly bad record; but I never knew a more sunny nature or a more generous one. And with all his bad history he was tremendously courageous and had as much endurance as any man I ever knew.

This boy broke his leg on the round-up. Van Dyke set it with splints. The operation was exceedingly painful. Perspiration stood out in beads on the waddy's forehead, but he never murmured. Nobody could be spared to look after him. He was put on his horse and traveled a hundred miles alone to the nearest town for medical treatment, to make sure the limb was properly set. He camped, picketed his horse, gathered wood, cooked food for himself, remounted, and rode hour after hour under a blistering sun, every motion of the horse racking the wounded leg. A few weeks later he was back on the job, ready for whatever more of experience a varied life might have in store for him.

Theodore Roosevelt lived among these roughriders of the plains and appreciated their fine manly qualities, the loyalty that moved them, the fortitude with which they faced pain and danger.

"Brave, hospitable, hardy, and adventurous, he [the cowboy] is the grim pioneer of our race, he prepares the way for the civilization before whose face he must himself disappear," the cowboy President wrote in appraisal of his former comrades.

6

The trail led through hundreds of miles of wilderness. Most of the thriving towns that now dot the map had not then been thought of by the promoters. Fort Worth itself was scarcely more than a whistling post in the desert. A store or two carrying bare necessities, a blacksmith shop, a few saloons—that was all.

During these early days of trail driving the fuel chiefly used was buffalo chips, dried dung found along the way. This gave out great heat. When soaked with rain buffalo chips made a smoldering fire that set the cook's tongue to blistering adjectives. Some of the first trail drivers to reach Abilene were asked by the farmers, "the fool hoe men," as the Texans called them, to bed the herds on their homesteads. A fair-sized bunch of cattle would leave enough fuel to last the granger an entire winter.

If there were heavy rains in the spring, as in '67, the dangers and difficulties of the trail were much increased. Storms meant stampedes, swollen rivers, rank and spongy grass. Between San Antonio and Abilene were many treacherous streams. The Colorado and the Brazos might be safely crossed and the drover find the Red a raging torrent nearly a mile wide. The Washita and the North Canadian were narrow, but both of them deep and swift. The Cimarron took toll of the lives of many cattle, horses, and men, and the Arkansas might be on a rampage disastrous to a herd.

The Cimarron had an especially bad reputation. During most of the year it is a sandy stretch with a small, sluggish current. Its bed is full of treacherous quicksands which dragged down buffalo, cattle, horses, and men. Cloudbursts near the head used to send the water down in solid sheets which had whipped up the sand from the bottom until swimming was almost impossible. The South Canadian and the Salt Fork of the Arkansas were much the same. All old-timers knew better than to venture into these streams when they were in flood. But not all of them followed their own best judgment.

Steinel, in his *History of Agriculture in Colorado*, tells of a foreman who was twitted by his men because he held

the herd at the Canadian waiting for the stream to sub-
side. They were in a hurry to get to Dodge. He listened,
then yielded with a grim face. "All right, we'll swim," he
said curtly, and plunged into the boiling water to lead the
column. The herd got across, but the foreman and his
horse went under. After the saddened cowboys recovered
his body they found in a coat pocket a letter from his wife
begging him not to try to cross any of the rivers when they
were high.

Often in the rainy seasons these streams would be so
high as to make swimming the cattle out of the question.
Not infrequently from ten to twenty different outfits
would be camped in the vicinity of the crossing waiting
for the river to go down, each hoping some other outfit
would be the first to try it and thus break the way for the
rest of them.

When low the rivers were mere trickles of alkali water,
the sand firm and safe. But at flood some of them were a
mile wide, a body of boiling, whirling, mud-colored water,
generally with a very swift current. The swirling stream
often dug deep holes where two hours before the bottom
was smooth. Cattle might be swimming quietly, and
suddenly right in their faces would break a succession of
huge waves that turned them into a fighting, milling mass
and often sent them back to the very bank from which
they had started.

Every year a number of men were drowned while crossing the herds under such conditions. It was no child's
play, this crossing a trail herd over the streams. A few
trail bosses hauled good-sized flat-bottomed scows on
their chuck wagons for these crossings. In these the men's
bedding, saddles, camp plunder, and food from the wagon
were easily and safely transported. Mostly, however, they
took a chance. If the river was up they lashed a couple
of big cottonwood logs on each side of the wagon to help
float it and then, with oxen straining at the yokes, cowboys with their ropes pulling from the saddle horn, and

others standing on the upstream side of the wagon to keep it from overturning, the wagon was generally got across in safety.

Huge "dugways" had to be graded down the steep banks to let cattle and wagons into and out of the stream. Often the cattle would be swept past the "going-out place" on the farther side and perhaps be carried half a mile or more downstream before they could climb out of the torrent.

All the old trail drivers tell stories of difficulties in getting herds across the rivers when the waters were high. Anything was likely to happen, for cattle are creatures of habit, and any new experience may bewilder them. Riders swam their horses on either side of the leaders to guide the point in the right direction. But a cottonwood drifting downstream might throw the swimming herd into confusion. G. H. Mohle mentions in *The Trail Drivers of Texas* being with a herd which found the Red, the North Fork of the Canadian, and the Arkansas all bank-full. The men had trouble getting the cattle into the water at the North Fork, and when they went in there was such a jam that the longhorns began to mill. Three horses and 116 cattle were drowned. E. A. Robuck dragged out of the Red River his unhorsed boss, Mac Stewart, a famous trail driver who later served ten years in a Mexican prison under a postponed death sentence for killing an officer with whom he had "a difficulty." No matter how great the peril, when cattle got to milling in a stream the cowboys had to ride in and break the mill. In this way many lost their lives.

Sometimes, instead of too much water there was too little. This was especially true of those who drove across the Staked Plains and along the Western trails. Many a herd was without water for days. The pioneer drivers, uncertain of the best route to follow, more than once, after two or three days without water, had to turn back and retrace the way. In such cases the weaker cattle perished and the stronger came at last to the watering hole with their tongues hanging out and swollen.

From the South Concho to the Pecos across the Llano Estacado was more than a hundred miles without water. It was a torturing drive. Usually it started about eleven in the morning and continued for two days with no respite. The salvation of the herd depended upon constant travel. Hour after hour the march across the hot desert continued. The men kept going by drinking great drafts of black coffee. By the close of the second day the cattle were half delirious. Their tongues were swollen. A constant distressed moaning came from the herd. The leaders and the drag could with difficulty be kept together. As they drew close to the Pecos nervous excitement swept over both cattle and the riders. There was always a danger that the tormented stock would break away and dash over some bluff in the haste to get to water.

A stampede could be caused by anything or nothing. It is on record that an old setting hen which flew cackling from her nest started one. The snapping of a twig, the lighting of a cigarette, the snorting of a horse, a sneeze, the unrolling of a slicker, were sometimes as disastrous as one of the sudden electric storms, likely to occur any time. These storms were extremely violent, and frequently cattle and horses were killed by bolts of lightning. One old trail herder became so well acquainted with the electricity that he writes in *The Trail Drivers of Texas* of flash lightning, fork lightning, blue lightning, and ball lightning rolling along the ground. The air would smell like burnt sulphur, and one could see the light playing about the horns of the cattle and the ears of the horses. Sometimes a bunch of cattle got the habit of stampeding, especially if it had some wild scary leaders, and after that the herders led an exceedingly active life. There was no speed limit in a stampede.

A herd in a panicky run, started from the bed ground
in the darkness of a moonless night, was a terrifying experience for a raw hand. A wilder scene can scarcely be
imagined. The ground shook with the thunder of pounding
hoofs. There was a peculiar rattle of horns and hocks
never to be forgotten. The waddy could scarcely see the
head of the mustang he was riding. If there was a storm,
with pelting rain, the artillery of thunder, and vivid
lightning flashes, the peril was increased, since it intensi-
fied the nervousness of the longhorns. The boy raced
beside them, at first busy keeping clear of the terror-
stricken animals. For if his horse fell in front of the
running mass of beef, every bone in his body would be
crushed. His companions were lost somewhere in the black
night. It was up to him, as far as he knew, to check the
run.

As the speedier ones forged ahead and the mass became
less packed, the cowboy closed in on the point, trying
little by little to crowd the leaders from their course and
gradually swing them into a circle to start a mill of the
herd. By this time he had learned that there were other
riders near, assisting him to check the rush.

A good deal of heat was developed by a trail herd in
stampede. On any hot day the lee flank of the drive was
unpleasant on account of dust and heat, so much so that
the waddies often exchanged places.

Sometimes a stampede lasted for hours. The cattle
might split into small bunches, and it would take days to
round them up again. Often a count later showed a good
many missing. Some, perhaps, had been killed, crushed to
death by the packed mass in a ravine they had crossed.
Others had run too far to recover or were hidden in some
unsuspected draw that had not been combed. In any
case the boss counted his losses and willy-nilly made the
best of it.

Usually stampedes did no great harm beyond running
the tallow off the stock. But sometimes herds bolted into

droves of buffaloes, and many were lost. Occasionally, when herds were bunched near a river crossing, cattle of different brands became badly mixed.

Nick Chaffin of Las Vegas, New Mexico, an old trail-herd boss, once told of a night on the trail when owing to high water ten or fifteen big herds of cattle were held up at the Red River crossing. There were also two or three herds of horses with from six hundred to one thousand in each bunch. They were, of course, held at such distances from each other as to minimize the danger of a mix-up if they ran. During the night a tremendous thunderstorm broke. It came up out of the southwest quietly enough, but as the great thunderheads swept across the face of the full moon the whole artillery of the heavens let loose in tremendous crashes, followed by a torrential rain. All the rest of that darksome night some three hundred or more cowboys did their best to hold the terror-stricken stock. At daybreak they found themselves in one great herd of about thirty thousand cattle and several thousand horses. The latter, half-broken mustangs, romped back and forth through the cattle, neighing for lost friends and adding to the devastating effect of the storm. It took ten long hard days to get the herds separated and straightened out. Even then every herd contained strays which should have been in other herds.

Ice-laden blizzards came down from the North and swept the herds before them. Sol West, the youngest man who ever bossed an outfit up the trail, ran into one of these. Not one of his riders was more than twenty years of age. It was at Hell Roaring Creek the blizzard broke, though all day the men could "feel it in their bones" that one was coming. The cattle drifted with the wind. Every horse ridden by the herders went down. The entire remuda, including sixty-five horses not under saddle during the storm, was frozen to death. The men escaped only by building a fire of blackjack. West was to have received one half the net profits of the trip. At the end of it he was handed seventy-five cents with a warning not to spend it in riotous living.

Except creek brush, there was no timber in the Indian Territory but the Cross Timbers, a strip running from the Arkansas line half across the Nation, about ten miles wide. After they had passed this wooded country the herds in the early days were likely to meet the buffalo moving northward for the summer. There were thousands upon thousands of these, and they were a constant menace to the integrity of the outfit, for if the cattle got into one of these drifts many of them could not be extricated. The bosses often sent men ahead to drive the buffalo away. In these great herds horses, elk, deer, wolves, and antelope were all mingled, as wild animals sometimes are when flying from a forest fire.

But somehow the trail herd roughed through to the journey's end. It might be depleted in number and in flesh, but it reached Abilene or Ellsworth at last.

As herd after herd pushed north the trail grew well defined. A million hoofs beat out the grass along this brown ribbon, several hundred yards wide, which was the connecting link between the producer and the consumer. The plodding armies filled the road with dust, later blown away by the wind, so that the trail was not as high as the surface of the adjoining land. Along the course of these great cattle paths—the Goodnight Trail, the Chisholm Trail, the Shawnee Trail, and others—might have been seen white skulls and bleaching skeletons of longhorns, barren bedgrounds, and sometimes a grassy mound where a rider had been buried—shot, drowned, or perhaps flung headlong from an outlaw horse.

7

The most famous of all these cattle roads was the Chisholm Trail. It was named for Jesse Chisholm, a half-breed Indian trader who dealt in horses, furs, hides, and

THE WHOLE RANGE COUNTRY
was strewn with their whitening carcasses.

THE COMANCHES
*and other plains Indians hunted the buffalo with bow
and arrow.*

WINDMILL

*in the Panhandle of Texas where once men had died
from thirst.*

THE WATER

*in this stock tank is piped eight miles from an old
mine tunnel in Arizona. The question of stock water
has always been a prime consideration.*

other marketable products. He was not a cattleman, except very incidentally. His genesis is traced in the *Memoirs of Narcissa Owen*, written by the mother of former United States Senator Owen of Oklahoma. He was the son of Ignatius Chisholm and Martha Rogers, the latter a sister of Sam Houston's Cherokee wife. Jesse was, she adds, a remarkable man who spoke fourteen Indian languages and was an interpreter between the tribes of the plains and the army officers at Fort Gibson.

The connection of Jesse Chisholm with the trail had nothing to do with cattle. He worked out the route to take supplies from the Arkansas Valley into the Indian Territory. It passed through Caldwell, Buffalo Springs, and Fort Sill.

When the first cattle began to move along this trail they found it well marked because it had been recently used by a band of poor terror-stricken Indians fleeing from death.

After the outbreak of the Civil War a large number of Indians fled north for safety. These included Shawnees, Delawares, Kickapoos, and Wichitas. They migrated because of fear of the slaveholding Indians, chiefly the Five Civilized Tribes. Leaving their homes on the Washita and Canadian rivers, these anti-slavery natives trekked about 1861 to a point on the Little Arkansas, where the city of Wichita, Kansas, now stands. They endured many hardships en route. When they arrived they were destitute and without supplies. The government gave them some tardy and insufficient relief, but during the first winter all their horses starved to death and many of the children perished from want and illness. As time passed, conditions improved for them, until in 1867 cholera swept over the plains and played havoc with these transplanted tribesmen.

The story of this cholera epidemic is one of tragedy and sorrow. It spared none. Military posts well supplied with surgeons and medical stores suffered alike with little isolated hamlets scattered along the Santa Fe Trail or the route of the new Kansas Pacific Railroad. The toiling hordes that were building the road died like flies. The emigrants crossing the plains in their covered wagons left new-made graves at every night's camp. Often the bodies were abandoned and left unburied by the living who feared even to go near the dead lest they themselves die. It was a year of stark fear all over the plains, and thousands of unmarked graves dotted the prairies along the Santa Fe and Oregon trails.

No sooner had the Wichitas started on their southward course than the disease broke out among them, even more violent and deadly than when they were in camp on the little Wichita. It followed them day and night. They plodded slowly along the Chisholm Trail, as it was even then called, horseless and afoot, hungry and discouraged, their course marked by new-made graves.

Every morning they left behind them some of their people carried off by this terrible scourge the white men had brought to them. At one creek so many died and the survivors were so helpless and discouraged that they moved off leaving the dead bodies unburied. On the map to-day, not far south of Wichita, Kansas, you will find Skeleton Creek, which received its name from the bleaching skeletons of those who died. Even after the Indians reached their old country the disease still cursed them with its unwelcome presence.

One wonders if the old men of the tribe recalled stories of the dreadful visitation of smallpox that the French explorers brought to the Wichita from the South, more than a century before, which decimated the tribe almost to a remnant. Little they owed the white man's civilization. It was a sad and sorrowful return over the Chisholm Trail for these red men of the plains. Jesse Chisholm gathered them about him, comforted and encouraged them, and endeavored to get them located on their old farms and hunting grounds.

Here they remained [according to a report of the Kansas historical society] until he [Chisholm] suddenly died on the North Fork of the Canadian River, in the Indian territory, March 4, 1868, of Cholera morbus, caused by eating bear's grease that had been poisoned by being melted in a brass kettle.

After the cattlemen on their drive from southern Texas to Kansas reached the Indian Territory they picked up this trail marked out by Chisholm and still fairly well defined, following it to the north. The Chisholm Trail proper was only 225 miles long.

But soon the whole trail north from Austin became known as the Chisholm Trail. It was as well marked as a road could be, since the hoofs of millions of cattle had laid out this path of empire. In *The Trail Drivers of Texas* C. H. Rust defines the course of this, the most traveled of all the cattle routes.

The Chisholm Trail began at San Antonio, Texas, crossed the Colorado River three miles below Austin . . . left Fort Worth on our right . . . crossed Red River at Red River Station . . . the Little Washita at Line Creek and then straight north to Abilene.

Not unnaturally the name of John Simpson Chisum, the owner of the famous Jingle Bob outfit, has been confused with that of Jesse Chisholm. In 1867 John S. Chisum drove his herds into New Mexico from Texas up the Pecos River and located ranches near the present town of Roswell. Within the next fifteen years his cattle had increased in numbers so greatly that he was the cattle king of New Mexico. He did not know himself how many cattle he owned, but a conservative estimate puts the total over seventy-five thousand. There was no other herd of this size in the world owned by a single man.

Chisum trailed many cattle to Arizona and to various points in New Mexico to fill army and Indian agency beef contracts. His name was famous all over Cattleland. Among those who did not know, it was presumed that the

Chisholm Trail was named in his honor. Such was not the
case. He never trailed a herd to the Kansas market.
This is indisputable. Of the hundreds of old drivers who
went up the trail and have recorded their stories, not one
went with or knew of any herd of Chisum's in Oklahoma or
Kansas. Charles Goodnight says that John Chisum never
drove a cow up the trail. Scores of old-timers substantiate
this. The coincidence of similar names and Chisum's
widespread reputation are alone responsible for the mistake which has identified him with this best-known of the
cattle routes.

Beyond question the trail was named for Jesse Chisholm, the old half-breed scout and Indian trader.

There were many songs of the Chisholm Trail sung
around the camp fires and by the cowboys circling the
night herds. The best known of them had hundreds of
verses, some improvised to suit the occasion, a good many
of these too Rabelaisian for quotation. It was sung from
the Gulf to Montana:

> Come along, boys, and listen to my tale,
> I'll tell you of my troubles on the old Chisholm Trail.
>
> *Coma ti youpy, youpy ya, youpy ya,*
> *Coma ti yi youpy, youpy ya.*
>
> Oh, a ten-dollar hoss and a forty-dollar saddle—
> And I'm goin' to punchin' Texas cattle.
>
> We hit Caldwell and we hit her on the fly,
> We bedded down the cattle on the hill close by.
>
> No chaps, no slicker, and it's pourin' down rain,
> And I swear, by God, I'll never night-herd again.
>
> Foot in the stirrup and hand on the horn,
> Best damned cowboy ever was born.
>
> Stray in the herd, and the boss said kill it,
> So I shot him in the rump with the handle of the skillet.

We rounded 'em up and put 'em on the cars,
And that was the last of the old Two Bars.

I'll sell my outfit just as soon as I can,
And I won't punch cattle for no damned man.

Many a Texas cowboy in striped trousers sang this ditty
as he headed north. Many a Negro rider—and most of the
colored boys were top hands, expert with rope and brand—
murmured it as he circled the herd. Often there was a
modification of it which ran:

Come a-runnin', all you cowboys,
  Come and listen to my tale
An' I'll tell you all a story
  Of the old Chisholm Trail.

I dumped my roll of beddin'
  Near the old chuck wagon's tail
For the outfit was a headin'
  Up the old Chisholm Trail.

Doan's Crossing, on the Red River, was the jumping-
off place into the great unknown. Here a post office was
established in the late '70's. A store had been built by J.
Doan. The first house was made of pickets with dirt roof
and floor, a buffalo robe serving for a door. It was used
both as a residence and a store. Later there was an adobe
store, and then a frame one. A log cabin was built for the
use of the family.

"We crossed Red River at Doan's store in 1877. It
consisted of three buffalo hides and a wagon sheet," Bob
Lauderdale recalls.

Some of the stations that grew up on the trail were dead-
falls of the worst kind. Whisky was a chief item in stock,
and gamblers and prostitutes lay in wait to fleece the unwary Texan. On the south bank of the Cimarron Red
Clark had a roadhouse called Long Horn Ranch. Across

the river was another hangout known as "Old Julia's Dead fall." It was a sink of iniquity.

Hundreds of cowboys in their high-heeled boots have clumped into a small combination store and post office at Doan's or at Denison or Fort Worth and asked for mail from home. If a letter was handed one he knew it was from the girl he had left behind in Texas. He looked around to make sure none of his companions had seen him get the precious message, and he never read it till he was alone. For the cowboy was then a shy soul, and he did not want to be "joshed." He might be a hair-trigger lad, ready to fight at the drop of the hat, but when he "went gallin'" he was anybody's game.

Though the dress of the cowboy was not as yet standardized, his riding equipment was much more so. He rode a stock saddle, heavy, broad, and double cinched, the details of cantle and seat determined by personal choice or the locality from which he came. A Brazos tree was at this time much in vogue as a framework for the saddle. The stirrups had heavy taps (short for tapaderos), necessary to prevent the feet of the rider from pushing through and getting snagged by brush. Two cinches were then customary in Texas but only one in California.

A rider's saddle was a matter of pride to him. Though he often came back home after a long trail drive in a roundabout way by rail and river, he always sacked his saddle and brought it with him. The last word in the degradation of a puncher, the fact which showed he was completely down and out, was the selling of his saddle. Finally the word became a bit of expressive slang. In *The Cowboy* Philip Ashton Rollins illustrates this by an anecdote. A Montana schoolboy, asked by his teacher who Benedict Arnold was, gave sufficient description of him by saying, "He was one of our generals, and he sold his saddle."

CHAPTER V. THE END OF THE TRAIL

T HE trail herders had lived hard for months. They had not for weeks at a time seen anybody except those of their own outfit. No liquor had been within reach, and they had been too busy to do much poker playing. Therefore they were ready for a spree by the time they reached the end of their journey.

The waddies usually lived at the cow camp, but the trail boss moved into the Drovers' Cottage, if there was room. This hotel was taken over by Mrs. Gore in the spring of '68 and run by her for years. Here buyers and sellers congregated as a headquarters at which to talk over sales. Mrs. Gore is still remembered by scores of old trail men for her kindness and her generosity. Many a sick Texan found in her a nurse and a friend. No cowboy was ever turned away because he was without money, and it is to the credit of the boys in the high-heeled boots that one of them would rather have lost his saddle than beat a board bill at her place. In the rather magniloquent expression so many old-timers used in writing but never in speech, she was one of nature's noblewomen.

Abilene was wide open. It gave the cowpuncher the keys of the town and told him to cut loose his dog. There was whisky by the barrel. The roulette wheel rolled day and night. Chuck-a-luck and Mexican monte were there for those who preferred them. Hard-eyed men with pallid faces, in Prince Albert coats and white shirts, most expert of finger, waited to accommodate those who wished to try their luck at faro and poker. The dance halls employed plenty of girls eager to treat the cowboy "like someone who had come," as one of them put it.

As soon as the herd was bedded down and guards set for the night those released from duty saddled up and rode to town. They had come up the trail like the buffalo, wild and woolly. They were long-haired and unshaven. The first thing they did was to go to a barber shop, the second to buy a new set of clothes from the skin out. The striped or checkered trousers, the run-down-at-the-heel boots, the hickory shirt, were all worn out and fit to be discarded.

The worst of the trail towns were Abilene and Dodge, and in their evil prime there was nothing romantic about them. Except when held down by officers who strictly enforced the regulations they were full of vice, lawlessness, and crime. The desperadoes and scoundrels with whom the West was afflicted for years after the Civil War flocked to them, drawn by the magnet of easy money. In the winter Abilene was deserted except for a few hundred permanent residents. In the summer its population was ten times as great. The buzzards were back on the job, thieves, swindlers, confidence men, killers, and courtesans. The best of the cowboys held aloof from them. The careless and the profligate allowed themselves to become victims. Drunkenness, lewdness, robbery, and murder became so common as to excite little notice.

The theory of the merchants at first was that the boom must be encouraged and that a wide-open town was good for business. But conditions became so flagrant that a check was necessary.

Man after man tried to fill the job of marshal and gave up within a few days. The carnival of license was too much

for them. It became a matter of pride among the wilder
spirits to mock the authority of an officer. An ordinance
was passed against the firing of guns in town. The posters
announcing this were shot to fragments. Two men were
imported from St. Louis to keep the peace. They left on
the next train. One marshal arrested a colored trail cook
and put him in the calaboose. His companions drove the
officer to cover and rescued the prisoner.

How far the cowboy on a tear went depended on the
amount of liquor he consumed and on his native taste for
trouble. Most of them made a good deal of noise, as college
boys do now after a football game, but held themselves in
hand and did not "get on the prod." That was all right.
Nobody objected to exuberance if it was good-natured
and without malice.

But quarrels flared up between the professional gamblers and the punchers. There were crooked games. Phil
Coe and Ben Thompson and other keepers of houses had
reputations as gunmen quick on the trigger. Texas sent up
the trail scores of hard characters who had signed up for
the drive. Difficulties were frequent, and the almost certain appeal was to the six-shooter. The words "a man for
breakfast to-day" began to be heard too frequently. The
city dads decided that in self-protection Abilene had to
have authority represented in the person of a marshal
with prestige enough to command respect.

From Kit Carson, Colorado, drifted Tom Smith, who
as marshal had achieved enviable distinction in that wild
end-of-the-railroad town. He applied for the job of re-
storing order. But he was so quiet, so soft spoken, had so
much the manner of a reserved self-respecting decent
citizen, that the mayor would have none of him. Mani-
festly he would not do. Abilene needed a hell-roaring
fighter to cow the bad men. The less diffident applicants
were chosen and failed, one after another. For want of
better Smith was at last appointed, hesitantly even then.

T. C. Henry, the mayor, asked him if he could stop the

disorder. Smith thought he could. How? The candidate said that drunken cowboys and guns were not a good combination; he would make everybody discard weapons in town. Henry looked at him in amazement. There was an easy confidence about this man that inspired trust. And yet how could any man separate either the Texans or the cormorants from their weapons? He told Smith he was appointed. "Make good!" he snapped.

Smith did, within the hour. He met Big Hank, a cowboy desperado. The trail rider strode up, a gun by his side.

"You the new marshal?" he demanded—"the galoot that's allowin' to run this town?"

Smith admitted identity and asked for the gun. Watching the marshal, to make sure he would not try a gunplay, Hank said he guessed there wasn't any bird alive could take his cutter from him.

The arm of the marshal traveled, but not toward a gun. In point of fact he did not have one. It moved swiftly toward the chin of the bad man. Smith stood an inch over six feet and he was muscled like a panther. When his fist landed on Big Hank the ruffian doubled up like a jackknife.

Swiftly the news spread. Hank was considered a tough proposition, but Wyoming Frank felt that he was more so. He roped a bronco and rode to town from camp. He boasted of what he meant to do, so that quite a bevy of spectators were present at the show-down. Frank swaggered toward the marshal, gun in hand. He got a little too close. Once more that chain-lightning right of the officer crashed to the chin. Wyoming Frank was down and out. He woke up in the calaboose.

Abilene opened wide its eyes. This was not the sort of thing it had been expecting. Unarmed men were not in the habit of walking up to ruffians garnished with six-shooters and knocking them cold. The courage of it won the heart of the cow town. Smith became the hero of the trail drivers.

The marshal was not trying an experiment. He had ruled at Kit Carson by the same method. Colonel William M. Breakenridge, now of Tucson, Arizona, says that Smith was the bravest peace officer he ever saw. He walked into danger so steady of eye, so unperturbed, that it vanished at his approach. Anybody, he said, could arrest a dead man; an officer was employed to bring lawbreakers in alive. Bill Tilghman held the same view during his forty years as a law enforcer. Like Smith, he fell a victim to his principles.

For six months Smith held Abilene down to a reasonable decorum. It was no Sunday-school town, but life and property were safe. The thugs hunted cover, and vice was not flaunted openly. With his deputy Smith rode out of town to arrest a man named McConnell who had killed a neighbor. As he walked up to the dugout where the murderer had taken refuge McConnell shot him down from a window.

All the decent men and women of Abilene mourned the passing of this gentle, soft-spoken athlete, the fair-haired young fellow with the gray-blue, unflinching eyes, always so clean of speech and so friendly of manner. He neither drank nor gambled, but even those who did recognized his value. Many years later the town erected a monument to his memory and carved its appreciation upon it.

THOMAS J. SMITH
MARSHAL OF ABILENE, 1870

DIED A MARTYR TO DUTY, NOV. 2, 1870

A FEARLESS HERO OF FRONTIER DAYS, WHO, IN
COWBOY CHAOS, ESTABLISHED THE
SUPREMACY OF LAW

Not one of all the many marshals of the border towns stands higher than Tom Smith.

Wild Bill Hickok. ex-marshal of Hays City, then the

terminus of the Kansas Pacific Railroad, was appointed to succeed Smith. At Hays Mr. Hickok had become supreme by the simple method of shooting down both personal and official opposition. He had killed there Jack Strawhan, Bill Mulvey, and three soldiers who seemed to be looking for a fight. This last annoyed the army authorities. They felt they could not have the troops at Fort Hays mustered out thus summarily. A hint had been given Mr. Hickok that it would be well to seek other fields for his peculiar talents.

Speaking at the dedication of the Smith monument, T. C. Henry took occasion to compare the two most famous marshals of Abilene. He did not deny the courage of Wild Bill, but said it was of a far lower order than that of Smith. This was true of the whole character of the man. Smith was genuine; Hickok, a poseur. Smith believed in law; Wild Bill wanted to be cock of the walk. Smith brought order out of chaotic disturbance; the administration of Hickok was a complete failure.

With Wild Bill as marshal the vicious element at once began again to run the town. Thuggery and murder thrived. Drunkenness and debauchery walked the streets. Personal encounters with Hickok were avoided, but life and property were at the mercy of scores of unprincipled scoundrels. As a result of this defiance of law the best citizens of the town and the adjacent farmers put an end to the local cattle trade. They notified drovers to stop coming to Abilene, that the trail herds were not wanted there. Abruptly the business ended. The herds went elsewhere, to Coffeyville, to Wichita, to Newton. Gambling houses and dance halls vanished within a week. This was in 1872. In any case the trade would soon have been lost. The extension of railroads had cut into the Abilene territory.

Wild Bill was an eye-satisfying spectacle. There is abundant testimony to that. Henry M. Stanley, Colonel E. C. Little, General Custer, and Mrs. Custer all agreed that he was one of the handsomest men they had ever seen. He was arrow-straight, easy, graceful, nonchalant, built like an Apollo. He dressed with great care and not at all flashily. His manners were quiet. The only flamboyant touch about him was the heavy brown hair that swept his shoulders. One of the best shots with a six-gun ever seen on the frontier, he could beat any other gunman to the draw and still fire with deadly accuracy.

Yet, in spite of all these accessories to the make-up of a dime novel hero, the Wild Bill myth has been shot full of holes by inquisitive historians. For character and courage Hickok does not compare with many other peace officers who reigned in the wild cow towns. The McCanles fight, upon which his reputation was originally built, instead of being a battle where he fought single-handed against a band of attacking outlaws and killed nine of them, was a cold-blooded killing done by Wild Bill and two companions with three men as victims who were probably unarmed and who certainly did not fire a shot.

Hickok was a man who did not take unnecessary chances. His pragmatic philosophy was that if a man was dangerous he could be arrested more easily dead than alive. This was a view quite commonly held by officers careless of human life.

Mr. Hickok realized that for him the price of life was eternal vigilance. This made him excessively wary. At Abilene he had a difficulty with Phil Coe, a Texas gambler, who ran in partnership with Ben Thompson a place called "The Bull's Head." Thompson tried to get John Wesley Hardin, the Texas killer, to assassinate Hickok, but Hardin told him that he was doing only his own killing, thank you. Trouble was looked for, and it came. Coe and Wild Bill met in front of the Alamo saloon. Both fired. Coe was mortally wounded. The marshal whirled at the sound of an approaching runner. The newcomer had a revolver in his hand. Hickok killed him. The man was Jim Williams, his deputy, coming as fast as he could to the assistance of his chief. There was some criticism of this proof of the shell game man's assertion that the hand is quicker than the eye. It was felt by a good many that Mr. Hickok might well have been a trifle less efficient, and that he was too careless of other men's lives. If so, he was at least very careful of his own—except on that last day at Deadwood, August 2, 1876, when he sat with his back to a door and was murdered by Jack McCall.

Though inclined to be sullen at cards when losing, Wild Bill had his good points. Sometimes he took an interest in young fellows for their good. He told Alfred Moye that the best way to beat the gambling game was to leave it alone. He gave the same advice to Harry Young and even hunted him up a job. Any down-and-outer could panhandle a dollar from the marshal.

In March, 1871, John Wesley Hardin started up the trail with his cousin Jim Clements. They were in charge of twelve hundred head of cattle. Manning, Gip, and Joe Clements, brothers of Jim, followed with another herd belonging to Doc Burnett, one of the earliest drivers. There was a warrant out for the arrest of Hardin. He was wanted in Texas for murder. On the way up the trail, according to his own story, he killed two Indians and five Mexicans. It is likely he was drawing the long bow, though there is evidence to support part of his claim.

Soon after reaching town Hardin had a run-in with Marshal Hickok. Notorious killers were wont when they met for the first time to eye one another like strange cats. So did these two watch each other while they shook hands warily and made small talk. Each knew that the other would not hesitate an instant to shoot him down if occasion seemed to suggest the wisdom of swift action. Hickok inquired about the killing of the Mexicans and showed a proclamation for Hardin's arrest. He explained that he did not intend to take the young fellow into custody. They parted on terms of ostensible friendliness.

The Texan spent most of his time in saloons and

gambling houses. The marshal had to caution him for being too noisy and for not discarding his revolvers. According to Hardin's story, written years later, Hickok attempted to arrest him and was caught at the wrong end of a pistol by the whirling gun trick. The marshal kept his nerve and talked the young fellow out of killing him.

Hardin had known many fast towns, but he thought Abilene the wildest he had seen. While there he did his share to make it wilder. A drunken man in a saloon expressed indiscreet views about Texas and its inhabitants. If he owned Texas and hell he would sell Texas and live in hell. As for Texans——

John Wesley interrupted: "Two Texans present."

Guns flashed. Hardin walked out of the place across the prostrate body of his foe.

He left Abilene, but heard in a day or two that a Mexican named Bideno had killed a cowman, Billy Coran, who had come up the trail with Hardin and was holding a herd at Abilene pending a sale. John Wesley got himself appointed a deputy sheriff and followed Bideno south. The Mexican was going fast, but the posse caught up with him at Bluff Creek. In a duel Hardin killed him.

He returned to Abilene, apparently under the impression that the Bideno matter had wiped out the indiscretion in the saloon. The cowmen seemed to be of that opinion. They raised a purse of about a thousand dollars for him.

Wild Bill dropped into a drinking place where Hardin was ordering wine in noisy celebration.

"You can't hurrah me," Hickok told him. "I won't have it."

The two killers looked steadily at each other.

"I haven't come to hurrah you, but I'm going to stay in Abilene."

Friends averted a breach, and Hickok drank with the group.

A few days later Manning and Gip Clements reached

town and hunted up their cousin. Manning told Hardin that he had killed the night before two of his riders, Joe and Dolph Shadden, who had been insolent, quarrelsome, and had confided to other waddies that they meant to kill Manning before they reached Abilene. If they made such a boast they were very unwise, for Manning Clements was one bad hombre.

John Wesley told his cousin that he stood ace-high with Marshal Hickok. After Clements had been arrested he arranged with the marshal to let Manning escape. Hickok attended to this, and Manning returned to Texas. So Hardin told the story.

Hardin was staying at the American Hotel. He charged that an assassin tried to kill him in bed, and he slew the man. Wild Bill and some officers came to arrest him. He slipped out of the hotel, jumped a horse, and left town. It seemed best to him to head for Texas *muy pronto*. His visit to Kansas and that of his cousin Manning Clements had been so devastating that wisdom counseled an immediate departure.

It may be mentioned here, as Mr. Hardin is galloping back to Texas out of trail history, that he came to the usual end of his kind, a swift and tragic death. John Selman, an officer and a killer, shot him in the Acme saloon at El Paso. George Scarborough killed Selman. Kid Curry rubbed out Scarborough. So the tale runs for most of the noted gunmen, whether they fought for law or their own hand. Hickok and Ben Thompson and Manning Clements, Pat Garrett and Billy the Kid and Jesse James, Dallas Stoudenmire and Tom Smith and Ed Masterson, Tilghman and Nixon, Sam Bass and Joel Collins, most of the Dalton and the Doolin gangs, Morgan and Warren Earp; the list of those who passed out to the accompaniment of roaring guns would fill pages. Slade and Longley and Brooks were hanged. The Horrells and the Marlows and Joe Hardin were lynched. Violence begets violence.

There were exceptions, enough only to point the moral.

Bat Masterson, Luke Short, Wyatt Earp, Mike Sughrue, and Doc Holliday died in their beds. Three of these were law officers, Luke Short a gambler ready to accommodate anybody looking for trouble, Doc Holliday a consumptive gunman none too scrupulous in his methods.

Since Hardin was only one of many wild young hellions who came up the trail it may be guessed that Abilene was a fairly live town. Anybody who felt wild and woolly and hard to curry could be accommodated instantly if he asked for trouble. Nobody but a fool would try to "run a blaze" in the trail towns. Bluffs were called promptly and explosively.

The cowboys danced in spurs, sombrero, and at first with pistols strapped to their sides. Later weapons were checked at saloons and trading stores as soon as the riders came to town. It was too dangerous for all concerned to leave them armed while in town and drinking. In his story of Dodge City Bob Wright says that these guns were sometimes piled up by hundreds in his store, to be reclaimed by their owners when the trail men were ready to leave town.

In 1869 about three hundred and fifty thousand cattle came up from Texas. Nearly half of them were shipped from Abilene, the rest from rival towns, such as Wichita and Ellsworth. The farmers around Abilene had a good market for all their produce, and they deserted their dugouts and got into new frame houses. Fences began to appear, and it became apparent that the days of Abilene as a longhorn cattle town were numbered. Several factors combined to push the trail to the West. The most important were the taking up of land by the farmers, the tax insisted upon by the Five Civilized Tribes, the quarantine regulations imposed by Kansas and Missouri and intermittently enforced by grangers with shotguns, and the better feed to be found in western Kansas and eastern Colorado. It was possible to evade the protective law which required that stock must have been brought north before the first of May by getting certificates from complaisant officials who engaged in the business of issuing these wholesale, regardless of the facts, but it was easier to drive farther west, where the question was less likely to be raised.

The price of steers steadily increased. By 1870 a seller could get from thirty to forty dollars a head for good four-year-olds delivered in Chicago, and if wintered in the North sometimes as high as fifty dollars. About the same number of longhorns left Texas that year as during the previous season, but the good prices so stimulated trade that in 1871 this was doubled. More than six hundred thousand came up the trail. One could stand on a hill and see in every direction herds pointed north. Those who have watched this sight will never forget the fascination of it. North, south, east, and west one could observe the dust rising from the long snaky lines marching resistlessly as fate to settle the wide ranges that were being taken from the Indians.

Unfortunately the season was a rainy one. There were many bad stampedes. The grass was rank and would not make tallow. Prices were low. Buyers were scarce. Many drovers had to hold their cattle over the winter unsold. They drove west to the buffalo grass and encountered more rain, frozen ground, heavy snows. The longhorns died by thousands. A great many of these were skinned, perhaps 50 per cent of those which failed to rough through. More than a hundred thousand hides were shipped East to tanneries in the spring. One firm put a herd of nearly four thousand on the Republican River and saved only a hundred.

Each trail town, as it burgeoned into prosperity, attracted the dance and gambling hall, the riffraff of the border, and lewd women. The newspapers of the country exploited this phase of the life. Young Easterners, new to the wild license of the West on a spree, exaggerated it in letters home. They conveyed the impression that the first question the citizens asked in the morning was, "How many killed last night?" It is true that there was shooting and plenty of it, but a quiet man who minded his own business was as safe as such a one is now in gang-ridden cities.

The new trail towns were as wild as Abilene had been, but a large percentage of the fighting was professional. Ben Thompson and his brother Bill, up from Texas like leeches to fatten on the spendthrift cowboys, terrorized Ellsworth the first year of the drive there, killed the sheriff, wounded his deputies, and left on the run. Newton, on the Atchison, Topeka & Santa Fe, had an even more sinister record. One gory night gamblers, cowboys, railroad men, and officers staged a battle memorable even for that time. McCoy says that eleven died with their boots on. Emanuel Dubbs records that he and his wife drove into Newton in a covered wagon on a sunshiny spring day of '71 to find the bodies of seventeen dead gamblers and cowboys lying on the floor of the Gold Room gambling house. No doubt both McCoy and Dubbs were referring to the same fracas. The memories of old-timers are often very erratic.

The Santa Fe Railroad reached Wichita in '72 and eighty thousand cattle were brought there. The glory of Abilene had departed. The hoe man and his fence and Wild Bill Hickok's lawless administration had put it out of business as a trail town.

This was the great era of transcontinental railroad building, and new cow towns were coming to the front every month. Hays, Schuyler, Sidney, Ogallala, Kit Carson, Denver, Cheyenne, Coffeyville, Miles City, Ellsworth, Trinidad, Baxter Springs, Julesburg, Dodge, Trail Town, each had its day. Around these towns trail history was written, a good deal of it punctuated with guns. It has been said that three mileposts of the cattle business were the six-shooter, barbed wire, and the haystack. The early days of the trail drives were the period of the .45. In many places there was no other law except the weight of a rough-and-ready public opinion. Often this failed to express itself on account of lack of leadership to direct it. But in the end law and order always caught up with the frontier. There came little red schoolhouses and Ladies' Aid societies and meetings of the G. A. R. By that time the frontier had been wiped out and with it the bad man who swaggered down the dusty streets of its cow towns.

CHAPTER VI. THE BUFFALO OR THE COW?

T HE forward sweep of the open-range live-stock industry was checked in the early days by barriers that dammed the flood. The high plains were Indian country. Even those who realized the value of the wilderness knew that there could be no occupancy of it until the nomadic life of the natives had been curtailed.

No compromise between white and red man could be permanent, since the ends sought were incompatible. The buffalo or the cow, the Indian or the settler—there was no middle ground. There had to be conquest, and there had to be defeat.

In this war for the range the cowman played an important part. It was for him that the buffalo country had to become Cattleland. Troubles with the Apaches and the Comanches and the Cheyennes came home closely to him, because he was always aggressively pushing his cows to the very edge of the red skins' hunting domain. These difficulties had to be determined before he could live in peace.

From the time of the first settlements by Europeans in America there has always been an Indian problem. To

what extent ought the priority rights held by the tribes
to be exclusive? That was a debatable question. Pioneers
pushing into the untrodden wilds held that the vast
domain over which Indians hunted once a year or not so
often could not be termed their property. Land was to be
used, and these roving hunters had no claim based upon
actual tenure.

The difference of viewpoint was not one that could be
settled on a basis of abstract justice, since human nature
is what it is. The inexorable fact was that the white would
not recognize an ownership founded upon a priority right
in a hunting preserve. If the country was desirable he
pushed into it, regardless of any treaty the Indian Department might have made with the tribes. These compacts
were ignored both by the pioneer and by the red man,
usually first by the former.

There was not wisdom enough on the part of the government or patience enough in the frontiersman's temperament to conciliate the native. The policy of the Indian
Department was disingenuous. No continuity marked its
dealings with the Indians. The commissioner was a
political appointee who entered upon his office with little
regard to what had been done by his predecessors. With
Satanta alone, chief of the Kiowas, not to go back of the
days of the buffalo hunters, five separate compacts were
made by five commissioners, prior to the Medicine Lodge
treaty, each ignorant, or at least regardless, of what the
others had done. The tribes failed to understand this
detachment from the past. They saw that each successive
powwow reduced their territory, and the only answer they
found to their bewilderment was bad faith on the part of
the United States. Why otherwise was it necessary after
an agreement had been signed that lands belonged to
them to have another conference to discuss how much of
these they might retain? It must be admitted that the
red man was justified in his fear of the future and his
distrust of the whites.

The conflict over the buffalo country was typical. At Medicine Lodge, for instance, peace delegates from the government met with the leaders of the tribes to iron out difficulties. Among those representing the United States were Generals William T. Sherman, W. H. Harney, A. H. Terry, and John B. Sanborn, as well as several civilians of note. The tribes involved were the Cheyennes, the Kiowas, the Apaches, the Comanches, and the Arapahoes. Satank, Satanta, Black Kettle, and Lone Wolf were their leading chiefs. They spoke with eloquent bitterness of the wrongs done their race. By the terms of the treaty, signed with impressive ceremonies, the Arkansas River was to be the dividing line. The Indians were to stay south of it, the whites north. The whole game country running up to the river was forever to be the property of the tribes.

Nearly two thousand Indians, the pick of the tribes, had accompanied their chiefs to Medicine Lodge. They were restive and unfriendly. Billy Dixon, the famous buffalo hunter, was present as a packer, and he wrote that the Indians were mentally very hostile. Even during the conference a battle seemed at any time possible. The description of one scene given in his Life is impressive.

I shall never forget the morning of October 28, 1867. At a distance of about two miles from our camp was the crest of a low swell in the Plains. The background was blue sky—a blue curtain that touched the brown Plains. For a moment I was dumbfounded at sight of what was rising over that crest and flowing with vivid commotion toward us. It was a glittering, fluttering, gaily colored mass of barbarism, the flower and perfection of the war strength of the Plains Indian tribes. The resplendent warriors, armed with all their equipment and adorned with all the regalia of battle, seemed to be rising out of the earth. Their number was estimated at 1500, but I cannot vouch for its accuracy.

As they came into plainer view, the Indians spread their ranks wider and wider, to create as profound an impression as possible, and inspire us deeply with their power. Now they could be heard chanting and singing. Having arrived within a quarter of a mile of our camp, the Indians charged like a whirlwind, firing their guns and brandishing them above their heads. The charge was abruptly halted, and the Indians stood at rest, waiting for the negotiations to begin.

The real grievance of the braves was the coming of the whites and the destruction of the buffalo. They knew that these meant an end to their free tribal life. With dread they watched the progress of the railroads. The protests of their able chiefs were filled with resentment.

The Kiowas and Comanches, at home on the headwaters of the Red, the Colorado, and the Brazos, wandered far afield in their raids and hunting expeditions. Sonora and Chihuahua heard with dread their war whoops. They roamed as far north as Dodge. They were expert horsemen, and the deer and the buffalo furnished them food, fuel, shelter, and clothing. From the Arkansas River through the Panhandle of Texas into Mexico a well defined trail showed their migrations.

Between these tribes and Mexican dealers at Santa Fe and Las Vegas there was a well established trade in horses and cattle stolen by the Indians from west Texas and Mexico. In the country around Tascosa and the present city of Amarillo, which was not yet on the map, were favorite meeting places for the raiders and the traders. Another was at the edge of the caprock, on the Pease River. For a decade after the cattle drives began, this trade in stolen stock was carried on extensively. J. E. Haley, in his book, *The X I T Ranch of Texas*, quotes from a personal letter of Charles Goodnight to the effect that the road was almost as plain as one to-day. It ran from Las Vegas to the Canadian, followed that river for a distance, and cut across to the Door of the Plains, a gap in the caprock which is a landmark. It struck the Palo Duro and ran beside it. So great were the gatherings on

the Tongue River that they gave the stream its name.
Spanish, English, and various Indian languages were
spoken by those engaged in barter. Goodnight estimates
that at least three hundred thousand head of cattle had
been run off from the Texas frontier during the war, and at
that time the trade was only well under way.

The conflict between the Indians and the pioneers was
irrepressible. After the Medicine Lodge treaty troops
patrolled the Arkansas to keep buffalo hunters from crossing into the country belonging to the natives, but it was
easy to avoid the soldiers. The real danger was from the
Indians whose herds they were depleting. The Comanches
and Kiowas were splendid warriors, of the finest physique.
General Nelson A. Miles defeated them disastrously a
year or two later, and they were confined to reservations.
But at this time the degradation of beggary, laziness, and
disease had not corrupted them.

It is difficult now to understand what a hunter's
paradise was this country south from Dodge City as far
as the Llano Estacado. It teemed with game. Probably no
such wild natural preserve has ever been known before.
The creeks tributary to the Arkansas were heavily wooded
with ash, box-elder, hackberry, cottonwood, and elm.
Beaver, muskrat, weasel, and otter were there in abundance, as were duck, geese, swan, and pigeons. On the
Canadian turkey could be found in flocks of hundreds.
The whirr of startled quail or prairie chicken aroused no
attention. Black and cinnamon bear, big gray wolves in
bands, wild horses, deer, and antelope fed on the rich
plains. There was a great covert for elk above the Hays
Crossing. Bob Wright says that for two hundred miles he
traveled along the Arkansas and never was out of one
continuous buffalo herd.

As early as 1846, George F. Ruxton, a young English
lieutenant traveling north from Mexico to the Bayou
Salado (now known as South Park), Colorado, where he
wintered, deplored the imminent passing of the buffalo.

At that time the bison had just abandoned their range close to the Rockies and for the first hundred miles down the Arkansas. More than one hundred thousand buffalo robes found their way to the markets of the United States and Canada.

Ruxton pointed out that individually the buffalo had a remarkable tenacity of life. Even when shot through the heart, he ran some distance, jets of blood pouring from his mouth. He fought desperately to keep from falling, feet braced as he swayed helplessly, sobbing, gasping for breath, until the legs collapsed and he went down with a rush.

The bison had its own peculiar habits. During the rutting season, while the calves were too young to look after themselves, the bulls kept on the outside of the herd watching for the attack of bands of gray wolves. All through the night could be heard the low roar of their lowing. After the young were able to take care of themselves the bulls deserted the herd and ranged apart. In spite of these precautions the wolves made great inroads on the herds, all the way from Texas into Canada. They pulled down the weak and the wounded as well as the calves.

It is impossible to estimate with any accuracy the number of the buffalo. The herds were migratory. With the coming of spring they moved north; in the fall they trekked to the South. There were such vast numbers of them that the prairies were black far as the eye could see. While a herd was passing, a railroad train was sometimes stopped for half a day at a time, and this was after the hide hunters had greatly depleted the supply. Horace Greeley guessed the total number at five million. General Sheridan put it at one hundred million. The estimate of Greeley is far too low. The firm of Wright & Rath alone shipped over the Santa Fe nearly a quarter of a million hides the first year they operated in Dodge City. Later, when the lean years hit Kansas, and buffalo bones, according to sarcastic outside comment, became legal tender there, the sale of these collected bones brought in two million, five hundred thousand dollars. This sum represented the bleached skeletons of thirty-one million bison, one historian figures. And Kansas was only one state where the buffalo roamed. It is likely that this estimate is much too high.

The Comanches hunted the bison on horseback with bow and arrow. These arrows could be driven at close quarters with astonishing force. The bullet from a big Sharp buffalo gun would not bore through two dried buffalo hides, but a Kiowa brave could send his arrow through one to the shaft. The Indian killed to supply his needs, though he was wasteful except when laying in a winter's supply of meat. He recognized that the buffalo meant for him most of the necessities of life, food, fuel, clothing, and shelter. It was essential to his existence as a nomad that the herds remain undiminished, and he contended scornfully that the methods of the hide hunters were cowardly and unsportsmanlike. These necessities were, however, a heavy tax upon the herd. It took from ten to twenty-five skins to make a tent, and these had to be renewed very frequently. Only the best of the animal was used for pemmican, which consisted of dried meat and fat pounded together and packed with hot grease in thin bags. The braves and half-breeds, mostly in the Northern country, who traded in pemmican killed several buffalo to make one sack of the food. The waste was enormous.

Mexicans used the lance very expertly while racing after the game. The whites of course employed rifles. The amateur and the sportsman pursued the buffalo on horseback.

This was the method employed by Buffalo Bill, though he was hired to kill for meat to supply the Kansas Pacific construction camps. The friends of Bill Cody and Bill Comstock had a dispute as to which of the two was the more efficient hunter. A contest was arranged and advertised by the Kansas Pacific, which ran an excursion train to the spot. The game was within easy reach. The party rode out to the nearest herd, and the two hunters began operations. Of the first bunch Cody killed 38, Comstock 23; of the second, Cody 18 and Comstock 14; of the third, Cody 69 and his opponent 57. Cody had killed the leaders and forced the others into a mill, while the other had followed the racing herd, shooting as he went. It is claimed that Buffalo Bill killed 4,280 in eighteen months for the railroad builders, but it is probable that a score of professional hide hunters can be named who did more deadly execution. Among these are such men as Billy Dixon, Emanuel Dubbs, Jack Bridges, Brick Bond, and Kirk Jordan.

The hide hunters who followed the herds as a business stalked their prey on foot. In his reminiscences of early days Dubbs describes the method of the still hunter, accurately if not grammatically.

Early in the morning after breakfast I would take my big fifty Sharp's rifle (long shell) using 110 grains of powder, my buffalo horse, two belts of ammunition, about eighty rounds, and start ahead of one wagon and team which generally consisted of one wagon and team and four men. Riding up on the windward side of the herd out of sight of the buffalo, jump off the horse when it was no longer safe to ride any closer, drop the reins over the horse's head, then walk as close as possible without frightening them, say three hundred or four hundred yards, then pick out the buffalo that was in the most favorable position, take aim, being careful to shoot just back of the fore shoulder so the ball would penetrate the lungs. The report of the gun would frighten the herd and they would start off at a tremendous speed. The next shot would not be fired at the herd but in front of them, the whistling of the ball and the dirt knocked up would turn the buffalo back, this would be repeated until I got the herd to milling, and until they got the scent of blood of the first buffalo shot. By this time their attention would be entirely distracted and the hunter could shoot them at his leisure.

Fort Griffin, on the Clear Fork of the Brazos, was one headquarters for the hide hunters. The town was supported by them. One season fifteen hundred hunters moved out from it to the range to kill. A correspondent for the Galveston *News* describes the activities.

We saw at Griffin a plat of ground of about four acres covered with buffalo hides spread out to dry, besides a large quantity piled up for shipment. These hides are worth in this place from one dollar to one sixty each. The generally accepted idea of the exciting chase is not the one employed by the men who make it a regular business. They use the needle gun with telescope, buy powder by the keg, their lead in bulk and the shells and make their own cartridges. The guns in a party of hunters are used by only one or two men, who usually kill a drove of 30 or 40 buffaloes on one or two acres. As soon as one is killed the whole herd, smelling the blood, collect around the dead body, snuffing and pawing up the ground and uttering a singular noise. The buffaloes pay no attention to the report of the gun, and fly only at sight or scent of the enemy. The rest of the party occupy themselves with "peeling." They are so expert that they can skin a five year old bull in five minutes.

Many carloads of meat, several consisting exclusively of buffalo tongues, were shipped to the Eastern market.

One of the authors remembers very clearly a carload shipment of half-frozen buffalo tongues and hind quarters received in Indianapolis late in the fall of 1875. They were bloody and far from appetizing, not covered or protected in any way, but dumped on the sidewalk in front of the commission house retailing the meat to local butchers.

But the amount eaten was an inconsiderable fraction of one per cent of the total. The carcasses were left to rot where killed and made a stench that could be smelled for miles. Never in the history of the world has there been a more prodigal waste than this ruthless slaughter. When the trail drives began the Western plains were covered with buffalo. Ten years later a few small scattered groups were making their last stand.

Slaughter is the word to use. With a needle gun, an improved Springfield, or a Sharp, the hunter could kill a small herd while the bewildered animals milled around helplessly, not knowing which way to run.

Naturally the buffalo hunter and the Indian cordially hated each other. The former was busily engaged in wiping out the means of subsistence of the latter. The braves had not much fear of regular troops, which did not have mobility enough to corner them. But they had a great respect for the buffalo hunters and were very wary about attacking them. The arms of these men were of the best, and they were trained to accuracy in firing.

Prior to 1870 only a man of great daring would venture south of the Arkansas to hunt. It was held by many to be almost sure death. But the hunters looked longingly across the Arkansas where the herds were more numerous. Year by year more hunters slipped across the line. By the spring of '74 the buffalo had left the range near Dodge, and it was necessary to give up hide hunting or go south. Already scores of men had made the attempt, had pushed into the Panhandle to hunt. Most of them came back alive.

One of these old hide hunters describes his fellows. They looked, he says, like desperadoes, unkempt, grimy, bearded, and often covered with graybacks. Each man wore a belt, was armed with a knife and two Colt's six-shooters. Quick to resent an insult, they were yet careful not to force an issue, since a quarrel meant the flash of guns. Dog fighting, they called a hand to hand struggle with fists. A woman's honor was "as sacredly preserved as if she had been in Paradise." Also they were loyal, brave, and honest, "God's true noblemen," in short.

This is a favorable picture. After he had been drinking, it is to be feared that sometimes the buffalo hunter forgot whose true nobleman he was. He was one tough hombre. He had to be to take his fighting chances with the Comanches, Kiowas, and Staked Plains Apaches. Death might jump at him out of the shinnery at any hour, night or day. It was necessary for him to be a good scout, to know how to read Indian signs, to be cool and as deadly as a rattlesnake when the appalling warwhoop of the savage burst on his ears.

Three or four buffalo hunters were more effective in a fight than a score of armed but untrained travelers caught by surprise. Bob Wright, from the top of his ranch house on the Cimarron, saw through field glasses a freight outfit of two or three hundred wagons attacked and destroyed by a band of Indians who charged down on them. The panic-stricken Mexican drivers were killed to a man. If this party had been hide hunters the Indians would never have attacked.

Like cowboys, cattlemen, and miners, the buffalo hunters were good and bad. The great majority of them were typical frontiersmen, no better and no worse than those engaged in other lines. Such men as Dixon and Dubbs and Rath were among the best of the pioneers, and this was true of thousands of those who "took the hides off'n 'em." Others were hard characters who later graduated into cattle thieves.

Adobe Walls was in the Panhandle, on the Canadian. This post had been built by Bent and St. Vrain, tradition says on the site of an older building, to trade with the Comanches, Kiowas, and Texas Apaches. In November, 1864, Colonel Kit Carson had a pitched battle here with the Cheyennes. The walls of the old adobe buildings, roofless but strong, still stood, a landmark on the prairies. They were about eight or ten feet high and from two to three feet thick, after the usual pattern of the adobe buildings of those days. Carson speaks of them in one official report as "Adobe Walls," in another as "Adobe Fort."

Under Carson's command were several hundred men,

of the First Regiment, New Mexico Volunteers, besides several scores of Utes and Jicarilla Apaches. Kit attacked, drove the Indians back, captured a village, then retreated hurriedly. His forces were in grave danger of extermination, and the old scout conducted a masterly withdrawal. One curious detail of the battle was that someone on the Indian side blew a bugle to sound the attack. It was never known for certain whether the bugler was a Cheyenne or a renegade white. Since the time of Carson the adobe walls had crumbled away and the roofs of the post had disappeared.

In the spring of 1874 A. C. Myers left Dodge with a hundred teams and as many men, to build for the buffalo brigade a supply station at Adobe Walls. Most of his men were hunters to whom it had become clear that the tremendous runs of bison were forever past on the north side of the Arkansas. The big kills of '72 and '73 had almost wiped out the herds in that vicinity.

The Myers party crossed the Arkansas at Dodge and camped the first night at Crooked Creek, the second at the Cimarron. The youngest member of the party was Bat Masterson, later well known as a fighting officer at Dodge and sheriff of Ford County. Other members of the party were the scout Billy Dixon, a saloon keeper James Hanrahan, the notorious horse thief Dutch Henry, and Bermuda Carlisle.

The hide hunters scattered. All the signs told them that the annual northern migration of the buffaloes was at hand. Scouts had seen them coming, a solid mass, thousands upon thousands. They had heard at early dawn the deep steady roar of the bellowing bulls. This trek of the herds was the great event of the year for the Indians. The bison came like bees out of a hive, incredibly numerous.

Myers put up a picket house for a store, Hanrahan built a sod cabin to be used as a saloon. O'Keefe ran up a blacksmith shop. Within a few days Rath & Wright, a merchandising firm of Dodge, constructed a sod store.

Rumors flew fast that the Indians were on the warpath. Some of these were verified. Two hunters named Dudley and Wallace were killed on Chicken Creek. Emanuel Dubbs lost three men on the Salt Fork of the Red and had to ride hard to save his own life. But the men at Adobe Walls were not disturbed. They felt that there were enough on hand to stand off any band of roving warriors that might attack. There were on the morning of June 27, 1874, twenty-eight men and one woman at Adobe Walls. Most of these were buffalo hunters, some of whom were expecting to leave at dawn with supplies for their camps. So secure did the hunters feel that most of them slept outside on the ground. The doors of all the buildings were wide open.

But for one strange thing the lives of all would have been sacrificed. About two o'clock in the morning there was a sharp sound like a rifle shot. It was the cracking of the ridgepole of the Hanrahan saloon. Since the building had a dirt roof there was danger that it would collapse and bury those inside. Dark though it was, the proprietor set about repairing the damage. All of those sleeping near were awakened and began to help. By the time a new ridgepole had been cut, put in place, and the dirt shoveled back upon the roof, the gray light of dawn was beginning to sift into the eastern sky. Some of the men rolled up again in their blankets; others thought it not worth while.

Someone glanced toward Adobe Walls Creek and gave a shout of dismay. Out of the fringe of timber poured on a wide front a rush of pounding cavalry. There rose in the air the hideous yell of hundreds of mounted Indians.

There was never a more splendidly barbaric sight. . . . Hundreds of warriors, the flower of the fighting men of the southwestern Plains tribes, mounted upon their finest horses, armed with guns and lances, and carrying heavy shields of thick buffalo hide, were coming like the wind. Over all was splashed the rich colors of red, vermilion, and ochre, on the bodies of the men, on the bodies of the running horses. Scalps dangled from bridles, gorgeous war-bonnets fluttered their plumes, bright feathers dangled from the tails and manes of the horses, and the bronzed, half-naked bodies of the riders glittered with ornaments of silver and brass. Behind this headlong charging host stretched the plains, on whose horizon the rising sun was lifting its morning fires. The warriors seemed to emerge from this glowing background.

So Billy Dixon in his Life described that magnificent charge. Each hunter fled for safety to the nearest building. All but two. The Shadler brothers were caught asleep in their wagon and killed instantly. Shortly afterward Billy Tyler was shot through the lungs and soon died.

The warriors charged so recklessly that they struck the doors of the buildings with the butts of their lances and rifles. Later, when it was clear to them that they could not win by a frontal attack, dozens of braves risked their lives gallantly to recover the bodies of those who had been shot down by the whites.

Curiously, in this second battle of Adobe Walls as in the first, a bugler sounded the charges for the Indians. He was killed later in the day by Harry Armitage.

The Indians were Cheyennes, Kiowas, and Comanches. The chiefs in command were Lone Wolf, Stone Calf, and Quanah Parker, a half-breed Comanche whose mother had been a white woman captured in a raid. Their medicine man had promised them an easy victory, but this was proving a costly battle for them. By noon they had given up their fierce charges. They withdrew to a distance. After a time the beleaguered men ventured out. They found thirteen dead Indians too close to the buildings for their comrades to remove. The horses and cattle of the whites had all been killed or run off.

The tribes had had enough. On the second and the third days bunches of Indians showed up on a bluff across the valley. It was at this time that Billy Dixon made his famous shot. With a .50 Sharp he drew a bead on one who was making a contemptuous gesture. The distance, afterward measured, was 1,538 yards. Dixon dropped and killed him.

Mrs. William Olds was the lone woman at Adobe Walls. She had come with her husband to run a restaurant for the buffalo hunters who would outfit there. It is on record that she showed a nerve of steel until the sad event which happened after the fight was over. Coming down from the lookout position, rifle in hand, Olds stumbled, and the gun went off. He was dead before his body struck the floor.

The fight at Adobe Walls did not affect the main issue. The hunters continued to cross the Arkansas into the Panhandle. The buffalo was doomed.

Y EAR by year the Texas cattle trail was bent westward by the advancing tide of settlement. The fences of the granger, as he pushed deeper into Kansas, deflected the herds from the first roads followed. Baxter Springs and Coffeyville had their day as cattle centers and resumed a more staid existence. The Chisholm Trail offered a route more direct, with better feed, fewer heel-flies, less timber and wider stretches of prairie, and no civilized tribes to tax the drover. Abilene and Wichita and Newton became unavailable as trade centers for the longhorn. So in time did Ellsworth and Caldwell and Hays City, Dodge and Ogallala, Sidney and Julesburg, Trail City and Kit Carson. The barbed-wire fence and the laws protecting the farmer made the way continually more difficult and at last blocked it entirely. The most westerly point touched by the Chisholm Trail was Fort Lyons, Colorado. More remote parts of the Rocky Mountain region were reached by extension drives over the Bozeman and other trails.

In these trail towns the Texan driver and the Northern buyer met to negotiate the transfer of the herds. Most of the contracts to supply beef for army posts and for reservation Indians were let to men who lived above the Mason and Dixon line. The war was so recent that the Texans, ex-Confederates to a man if they had been old enough to bear arms, did not find it feasible to deal directly with the United States government. There was a prejudice against them at first, one which they returned with interest. Therefore the beef contractor was a middleman, very likely one who had served as an officer in the Civil War on the Union side.

Often the buyer went down the trail from Dodge or Ogallala or Denver several hundred miles to meet the herd of the drover with whom he had been dickering. He might spend a day or two with the outfit. If he wanted the cattle driven to the Black Hills or to Miles City he would probably engage the Texas cowboys to continue with the longhorns until they reached the journey's end. In the early days the buyer brought money with him— gold in a belt around his waist or silver on a pack-horse—to pay for the cows. But after the banks began to function in the cattle trade the business was done by means of paper.

The westward push of the farmer was more rapid east of the hundredth parallel. Lack of sufficient rainfall beyond that latitude made farming at first unprofitable. For this reason Dodge was a trail town longer than any of its rivals. The big cattle drives began there about 1875, following the extinction of the buffalo, and for ten years the town held the trade. More cattle were driven to Dodge than to any other town in the history of the movement.

Each of the towns named was wild and wide open. Each in turn was exploited as the world's worst. When the gamblers, sporting women, and other parasites upon the cattle trade moved en masse from Julesburg to Cheyenne they went on flat cars carrying their equipment with them. Samuel Bowles described this migration as "hell on wheels."

During its heyday one of these towns was as like the others as a pea in a pod is like its neighbors. It began with tents, sod houses, and small rough frame buildings.

As civic pride developed, the false fronts peculiar to the prairie country began to appear on the business street. Every other shack housed a saloon, a dance hall, or a gambling joint. These houses sometimes chose picturesque and telling names, such as The Last Chance or The Road to Hell. Hotels and dance halls and business houses, catering to the visiting trail men, were called The Alamo, The Lone Star, or The Longhorn.

The main thoroughfare was busy as an ant hill, buying, selling, trading, outfitting, and restocking. It was jammed with people moving to and fro, riders weaving in and out, horses tied to hitch racks, freight outfits unloading. There was much drinking, shouting, swearing of mule skinners. The atmosphere was one of boisterous heartiness. Even the profanity had the crisp cheerful robustness of the outdoors.

Dodge City was probably no worse than its neighbors, though it was wild for a longer period, since prior to the cattle trade it had been coincidently the end of the railroad and the center of the hide hunting trade. Beyond it lay the grama grass, the dangerous wilderness. It was the jumping-off place. The railroad graders were a tough crowd. They worked hard and played hard. The same is true of the buffalo hunters. Everybody had money to spend and plenty of it. A good hunter could make a hundred dollars a day, and often the temporary owner of this income was not satisfied until it had been dissipated. Saloon keepers, women beyond the pale, and professional gamblers, pallid of face and cold of eye, with derringers under the long tails of their coats, gathered like buzzards to feast on their prey. It was the spirit of the happy-go-lucky Esau of the plains to spend lavishly. As soon as the cowpunchers began to reach Dodge many of them joined in the carnival of license.

Roll yore tails and roll 'em high,
We'll all be angels by and by,

they sang. Occasionally one of their high-rolling tails got caught in a crack. But that was to be expected. To buck the tiger, to dance with painted women, to swagger from saloon to gambling hall, spurs jingling on their dusty high-heeled boots, was meat and drink to the lads just released from months of hard work on the trail.

But not to all of them. Even in those early days some of these youngsters were sober and reliable youths. A certain percentage of them did not drink at all. These were either members of churches or youths with old heads on young shoulders. It is worthy of note that a great number of the lads who went up the trail later became active in church work and in some cases leading prohibitionists.

Most of the cowboys were young, not older in years than the average college boy of to-day. Already they had lived a lifetime of experience in meeting the hard, rough conditions of the frontier. They had fought blizzards, run stampedes, faced hostile Indians, and held their own with the tough characters of the border. But in spite of the fitness to meet their environment forced upon them by the barbaric vigor of the country they were when out of the saddle as unsophisticated as schoolboys, full of a high-spirited desire to have a good time. Just as college students feel they own a town after a football game, so the trail riders ignored rules imposed upon them by the authorities. If a herder grew boastful under the influence of bad liquor he wanted it known he had money to throw at the birds, had cut his teeth on cartridge shells, and could whip his weight in wildcats. Most of the cowpunchers were good lads, even though given to practical jokes, horseplay, and at times unrestrained gayety. But there were exceptions who gave the class a bad name, killers and thieves who had gone up the trail for the adventure of it, such men as the James brothers and Hardin and the Bass gang.

Dodge was a high tariff town. Nothing could be bought for less than twenty-five cents. Two bits was the cost of a drink or a shave. Everything else was in proportion.

Business boomed. The Dodge House and the Alamo were always full. The overflow slept on the sawdust which covered the floors of the saloons or on the prairie. Even this last innocent occupation had its dangers. During the first year of the existence of Dodge ten men died from the bites of skunks which attacked them while they were asleep.

Front Street was the chief business thoroughfare. It ran parallel to the Santa Fe tracks. To the north, on a hill, lay the residence section. From this eminence one could see a dozen herds being held outside of town. The stockyards were crowded to the gates. Clouds of dust at the far horizon showed where other herds were pointing north. The famous cemetery, Boot Hill, dominated an adjoining rise, the highest point in town. Here were buried the men who died with their boots on. Lumber was scarce, and most of them were laid away without coffins. About twenty-five died from bullet wounds the first year of the town's existence. South of the tracks, between the railroad and the Arkansas River, lay Hell's Half Acre. Here the hurdy-gurdy houses, the brothels, and the worst of the gambling houses did their roaring business.

No weakling made good at the job of maintaining order in such a town as Dodge. A marshal took his life in his hands. Tom Smith and Ed Masterson and T. C. Nixon and Tom Carson paid the price in full, shot to death by desperadoes who disputed their sway. The story of the marshals of the trail towns would be an interesting one. The railroad graders were notoriously rough, but scarcely more so than the freighters. Many of the gamblers, such as Ben and Bill Thompson, Wild Bill Hickok, Wyatt Earp, Luke Short, and others had achieved reputations as gunmen. The buffalo hunters were a cool, hard, hair-trigger group of individualists who did not choose to be "ridden herd" on. Outlaws like Sam Bass and Joel Collins could look any officer in the eye and tell him to hunt a hotter climate. To rule in such a town took a man with nerves of steel and will of iron. Men without fear were chosen as marshals. Killers had the preference because their prestige would tend to make lesser bad men careful as to how they violated the regulations laid down.

Even a partial list of the peace officers of Dodge reads like a roll of honor among the gunmen of the Southwest. Bridges and Brooks and the Mastersons, Wyatt Earp, Ben Daniels, Mysterious Dave Mather, Pat Sughrue, Luke Short, Billy Tilghman, Harris and Bassett and Nixon. What an aggregation of fighting men, every one famous in a day when gameness and skill with deadly weapons were taken as a matter of course! They had to be efficient with the Colt to live. In that they were alike. In other respects they greatly differed. Some of them were cold-blooded killers, callous and treacherous as Apaches. Mysterious Dave had that reputation. Most of them took no needless chances. When in doubt they played trumps; that is to say, they "came a-foggin'," not waiting for the other party to get into action. A few of them never drew a weapon unless driven to it. They preferred to run the risk of being shot down rather than kill desperadoes who might be arrested alive.

It was a chancy business, this one of being a symbol of the law in these border towns. For any time a drunken man had "hell in his neck" he might start guns blazing.

Consider the case of Ed Masterson, marshal of Dodge, a younger brother of the more celebrated Bat. Bob Shaw met Texas Dick in the Lone Star dance hall and mentioned balefully that the latter had robbed him of forty dollars. Dick replied with blistering epithets. At this opportune moment Marshal Masterson made debonair entrance, announced that the law had arrived, and mentioned that both gentlemen might consider themselves under arrest. Shaw, originally from Missouri, took an exception, also a pot shot at the Texas cowboy and another at the marshal. Mr. Masterson, by way of reproof, tapped him ungently on the head with the long barrel of his .44

but failed to subdue the debt collector. The next bullet struck the officer in the breast and came out under the shoulder blade. Masterson fell, coolly transferred his six-gun to the left hand, since the right was temporarily paralyzed, and punctured one Shaw leg and one Shaw arm. During this very short difference of opinion Texas Dick stopped a bullet with his right groin and Frank Buskirk one with his right arm. Frank was an innocent bystander who had not found a window to dive through when the band began to play. After the smoke screen lifted, Mr. Masterson could be seen on the floor riding herd on his prisoners. Result of this brisk encounter, four casualties, none fatal. Mr. Shaw went to jail. His guess about the non-arrival of the law was an erroneous one.

One of Edward J. Masterson's adventures with roistering ruffians did not end so pleasantly. On April 9, 1878, he undertook to arrest Jack Wagner and Alfred Walker, who were terrorizing the town. They killed him. Presently Bat Masterson arrived and was greatly shocked at what had occurred, but not shocked enough to prevent immediate action. He saw to it in person that Wagner and Walker were at once made ready for the undertaker. Bat was no amateur with a Colt's .44. He was a graduate of the frontier school of experience which kept open session 365 days every year.

Along Front Street and the leading thoroughfares of Dodge barrels of water had been placed at convenient intervals to use in case of fire. These barrels were very helpful to duelists taken at disadvantage. An unhappy combatant could duck behind one of them to escape bullets whistling past his ears. Billy Brooks found refuge there when Kirk Jordan, a hardy old buffalo hunter, went after him with a Sharp. Billy had been a high-stepping gunman since his arrival. He had left more dead and wounded in his wake than any other of his ilk to date. Kirk was not interested in Brooks' reputation. He had fought too many Indians to care about trifles like that.

When he got ready he went gunning. Mr. Brooks decided he did not like the climate of Dodge. He left between sunset and sunrise. A rumor drifted back a year or two later that his career had been terminated by vigilantes who tendered him a necktie party.

It must not be assumed that even the most notorious of the gunmen spent their time looking for victims. Most of them were quiet, cool men who never hunted trouble and were quite willing to sidestep it if possible. They were friendly and amiable companions, ready to join in any practical joke that might occur to them. Bat Masterson was especially given to this form of humor. Old-timers in Dodge still tell stories of his pranks. It was the day of youth. Though it must be conceded there was plenty of vice in Dodge there was also a great surplus of innocent, good-hearted fun. The place was riotous with life.

The Reverend F. L. Young, a Methodist minister who lives at Bandon, Oregon, moved in 1873 with his father to a homestead halfway between Hays and Dodge that later became famous as the Buttermilk Ranch. He helped lay out the last deadline west of which all Texas cattle must be kept unless they had been out of the Lone Star State a year. Riding for an outfit camped on the Saw-Log, one day Young waved *adios* to a bunch of his companions riding into town for a spree. Next morning he learned that seven of them had been wounded in a desperate battle with gamblers.

But sometimes the cowboys were not fighting. They were attending church services. The first sermon ever preached in Dodge was by a Methodist presiding elder, John W. Fox. He hired a hall and advertised the services by personal announcement at saloons and gambling halls. The building was jammed. After preaching he administered the Lord's Supper, asking those of his faith to come forward and commune. There was a moment's silence before a cowboy, half seas over, in chaps and spurs, jingled forward, took a square of bread, and drank a whole glass of the wine. When the collection was taken up this cowboy emptied both trouser pockets of all the money he had and poured this into the hat. "I never bum my drinks," he announced aloud.

During the early days of the cattle drives the cowboys took their mounts back to Texas with them, but as the cattle country in the North became dotted with ranches there was a demand for cow ponies. Not only did the drivers sell the remudas with the herd, but scores of herds of horses were driven over the trails. More than a million traveled north on the hoof while the trail was open.

Naturally the horse thief became busy. Broncos are much more easily driven away than cattle because they travel so much faster. Around Dodge gathered a large group of horse thieves, who also did a less thriving business in cattle. The king of these was Dutch Henry, one of the defenders of Adobe Walls against the attack of the plains Indians. Henry was a likable ruffian and made many friends even among respectable people. He had the audacious courage that always appealed to the West. His chief lieutenant was Tom Owens. The depredations of these outlaws were so bold and so great a tax on industry that the citizens of Dodge and Hays organized posses to wipe out the rustlers. There was a pitched battle. Several rustlers and some members of the posse were shot. Owens fell, shot from his horse. Dutch Henry escaped, though he had been wounded six times. He vanished from Kansas. Later he appeared in the Panhandle, a reformed man. He moved to Colorado, where he lived a very quiet life until his death. His neighbors did not know that this gentle, pleasant old gentleman was the notorious Dutch Henry whose reputation at one time was broadcast all over the border country.

2

This was the day of the stage and the train robber. During the turbulent frontier times they flourished like green bay trees, though the careers of all of them were short. The pioneer stood for law and order. When the outlaws became too great a pest they were extinguished by officers or citizens as daring as themselves. Stage robberies had occurred from the time of the first Western frontier. The holding up of trains began almost as soon as the steel lines pushed into the wilderness. The James and Younger gang set a precedent which was followed by Sam Bass and his friends, by the Daltons, the Doolins, and by scores of others from Arizona to Montana.

Sam Bass was a cowboy. The story of the exploits of his gang has become as much a tradition in Texas as the murderous deeds of Jesse James in Missouri or Billy the Kid in New Mexico. Even to this day many men who knew these bandits or have listened to tales about them are apologists for their actions. They say that Jesse James or Cole Younger or Billy the Kid, as the case may be, was driven to crime by outrages committed upon relatives or by the broken faith of others. A maudlin public sentiment has invested these desperadoes with the reputation of Robin Hood. None of them deserve this tender regard for their memories. All had "gone bad." They fought against society for their own ends, and it became as necessary to exterminate them as it is to destroy wolves in the hills.

It may be admitted that Sam Bass had none of the savage cold-blooded will to kill that possessed Jesse James. He drifted into outlawry because it was the line of least resistance. According to the ballad, he

... was born in Indiana, it was his native home,
And at the age of seventeen young Sam began to roam.

Sam first came out to Texas a cowboy for to be—
A kinder-hearted fellow you'd seldom ever see.

Sam worked for Sheriff Everhart of Denton County, but he was too wild even for a cowboy. Upon a race horse that he loved he rode to San Antonio. This was in 1877.

The town was full of cattlemen about to take the trail. One of these was a cowman, Joel Collins, ready for a drive to Deadwood, South Dakota. He needed a point man, and he hired young Bass. It was a long grueling trek to the mining town in the Black Hills, and by the time they reached it the riders were all set for a wild spree.

Collins had bought the herd on credit, but he threw in with his boys, drank wildly, and gambled away the money received. The man was desperate. His friends in Texas had trusted him, and he had betrayed them. He induced some of the men who had gone up the trail with him to join in robbing two or three stages. These enterprises held little profit. Collins decided to play for bigger stakes. He and his band rode down to Ogallala, Nebraska.

At Big Springs they held up a Union Pacific train, took from the express car $80,000 in newly minted gold pieces, and robbed the passengers of $5,000 more. The loot was cached and before dawn the bandits were back in bed at Ogallala. Hundreds of cowboys were in town, as well as scores of the border riffraff. Only one man suspected the Collins outfit, a clerk in the outfitting store which they frequented. His mistrust was so active that he hired a horse and followed the Texans down the trail, hid in the brush near their camp, and actually saw them divide the money. The robbers split into three parties. Sam Bass and a cowboy named Davis headed for north Texas, Berry and Old Dad Underwood for Missouri, and Joel Collins and Bill Heffridge for San Antonio.

Meanwhile the clerk posted back to Ogallala with the news of what he had seen, and posters were sent out everywhere describing the outlaws. Collins and his companion drifted south, quite unaware that they were suspected. The leader fell into talk with a man, mentioned that he was a cattleman, and even gave his name. An army officer with a detachment of soldiers rode after and stopped the two outlaws, charging them with the crime. When Collins found he could not laugh off the suspicion, he made a swift characteristic decision. He looked at Heffridge and nodded. Their six-shooters flashed into the air, and both of them fell riddled with bullets from the weapons of the troopers.

The other four reached their destinations. Old Dad escaped from the country. Berry was killed by a sheriff's posse. Bass and Davis hid out in the chaparral. The chase was too hot for the latter. He emigrated to South America swiftly and silently. Bass stayed to organize another gang.

He held up train after train. The Texas Rangers and a dozen sheriffs were watching for them. One of the outlaws, Arkansas Johnson, was killed in a fight with some of the Frontier Battalion. The three others, betrayed by a confederate, were cornered at Round Rock, where they had gone to rob a bank. Two local officers had been warned that the Bass gang might arrive. They attempted to arrest the suspected men, and both officers were killed. Dick Ware, a Ranger, wounded Bass so badly that he could not mount his horse. The third bandit, a boy named Frank Jackson, held the Rangers back while he helped his chief to the saddle, after which he swung to the back of his own horse and galloped down the street, a dozen bullets singing past him.

Bass could not travel. He insisted that Jackson save himself. The boy escaped and went into hiding in the elm bottoms of Denton County.

Two or three days later Bass died. He was buried at Round Rock beneath a stone upon which had been cut these words:

SAMUEL BASS

BORN JULY 21st, 1851
DIED JULY 21st, 1878

A BRAVE MAN REPOSES IN DEATH HERE.   WHY WAS HE NOT TRUE?

This might justly have been carved upon the graves of ten thousand wild and reckless souls who traveled a path similar to that which Bass rode.

As for Jim Murphy, the member of the gang who betrayed the others, he took poison and ended his life. The ballad makes comment on his probable future.

. . . he sold out Sam and Barnes and left their friends to mourn—
Oh, what a scorching Jim will get when Gabriel blows his horn.
Perhaps he's got to Heaven, there's none of us can say,
But if I am right in my surmise he's gone the other way.

3

It is easy to draw a picture of Dodge that is entirely out of focus. The little town was explosively vital. Most of its residents were red-blooded outdoor men. The dry clean air of the plains was a tonic for those whose lungs were affected. Those who came to die of tuberculosis soon found themselves in the pink of condition. Rich life renewed itself in their veins. Naturally they took on the color of this happy-go-lucky West which had saved them.

The aim of one part of the population was to amuse and interest the gawky lads who high-heeled along the streets with the dust of the trail still in their throats. It was with them a cold business proposition of separating the sucker from his money. Some of them had no scruples as to the means they employed, though there were honest gamblers, decent bartenders, and kind-hearted prostitutes. Any song about home and mother, sung by a drunken ne'er-do-well in a throaty tenor, would bring lumps into the throats of cowboys and sporting women.

But side by side with this life of license was another and totally different one. Some of the business men of Dodge were Christians and supported churches as soon as these could be organized. They worked for civic righteousness, Sunday closing, the abolition of the red-light district, local option. Their efforts at first seemed to show no results, but in time they accomplished their objects. The children of the citizens went to good schools and saw nothing of the

and though many twos and threes and some yearlings went along they were all fours by the time they reached the trail's end. The cowboys claimed they aged rapidly en route.

On the western trail, up the Pecos and across the Ratons, Loving and Goodnight early discovered a demand for breeders as well as feeders. They took cows to Colorado. Scores of calves dropped on the way had to be killed, since the outfit had no facilities for carrying them. The market for breeders was a local one, based on the gold discoveries near Denver. It was limited to farmers in the territory of Colorado, who had gone into the business of raising food supplies for the new mining towns, a population of not more than thirty thousand in 1866, and very much less than this at the time Loving took his first herd through. Cows were much more difficult to drive than beef stock, and many trail men would not at first bother with them. Of course "grown stuff" was more easily handled than young stock.

The imperative demand for cows to stock the great ranges along the Rockies came later. No Texan could have anticipated the amazing market that was to develop so swiftly, a market that had its roots in changing conditions that were to win an empire out of an untrodden wilderness.

The push of the railroads into the trans-Mississippi deserts made possible a contact between the crowded population of the East and the rich grass lands of the West. Four transcontinental lines were building, the Union Pacific, the Santa Fe, the Southern Pacific, and the Northern Pacific, and these made millions of acres accessible to home seekers. The end of the war had released from the Union army thousands of men too restless to settle down in the quiet communities where they had been brought up. The West became to them a golden opportunity, and they turned their faces toward the setting sun as quickly as they could. Simultaneously, the industrial centers of the country developed amazing energy, much of this along

lines which affected the rising cattle trade. Hardly had
Lee surrendered before the Union stockyards were built
in Chicago. Two years later Armour and his partner put
up a modern packing plant. By 1871 refrigerating cars
were running to the consumers' market, and shortly after
this beef was being canned much as it is now. All of these
innovations increased tremendously the demand for beef.

But when Goodnight first drove a herd into Colorado
the only evidence of this amazing revolution was the railroad roadbed which had barely begun to move forward
from "the river," as the Missouri was always called in the
Rocky Mountain region. Only a thin trickle of hardy
pioneers were pointing the way into the wilderness. Nobody could have foreseen that they were the forerunners of
millions. Nor could one have predicted the rapid extermination of the buffalo and the consequent entire break-up
of the free tribal life of the Indians. Already both of these
were under way. The remarkable and unexpected rapidity
with which they were consummated was characteristic
of the whole settlement of the West.

The historian Bancroft tells a story that one finds current, with differing details as to names and places but
almost identical as to date, in Kansas, Wyoming, Montana,
Idaho, and other states. The discovery of the nutritive
values of the grasses of the Platte Valley in Colorado
during the winter was made, he writes, as early as 1858
by A. J. Williams, a freighter who turned his eighteen
oxen loose in the fall near old Fort Lupton because he had
no feed. He expected them to die. In the spring he found
them sleek and fat. Williams made no practical use of his
knowledge until after the war when he drove fifteen
hundred Mexican cattle into the valley.

It happens to be on record that in 1843 the explorer
Fremont found hogs and cattle ranging at the very spot
which afterward became known as Fort Lupton. It was a
trading post and ranch owned by Lancaster P. Lupton,
formerly a lieutenant in the United States army. The trap-

pers at Fort Bent had four years later "a tolerable supply of cattle, horses, mules, etc." Gunnison found in 1853 a herd of cattle and horses feeding on the wagon trail which led across the Raton Pass into New Mexico.

Evidently Bancroft was not aware of this or that Loving trailed a herd from the Panhandle to Pueblo in '59 and wintered it in the Arkansas Valley, or that John Dawson drove one to the Cherry Creek camp at Denver the same year. If Texans were willing to risk wintering their herds in Colorado they must have known it was feasible. Certainly there was no need for Williams to wait until 1866 to put into practice his information, for by that time an official report shows that Colorado had twenty thousand cattle, most of them not Texas imports but bred from stock brought across the Overland Trail. By this time more than seventy thousand acres of land in the territory were planted to crops. Farms were beginning to dot the valleys of the Arkansas and the Gunnison, and ranches to fringe the plains of Arapahoe, Douglas, El Paso, and Pueblo counties along the eastern side of the Divide. Close to Denver there were scores of farms with land under cultivation, running into thousands of acres. The Hermosilla Ranch, on the Las Animas grant, had in 1868 more than fourteen hundred acres in corn, wheat, oats, and beans.

Small cattle owners bordering on the Overland Trail in various territories had proved, long before the discovery of gold in the Pike's Peak region, that it was practicable to let cattle rough through the winter without hay. Most of these early ranchmen in the North were old frontiersmen who had been bullwhackers or trappers and now made a living by catering to the needs of the man with the covered wagon. They raised vegetables, cut wild hay, and exchanged new oxen for travel-worn ones for a consideration. Horace Greeley mentions seeing herds as far West as Utah in 1859. Russell, Majors & Waddell used in '58 more than twenty-five thousand oxen freighting over the plains. Many of these subsisted through the winter on the thick wiry buffalo grass that covered the prairies west of the 96th parallel. In *Beyond the Mississippi*, written by A. D. Richardson in 1859, the author mentions that the farmers in the San Luis Valley did not feed their stock in winter, but let it rough through on a wild sage.

As early as 1861 Samuel Hartsel of South Park, Colorado, started a herd of registered bulls and cows and three years later brought in 148 cows and several bulls of the shorthorn breed, all eligible for registry, according to Steinel's *History of Agriculture in Colorado*. The same year the pioneers of Denver were looking to farming to supplement mining and proposed the organization of an agricultural society.

As has been said, the tides of tossing longhorns pouring out of Texas were not haphazard in the direction they took. Their course was determined by forces beyond the control of the bearded drivers, by the push of economic law. Because the Pike's Peak gold rush had already brought a considerable population to Colorado, it was naturally the first of the Western states to feel the impact of the Texas invasion of breeders. The current swept into the future Centennial State because there was a market.

John W. Iliff, later known as the cattle king of Colorado, had already become the biggest cowman in the territory when he bought the Goodnight herd. His stock increased rapidly until his cattle ranged along the South Platte for seventy-five miles. Iliff protected himself from competition of the small nester by getting control of the streams. The land could not be bought from the government, but it could be homesteaded and preëmpted. Sometimes he bought from settlers. More often he evaded the intent of the law by getting his own cowboys to take up claims along the river and buying them out for nominal sums as soon as they had proved up. Scores of big cattle outfits adopted this method of holding the range. It was held by them to be an entirely legitimate practice, even though technically illegal.

THE OLD LONGHORNS
have been replaced by cattle of superior blood and breed.

Taken in the stockyards at Fort Worth, Texas, 1898.

THESE OLD CORRALS AND WHITENING SHEEP BONES SAY, "KEEP OFF THE GRASS"

The value of the range was measured by the accessible water. Anyone controlling the water supply practically owned all the contiguous country whether it was legally in his name or not. During the years when the cowman was lord of the domain he and his neighbors made their own rules and later incorporated them into law. The basis of the code was that the dry plains were for grazing only and that the question of the Western public lands must be considered primarily from this viewpoint. Priority of occupation invested locators with validity as much as though they were confirmed by statute. The cattleman respected the rights of his fellows, and stood with them against the rustler and other evils that threatened their common welfare. Even in the North the big ranches took on certain feudal aspects. The riders shifted at will from one outfit to another, but while employed by one brand they were loyal to it often to the point of lawlessness. They fought brand blotters and homesteaders no less than they did wolves and blizzards.

The courts accepted to a certain extent this assumption of a feudal right in lands adjacent to those actually owned. A Colorado outfit sold to an English company a ranch on the plains described as having 150 by 120 miles of free range with exclusive right thereto, 3,000 acres of freehold pasture, 9 miles of river front and tributary streams, and 9,000 head of graded cattle. The purchaser brought suit and gained judgment, on the ground that false representations had been made as to the extent of the seller's rights.

Through the Commissioner of the Land Office during the Hayes Administration, the cattlemen attempted to settle the question of the grazing lands by permanent legal sanction. The Secretary, backed by an indorsement of the President, recommended that the public domain west of the 100th parallel (which runs through Dodge City, Kansas) be not minutely surveyed but be thrown open to sale in large lots. He referred to this country, formerly called the Great American Desert, as barren lands, unsuitable for agriculture without irrigation. Congress, always jealous in regard to the public lands, vetoed the proposal. The members of both houses who represented the Middle West had seen the granger within ten years push across and farm large sections of Kansas, Nebraska, and the Dakotas in spite of the opposition of the cattleman. They had no desire to antagonize home seekers.

Except in certain congested spots America was still rural, and the last decades of the nineteenth century were marked by an eager desire among hundreds of thousands for the new lands opening up. This absorption in our own undeveloped natural resources was a distinguishing characteristic of the people. It localized the national thought and kept the United States from being world minded. Among most of the citizens very little was known of Europe except in a hazy way. Even England was only a figment of the imagination, a figure of straw set up as a traditional enemy to furnish Fourth of July orators an opportunity for twisting the Lion's tail. The burden of their song was that we had whipped Johnnie Bull twice and were ready to do it again if he hadn't had enough.

The Texas steer did not get into Colorado without protest. Newspapers grumbled about it. Stockmen met and passed resolutions. The territorial legislature in 1867 put this feeling into an act prohibiting the importation of Texas cattle into Colorado. But there was money in the Southern cattle trade, and the law fell at once into desuetude, though more than a thousand head of local cattle died from Texas fever in Douglas County alone.[1] A band of armed farmers stopped one herd, killed some of them, and stampeded the others. This outbreak precipitated a conflict that resulted in the repeal of the prohibitory law by the legislature of 1870.

The pasturage on the plains along the eastern slope of

---

[1] This and some other statements regarding the early cattle days in Colorado are derived from Steinel's *History of Agriculture*, published by the Colorado Agricultural College.

the Rockies was excellently adapted for both summer and winter grazing. Grama grass, dried on the stem, curled up and made good hay for stock-rustling feed. One season in Colorado added nearly two hundred pounds to the weight of a longhorn and did a great deal to improve the appearance of his hips, belly, ribs, and general ensemble. The evidence of the swiftness with which information of this traveled may be found in the tremendous increase in the number of cattle in the Territory of Colorado. Within three years this was fifty-fold. The twenty thousand in 1866 had jumped to more than a million. Charles Goodnight was the first Texan to go into the ranging of cattle in Colorado. He bought in 1868 a large tract of land near Pueblo, and three years later another ranch forty miles from Trinidad. He had made on the trail seventy-two thousand dollars and this sum he invested in these two ranch properties and the cattle with which to stock them.

The great bulk of the cattle in Colorado in 1869, however, did not belong to Colorado ranches but were passing through on their way to a beef or a feeders' market. From Kit Carson the first carload rolled east in '69. Within three years more than four hundred cars of cattle moved out of the railroad yards in Denver and almost as many from Deer Trail, Cheyenne Wells, and Kit Carson combined. Most of these went to Kansas City, Omaha, and Chicago. By this time the raising of cattle began to take on the dignity of business rather than the glamour of an adventure. The Colorado National and the First National banks of Denver were financing the buyers, and the Kansas City banks were also making cattle loans. To lend money on cows held an element of unusual hazard, since the property could be driven away on the hoof and disposed of by an unscrupulous dealer. The banks loaned on the character of the cowman, usually a first-class basis for trust. A stockman had to build up a reputation for honesty as a financial asset. If there was anything shady in his business record the banks would have nothing to do with him.

As McCoy put it, a drover held his fortune by a thin and brittle thread. Market prices fluctuated greatly. Large sums could be made or lost very easily. The banker was a Westerner, as was his client. To build up the country he had to take a chance with the cattleman. But the odds were heavy enough at the best. He dealt only with men whose word was as good as a bond, men who were never known to have blocked a brand or bought a "wet horse," a phrase used for an animal which had been stolen in Mexico and swum across the Rio Grande.

There was no permanence in any aspect of the cattle trade during the early days of the drives. Swift changes were characteristic and business adapted itself to them with great rapidity. Even before the end of the Civil War decade Chicago was realizing a great impetus, owing to the fact that the importation of Texas stock reduced the price of beef and made it possible for the artisan to eat meat. Kansas City and Omaha had, with the building of the Union Pacific, become rival shipping centers, just as the railroads which supplied these towns had become transportation competitors. The threat to the trade at first monopolized by the Kansas Pacific and the Hannibal & St. Joe developed force as the plains of the North began to fill with cattle. The Rock Island and the C. B. & Q. fitted in as part of the connecting system which helped to make Chicago the largest nucleus of the middleman.

The quickness with which the Northern plains were stocked is shown by the short life of the different trail towns. Westward across Nebraska the shipping points moved on the Union Pacific from Schuyler to Kearney to North Platte to Ogallala to Sidney, and then beyond the Wyoming line to Laramie and Rawlins. The farmer had arrived, and while Ogallala was still booming with trail trade, Kearney was sending fat hogs to the Chicago stockyards and farm produce to commission men.

More cattle came up the trail in 1871 than in any other

year. The settlement of the river valleys in Nebraska, Colorado, and Wyoming made an imperative call for the longhorn. Unfortunately the demand was discounted by the vast number of cattle that poured north. There were not settlers enough to absorb the herds brought up the trail. One driver sent eight hundred longhorns as far as Virginia City, Montana. Others traveled nearly as far to find a market. Scores of owners took losses, but the year demonstrated beyond question that there were thousands of miles of unused range in the Northwest that would make rich feeding ground for cattle. Far-sighted men realized that the country of the Cheyenne and of the Sioux, at present too dangerous to penetrate, would soon become feeding ground for the stock of whites. As yet, however, the government had failed to subdue these tribes. They held a country, by treaty title, from the upper Missouri west to the Big Horn Mountains, that was larger than New England.

The financial depression of 1873 hit the cattle market hard, as it did all lines of business. The immediate cause of the panic was the suspension, September 18th, of the great banking house of Jay Cooke & Co. This ushered in a train of disasters that paralyzed the activities of the nation. The banking system was shaken to its center. Manufacturing plants shut their doors. Hundreds of thousands of workingmen were thrown out of employment.

Most of the drovers had not yet disposed of their holdings. They were doing business on credit and were not prepared to meet the strain. Banks could not renew loans, and many of them went down in the general crash. The cattleman did not know which way to turn. In the aggregate millions were owed by trail men, and there was no demand for the longhorns. To make matters worse there had been a short corn crop and the Mississippi states did not need feeders. The herds were sacrificed for whatever they would bring. Many thousands were slaughtered for hide, horn, and tallow. Everybody who touched stock lost money: the owners, the drivers, the shippers, and the ultimate buyers.

Even McCoy, who had done more than anybody else to develop the Texas trade, threw up his hands and cried, "Enough!" Along with many thousand other dealers in cows he had gone bankrupt. The Northern range did not need any more longhorns, he admitted.

He was both right and wrong. The business of ranging cattle in the North had reached a stage where it no longer needed scrub cows and calves for stocking purposes. The riffraff odds and ends which the Lone Star State producer wanted to get rid of could not be sold at the trail's end. The market in future would be for good stockers and fairly well matured steers ready for conversion into beef. McCoy was wrong in thinking that the days of trail driving were past. From three to five million cattle were still to come up the trails before the fences barred the path as a reminder that economic conditions had changed the status of the cow.

So unsuspected was the impending depression of '73, prior to the failure of Cooke, that a day or two before the suspension of the big banking house cattlemen met in Kansas City to form a Live Stock Men's National Association. This went down in the smash. It was twenty years before another one was formed.

The years 1874 and 1875 were dull for cowmen. The country was recovering from the shock of the panic very slowly. Business was cautious and times hard. During those two years not many more than three hundred thousand dogies went up the trail.

But during those years the foundations were being laid for a tremendous expansion of the live-stock industry. On the heels of the panic, in part because of it, the Western migration increased greatly in volume. Poor people, unable to get a foothold in the Middle West, where land had become comparatively expensive, moved in covered wagons past the last fringes of settlement to the range from which the buffalo was vanishing. The glamour of the new country was luring the "mover." Fortunes were to be made in cows. Instead of a steer netting ten or twelve dollars, as he did in Texas, he would fetch twice as much in prime condition at the river markets. So the word went from mouth to mouth. Moreover, the cattlemen were seeking new pastures. Near neighbors irked them. They wanted elbow room, a range where they would not be crowded. So they abandoned eastern Nebraska and Kansas to the farmer and pushed toward the setting sun. The Indians had been removed from the central plains, and the buffalo had vanished from this part of the country. Colorado cowmen pushed into the eastern part of that state to take up the land left vacant by them. Great tracts were being occupied in Wyoming, Dakota, and Montana, and lesser sections in Idaho and Utah. The buffalo and other native grasses of Wyoming were very nutritious and made high-grade beef. Some claimed that an immature Texas steer could be put on the range there and add four hundred pounds in a season. In spite of the cold Montana winters it had been proved that cows could rough through very well and come out in fair condition. Many Texans were either moving north or establishing feeding ranges there. The big companies had not yet reached their zenith, but they too later bought ranches in the Northwest as supplementary to their Southern ones.

The great boom in cattle was not to come for some years, but the factors which made it possible were operating now. Iliff went on record as saying that this was the greatest opportunity for investment ever offered, that the losses were almost nothing and the profits immense. How was it possible for him to guess, as he rode across the vast domain with scarcely a fence between the Arkansas and the North Platte, that within a very few years the grass would be greatly injured by overfeeding and the market depressed by overproduction?

A wealth of forage grasses originally covered the great plains; nor does this appear to have been greatly affected by the quantities of wild game which roamed the country.

In the time of the Spanish explorers Coronado crossed the plains at the head of an army of troopers and of Indians, herding a thousand horses, five hundred cows, and five thousand sheep, leaving so little sign that the path had to be marked for the rearguard by buffalo heads. The long grass hid the marks of thirty thousand feet. This condition remained true until the coming of the whites for settlement. In 1868 General Luther P. Bradley, reporting to the War Department, comments on the abundance of the feed.

I believe [he wrote] that all the flocks and herds in the world could find ample pasturage on these unoccupied plains and the mountain slopes beyond; and the time is not far distant when the largest flocks and herds in the world will be found here, where the grass grows and ripens untouched from year to year.

This fine range stretched, though interrupted by much desert country, from the Mexican border to Canada. An observer writing in 1898 quotes a stockman who traveled with a herd through San Saba, Tom Green, and Taylor counties, Texas, in 1867, as saying that the grass was everywhere from one to three feet high and that the range would have supported 300 head of cattle to the square mile.

Now at the end of thirty years almost every condition has changed [the observer makes comment]. The carrying capacity of the range has steadily decreased until it is an exceptional property that can carry one head of stock to five acres. . . . It is often considered not the best policy to put on more than 50 cows to the section of 640 acres.

Writing of the Little Missouri River country in South Dakota, John Clay, in his book, *Life on the Range,* shows that the feed in that country was as abundant:

What a wondrous country it was for grass. There was nothing but grass and then more grass; the blue joint with its ripening heads, good as corn for fattening. Mossy stretches of buffalo grass made unexcelled winter feed. Never before or since have I seen such fat calves, cows, steers, and heifers; all were fat. And then to think that three years from that time this fair land should be as bare as Sahara.

The grasses were described as inexhaustible by scores of travelers, but the greed of the white man to make money as quickly as possible was a factor destructive enough to change the situation radically.

All this natural gazing land attracted the rustler as well as the honest cowman. One Colorado gang had its headquarters at a place near Julesburg known as Robbers' Roost. The settlers found evidence, raided and destroyed the hang-out, and drove the thieves out of the country. Goodnight had to fight against numerous groups of rustlers operating around Trinidad. A score of other nests of brand blotters were wiped out. Bijou Basin cattlemen hanged three men on Kiowa Creek for mavericking a calf. But rustling was and is a persistent evil. Wherever there has been an open range the outlaw with a rope and a running iron has dodged in and out of the chaparral. Even to-day, with Cattleland thoroughly tamed and gentled, the stock lifter still pursues his nefarious calling. In spite of the most careful precautions thousands of cattle are stolen every year in the West.

A rough and wooded country offered a better field for the rustler than the open plains. In a pocket of the hills, a cañon, or a heavily wooded draw, he could lie concealed while he watched for inconvenient intruders. It was a chancy business, this lying out in the mesquite to steal other men's stock. In the early days the law could not usually reach the waddy who was swinging a wide loop. If it dragged him into court he was likely to be acquitted by a jury none too sympathetic to the big outfit he had robbed. But justice did not wait on law. The raider knew he was suspected and that if he should be caught with the evidence on him he would be given short shrift. Indignant cattlemen would not turn him loose to renew his thefts, but would hang him to the nearest cottonwood. Knowing this, he was a desperate man, and if cornered would fight to a finish while guns blazed. He took as few chances as possible. A good many cowboys riding range have been shot down because they came too close to rustlers at work or in hiding.

The outlaw operated in different ways. He burned brands, changing the original one by the addition of another stroke or two from a hot running iron. He mavericked calves not yet marked, often large ones overlooked in the round-up, and drove them from their mothers. He beefed steers and sold them to butchers in small towns who did not question ownership too closely.

Sometimes the rustlers worked in gangs, boldly and swiftly, defiant of the cattlemen. Billy the Kid and his companions would ride across the line from New Mexico, pick up a bunch of cows, and head for home through the chaparral. Traveling all night over a country scarcely settled at all, they usually reached their own range undisturbed. If seen and pursued, they were prepared to fight it out with the cowboys on their heels.

Because the odds favored the thief as against the honest man, line riders went armed and were quick to shoot. Anybody found in or near the pasture had to show cause for his presence or take the consequences. If the range was one subject to frequent depredation a check was kept upon any chance visitor. Word was passed around the ranch about his personal appearance, the color and brand of his horse, the story he had told, explaining his presence. If the boss was not satisfied he hinted broadly that the man had better "drag it."

This suspicion of unknown visitors was not usual except in a region infested with rustlers. The custom of the range was open-handed hospitality. "'Light, stranger, and give yore saddle a rest," fell heartily from the lips of men in Cattleland. A puncher "riding the chuck line" [out of a job] was always invited to sit on his heels, eat chuck with the outfit in camp, and stay until he wanted to go. If he came to a dugout far from the home ranch and found the punchers out, he made a fire and cooked a dinner, being careful always to leave as much fuel as he found. What he ate was negligible. It was his for the taking. He was welcome to whatever he found. This was so much a matter of course that anyone offering to pay for what he had received became at once an object of scorn.

Even now the spirit of this friendliness persists in out-of-the-way ranch country. The cook of one outfit in Montana kept check recently and found that chance guests dropping in had eaten more than three hundred meals during the year.

2

The currents of the Texas cattle drives followed the lines of least resistance. They poured out of the Lone Star State, not only to get in touch with a market, but to relieve the pressure of a glut too great for the feeding capacity of the range. Driven by this urge for more pasturage, cowmen pushed across the Staked Plains and settled in New Mexico along the Pecos River before any of them moved his herds into the country about old Tascosa. Chief of the Texans adventuring across the line was John S. Chisum. By way of the Horsehead Crossing, in 1867, driving ten thousand longhorns, Chisum pushed into the Pecos Valley to pastures new.

Most of the Lone Star State cattlemen, looking for a market, drove their surplus stock to it across many hundred miles of hardship and danger. Chisum went them one better. He was a bachelor, and his home was under his hat. Lock, stock, and barrel, he moved from the Concho River to a strategic point from which he could reach out to many markets. With his loaded wagons, his great remuda, the immense trailing herds guided by unkempt bearded riders, the trek of the Jingle Bob must have been as impressive as that of Abraham in Scriptural days.

Chisum located the buyers he was seeking. On the Pecos he was within driving distance of Tucson and Prescott, in Arizona; of Santa Fe and Albuquerque, in New Mexico; of Trinidad and Denver, in Colorado. If the Apache reservations were close enough to suggest peril, they were also near enough to make them easy of access to a cattleman bidding on the government beef contracts for the Indians. At convenient distances three or four military posts ringed the district where his cattle ran.

The owner of the Jingle Bob found his markets, and with them dangers enough to daunt a less resolute man. From Fort Sumner he secured a contract for the delivery of ten thousand beeves to feed the Navajo Indians held there. More than half the herd set aside for this purpose vanished from the range, stolen by rustlers in the wholesale trade. Apaches ran off an entire drove going through the Guadalupes. Mexican vaqueros preyed on his outfits. The cowboys of Chisum were as lawless as the men opposed to them. They fought for years, killed and were killed, went their appointed way with the rollicking mirth of boys and the savage harshness of frontiersmen trained to hold life lightly. And always the herds of Chisum grew and grew until they became so great that he did not know even approximately how many he owned.

He established his main headquarters near where the city of Roswell, New Mexico, now stands. It was such a center of life as a feudal lord of the Middle Ages might have owned, except that a long one-story adobe house, with wide porches littered by saddles, spurs, quirts, and other paraphernalia stood in place of the moated castle. The hospitality was regal. All comers were served. Every day a score of guests, most of them uninvited strangers passing through the country, sat down at Chisum's tables and ate of his abundance. He planted orchards, irrigated fields. From the desert he salvaged hundreds of acres for raising wheat and alfalfa. The cottonwoods that even to-day run from the road to the house to form a noble avenue were brought by him two hundred miles and set out under his supervision.

John Chisum's brand was recorded in San Miguel County, New Mexico, on May 29, 1872. This county then extended all the way down the east side of the territory to the southern line. The brand was a long straight bar (——) on the left side from shoulder to tail. In 1879 the brand was re-recorded and the letter U on the left shoulder added to the long bar. The earmark, a jingle bob in each ear, was for the first time made part of the record. The Chisum holdings were closed out in 1892. Most of the land passed into the hands of the Hagerman family.

The Chisum jingle bob was so outstanding as to have given a name to the herd. It was made by cutting into each ear on the upper side, close to the head and far enough in to sever the "backbone" of the ear, thus causing the flaps to hang down along the face as in the case of the long pendulous ears of the Angora goat or those of the pure-bred Brahman cattle. Frequently the flaps were frozen off in cold weather. The jingle bob was the homeliest earmark ever put on a cow.

Chisum was monarch of all he surveyed. In the part of the Pecos Valley where he lived his word was law. All over Cattleland men talked of him and his jingle bob. No other man held title to as many cattle as he. The number of his retainers ran into the hundreds. From Texas he brought his brothers and his relatives to bask in his opulence.

Yet there was a fly in the ointment of his content. Nesters here and there along the river, small cattlemen in the hill pockets of the tributary streams, were as disturbing to him as virulent mosquitoes to a thin-skinned man. They too had been driven out of Texas by the need for more range. To Chisum it seemed that their herds increased beyond reason, and at his expense. They were, he held, thieves without qualification.

The nesters had their own view of the Chisum régime. The Jingle Bob riders were arbitrary and overbearing. With their lord's iron they branded all the calves they found. From the best grass and water they pushed the stock of small owners, regardless of priority. The small owners said flatly he was as much a rustler as any fugitive who had taken to unlawful ways and was on the dodge in the chaparral.

So they contended, and since they were frontiersmen, hardy veterans of the Civil War, they drew together to defend what they felt to be their rights. In the person of Major L. G. Murphy, an ex-army officer who had located at Lincoln, New Mexico, they found a leader. Murphy ran a store and freight outfits, filled cattle contracts, gave advice and credit to the men who had settled on the Hondo, the Bonito, and the Ruidoso. With his partners Riley and Dolan he controlled the trade of the mountains.

He and Chisum eyed each other with suspicion and distrust. Go-betweens fanned their jealousy to an active hostility which eventuated in the Lincoln County cattle war, the most bloody page ever written in the history of cattle in the United States.

Looking back on it now, this "war" stands out only as an acute and early outbreak of a condition which later disturbed the whole high plains country, the conflict of interests between the rival claimants for free grass. It was born of cause and effect, and it differed from other such struggles only in that it was more dramatic in its contempt for law and more reckless in its disregard for human life.

A tenderfoot, Alexander A. McSween, had come to Lincoln. About the same time John H. Tunstall arrived from England. They went into partnership, backed by Chisum, and opened a store and bank at Lincoln. This invasion of his territory was bitterly resented by Murphy and his allies, one of whom was a prominent lawyer, politician, and official of New Mexico.

Neither McSween nor Tunstall was fitted for leadership in such a ruthless campaign. The former was a lawyer, pious, subtle, possessed of none of the stark courage necessary to control his own hired killers and to oppose the hardy ruffians imported by the other side as "warriors" to take part in this savage feud. Tunstall was a red-cheeked Britisher, fond of adventure and big-game hunting, a genial, open-hearted gentleman who to the day of his death failed entirely to understand that he had become involved in implacable warfare.

From all the frontier states and territories, but more particularly from Texas, outlaws and road agents, stock thieves, ruffians, and murderers gathered in New Mexico to take part in the carnival of crime about to begin.

There had been frequent collisions between the two parties, but the outrage which served as a declaration of war was the murder of Tunstall. At this time William H. Bonney, later known as Billy the Kid, the most notorious rustler and killer of New Mexico, first comes into the picture as a cowboy working for the Englishman. He was a lad not yet eighteen, but in his wanderings he had already left behind him a trail of blood.

Tunstall was killed by a posse led by Billy Morton, sent from Lincoln to attach some horses owned by the former. There was no justification whatever for the murder. The posse took the horses unopposed. With great difficulty Tunstall's foreman Brewer and Billy the Kid, having learned of the approach of the Morton party, had persuaded their employer that it was not safe to stay at the ranch. It took them hours to bring his stubborn mind to accept this, and even then he was not at all convinced. He had not injured any of these men. Why should they want to do him personal injury? The posse pursued. When Brewer and young Billy saw that cloud of dust in the rear they knew what it meant. Again the obstinate streak in Tunstall dominated him. He refused to run away. His companions left him hurriedly, and as soon as the pursuit reached him he was shot down.

The killing of Tunstall set a match to a powder magazine. Feeling ran so high that it was dangerous to be a neutral. Armed men rode the streets of Lincoln, watching one another with wary, smoldering eyes.

The party of the dead Tunstall struck swiftly and savagely. But they moved under some faint color of law, as did most of the ruffians during this bloodthirsty campaign. Sheriff Brady was friendly to the Murphy faction, so Brewer had himself appointed a deputy by a justice of the peace. He gathered a posse that included as many murderous ruffians as had been in the Morton party. It included Frank McNab, Doc Skurlock, Charley Bowdre, Fred Waite, and of course Billy the Kid. Among them was an Irishman named McCloskey, who should never have ridden with such a pack of avenging wolves.

The posse rode far before it flushed its game. Well down the Pecos Valley it jumped Billy Morton and Frank Baker, the latter also one of the group who had killed Tunstall. The two men fled, holed up in a dugout, and stood off the Brewer gang until their ammunition was exhausted. Under a promise of safe conduct to Lincoln they surrendered.

Both Morton and Baker knew to what a frail reed they were trusting. They had ridden the range with several of their captors, had swapped stories at friendly camp fires, enjoyed with them practical jokes played on one another. Nearly all present were boys not yet of age. But none of this mattered. The death of Tunstall stood between them. The captives knew that they had to pay a debt of vengeance.

The party spent a night at the Chisum ranch. Both of the condemned men wrote letters of farewell to relatives. It chances that the one from Morton has been preserved. In it he discusses quite coolly the probabilities, tells his version of the trouble, gives information as to what property he has, and signs himself "Yours respectfully." There is not even a faint suggestion of fear in the remarkable document. It is as quietly written as though he were describing an election in which he was casually interested. Though he knows he is marked for death he faces the fact with imperturbable courage.

There was a girl at the ranch, John Chisum's niece. Baker left his watch with her to be sent to his sweetheart. Morton shook hands with her before he walked out to climb into the saddle. Miss Chisum knew as well as he did that this was the last ride he would ever take. There was nothing she could do about it, no way she could save these two boys caught in the toils of their own ruthlessness.

In some cañon, on the way to Lincoln, the two prisoners were shot to death. McCloskey was a friend of Morton. He protested at the slaughter of men who had surrendered under a pledge of protection. He tried to defend them, and he was himself killed.

Lincoln County had become an armed camp. Men were dry-gulched by unknown assassins. Others were shot down among the jack pines that dot the red arroyos. Settlers were careful where they rode and when. They ventured from their cabins warily. Meanwhile the leaders of the factions on both sides were busy writing letters to various local newspapers explaining how spotless they were and how villainous was the enemy.

Court began at Lincoln April 1st, but Judge Bristol had not arrived. Sheriff Brady, his deputy George Hindman, clerk of the court William Matthews, and old Dad Peppin started for the courthouse to post a notice of postponement. There was a roar of guns from the adobe wall adjoining the McSween store and house. Matthews and Peppin escaped, but Brady was killed and his deputy fatally wounded. The hired "warriors," Billy the Kid, McNab, Tom O'Folliard, Charley Bowdre, and Fred Waite, had ambushed the officers. Billy and Waite ran forward to gather the weapons of the fallen men and were both wounded by Matthews.

The bodies of the dead men (so says a newspaper report of the affair) were still lying in the street when McSween and Chisum rode into town a few hours later. Nobody had cared to run the risk of removing them. The implication of the reporter that these two leaders were directly responsible for this crime is not warranted by any known facts. Chisum in particular tried to wash his hands of the whole factional warfare that had arisen so explosively. He wanted nothing to do with it. He had sowed the wind, but he did not want to reap the whirlwind. It is probable that both he and McSween were appalled at the work of the killers they had employed. Their weak justification was that they had hired men to protect them, for defense and not attack. This was the position also of the leaders of the other side. It was wholly untenable. They must have known when they employed men with such brittle tempers and murderous psychology as these desperadoes had that conflict could not be avoided.

On the Ruidoso lived a little ranchman known as Buckshot Roberts. He had been a soldier and a Texas Ranger, and his cognomen had been given him because he still carried in his body so many leaden souvenirs of past engagements. The man was of no importance in the community. Nobody gave his opinion or his personality much weight. He was not outstanding in any way, except in the hour of his death, when he fought the most desperate battle against overwhelming odds ever known to have taken place in the West outside of Indian warfare.

Fourteen men rode up to the agency at Blazer's Mill one day and found Roberts there. Four of them—the two Coes, Frank and George, Bowdre, and Doc Skurlock—were neighbors of his on Ruidoso Creek. But there was no neighborliness in the call they made that day. The newspapers charged that these "regulators" had come to get Judge Bristol, but not finding him there contented themselves with Roberts. Brewer was at the head of the party, which included Billy the Kid, McNab, O'Folliard, Waite, French, Brown, and others.

The killers closed on Buckshot. He fought back, coolly, steadily, with an amazing valiance. Standing there in the open, shot through the stomach at the first fire, he wounded George Coe and Middleton, then struck Bowdre on the buckle of his belt with a bullet that just missed killing the man. So steady was the blaze of his rifle that the regulators broke and fled for cover.

The ex-Ranger retreated into a cabin, bolted the back door, and dragged a mattress to the front door. Behind this he lay with his own rifle and an old Sharp's buffalo gun which he had found on a rack. He stood off the thirteen gunmen (Frank Coe claimed he was not one of the attackers) for hours. Exasperated at so stubborn a defense, Brewer ordered Dr. Blazer to force the defender to leave the house. Major Godfrey, the Indian agent, was present. Neither Blazer nor Godfrey would assist the killers.

"I'll get him myself," Brewer cried out with an oath.

He crept, by a roundabout way, to a pile of saw logs nearly two hundred yards from the cabin. His first shot at Roberts missed. Again he raised his head from behind a log to take aim. He fell back dead, struck by a bullet between the eyes. The besieged man, wounded to death, burning up with fever, still indomitably game, had focused his whole strength and mind on that one shot.

The killers quit—quit cold. Billy the Kid and his desperadoes rode away and left the field to the dying man. Buckshot Roberts had been too much for them.

The little Texan passed away next day.

There were indictments now and then, but indictments were only bits of paper. The war continued until a pitched battle was fought at Lincoln. It lasted two or three days, and during it half a dozen men were killed, including McSween himself.

Echoes of the cattle war reached Washington. In Oc-

tober, 1878, General Lew Wallace was appointed governor
of New Mexico with instructions to stop the feud. Murphy
had died. McSween had been killed. Most of the other
leaders were temporarily bankrupt. For lack of fuel the
war died down.

General Wallace declared an amnesty for those who
would surrender and give guarantees of good conduct.
He went personally to Lincoln to see the parties involved.
Billy the Kid had a personal talk with the Governor, half
accepted his offer, but was too much the outlaw to make
good as a law-abiding citizen. He turned his back on society,
stepped definitely outside the pale. Within two weeks of
the day Wallace talked with him he killed in cold blood
an Indian agency clerk named Bernstein. About himself
he gathered a gang of dangerous riffraff, such men as
Skurlock, O'Folliard, Bowdre, Middleton, Billy Wilson,
Tom Pickett, and Dave Rudabaugh. They rounded up
cattle in the Panhandle and ran them across the line into
New Mexico. They picked up horses at White Oaks, at
Agua Azul, at a dozen other places, and either sold or rebranded them. From Apaches and whites they stole indiscriminately. Occasionally they had brushes with hastily
organized posses. Twice Billy the Kid had horses shot
under him, and twice during the next few months he kept
his hand in by snuffing out the lives of men who offended
him.

Both New Mexico and Texas had had enough of the
young ruffian. Lincoln County elected a lank Texan, Pat
Garrett, to stop the depredations of the gang. The Canadian River Cattle Association appointed John W. Poe,
later a well known banker at Roswell, to coöperate with
Garrett in an attempt to stop the wholesale rustling of
Panhandle stock. Both Garrett and Poe were quiet, cool
officers, willing to take a fighting chance with the Kid
and his gang regardless of Billy's reputation as a killer.
They were Texans, from the Panhandle, men used to

sleeping on a cold trail, determined and resourceful. Of Poe it is certificate of efficiency as an officer to say that he had been marshal at wild Tascosa and had made good.

At the head of a posse, Garrett arrested young Bonney and several of his gang, after having killed two of them, O'Folliard and Bowdre.

Rudabaugh was tried, convicted, sentenced to be hanged. He escaped from prison and vanished. The same sequence of events took place in the case of his leader. It was for the murder of Sheriff Brady that Bonney was condemned.

Billy was taken to Lincoln to await execution. He was kept in the courthouse, which had formerly been the Murphy store. His guards were J. W. Bell and Bob Ollinger. Between Billy and Ollinger there was a bitter hatred.

Bell was a little lax, and his prisoner took advantage of this to get hold of a six-shooter. He killed Bell, stepped into a room used as an armory, picked up a double-barrel shotgun loaded with buckshot, and passed quickly to a window opening on the yard below and commanding a view of the street.

Lincoln had and still has one business street, the one into which Billy now looked down from the window. It has heard the roar of many guns. Here Sheriff Gillam, his deputy Martinez, and Ben Horrell were left dead after a pitched battle. Here Billy and his companions ambushed and killed Sheriff Brady and his deputy Hindman. Here was waged the three-day battle, watched by two troops of United States soldiers, in which McSween and half a dozen others were shot down. Once again it was the scene of swift and violent death.

Ollinger was at the hotel across the street when he heard the sound of the shot which killed Bell. He decided to investigate. As he crossed the road a jocund jeering voice hailed him from above. He looked up, to see his enemy grinning at him. In the boy's hands was the gun that Ollinger had loaded with buckshot before Billy that very

morning, remarking at the time that he hoped some condemned rustler would try to escape and give him a chance
to use it.

As the shotgun roared, Ollinger pitched to the ground.
He was dead before his body struck the dust.

Billy loitered around for an hour or two, in plain view
of all who cared to see, while a blacksmith knocked the
shackles from his limbs. He was full of merry quips about
the scheduled hanging that would have to be adjourned
sine die. Commandeering a horse, he rode gayly out of
town, free once more to go wherever fancy dictated.

Garrett and Poe took up the chase again. They learned
that Billy was at Fort Sumner, and they rode to the old
town. Their man was staying at Pete Maxwell's house.
He stepped into Maxwell's bedroom while Garrett was in-
quiring about him. In two seconds the sheriff had terminated Bonney's nefarious career.

That was the beginning of the end of open outlawry in
New Mexico. Garrett drove the rustlers to cover in the
chaparral. He harried them from gulch to arroyo, from one
hill pocket to another. Poe succeeded him as sheriff and
kept up the good work. It was men like these officers, who
carried law into the jungle at the continual risk of their
lives, that made the frontier safe for honest settlers against
miscreants such as Billy Bonney.

3

Even though the trail trade was taking a steady stream
of longhorns from Texas, the state was still bursting with
cattle for which there was not sufficient range. The grass
was already beginning to show the result of overfeeding.
There had to be an escape, of breeders as well as of beef
stock.

By the middle seventies the buffalo kill in the Panhandle
had been great enough to mitigate the Indian menace, and
cattlemen were examining its possibilities. The great river

of migrating longhorns swept up the Red and the Canadian rivers toward the Staked Plains.

The first man to run cows here was Charles Goodnight. Caught in the panic of '73, he had salvaged out of the wreck of his property eighteen hundred longhorns. These he drove from his Colorado ranch on the Purgatoire to the Palo Duro, where he made camp with his covered wagons, his herds, his family, and his retinue of retainers. He had followed an old Indian trail which led into the Palo Duro cañon over the caprock. The wagons had to be unloaded, taken to pieces, and lowered by ropes to the valley below. The provisions and household goods were let down the rocky walls by the same method. Near the mouth of the gorge Goodnight made a dugout and with the aid of his young wife started to rebuild their shattered fortunes. The valley of the cañon, miles wide and very deep, was an ideal range for cattle. Nature had fenced it with walls hundreds of feet high.

Goodnight had traveled the Panhandle in every direction and knew it better than any living white man, with the possible exception of one or two old buffalo hunters such as Billy Dixon. He had picked for his ranch the choice location of the hundreds of miles available. But he had to face many adverse factors. Buffalo had their habitat on his range and had to be driven away. In Tule Cañon, an offset of Palo Duro, more than fifty thousand wild mustangs ranged, Goodnight estimated. These interfered greatly with the cattle. The tribes were still hostile. As late as 1878 the United States military department of Texas reported 46 white men killed and 6 wounded, most of these stockmen, the work of the Indians.

Satanta and Quanah Parker came down to drive Goodnight away. They stayed to eat the cattle he offered and to smoke the pipe of peace. The meeting of these three men, all of them with the poise and dignity given by perfect physiques backed by intelligence and moral force, must have been an interesting one. Goodnight stood six feet in his socks and weighed 225 pounds without a superfluous ounce. He was a magnificent rider and a dead shot. In those days he had a remarkable resemblance to General Grant. That he impressed the chiefs of the plains Indians there can be no doubt.

This was in November, 1876. Shortly afterward Thomas S. Bugbee became the next-door neighbor of the Goodnights. A mere eighty miles or so separated the families. The nearest settlement to the east was Henrietta, 200 miles distant from Goodnight.

The Llano Estacado was still black with the buffalo. Where the city of Amarillo now stands thousands of them grazed. These first two cattlemen had to send out riders every day to drive them back both to save the feed for their stock and to prevent cattle from moving away with the wandering wild herds. Within two or three years the buffalo had vanished.

A great freshet of longhorns, most of them from "down in the skillet," poured into the watersheds of the Red and the Canadian. The Comanche and his allies had lately been subdued. Most of the new settlers had lived on the frontier and known what it was to fort up against an Indian attack. They were not of a type to be afraid of the plains warriors, but until the latter had been forced to reservation life, running cattle on the Llano Estacado had not been feasible. Now the Comanche and the Kiowa were no longer so great a menace, except for occasional bands of raiders on the lookout for stock to steal. Near Tascosa George W. Littlefield located with his brand, the L I T. Berry and Boice started the 777 ranch east of Buffalo Springs. The Scissors (✂), the Turkey Track (⋀), the Diamond Tail (◈), the T, Anchor (⊥), and the Hat (⌒) brands began to operate in the Panhandle. Henry W. Crosswell ran his Bar C's (ᴄᴄ) on the Canadian near Adobe Walls, assisted by his foreman Tom McGee, who was later, when serving as sheriff, killed by train robbers.

The only town in the western part of the Panhandle at

this time was Tascosa, and all of its inhabitants could have squeezed into a good-sized room. It had been a trading point in the old days between the Mexicans and the Comanches, a rendezvous where they met to exchange wares. Clarendon had a dugout or two. Due east of Tascosa was Mobeetie, the official center of Wheeler County. Since Wheeler was the only county in the Panhandle that had been organized, the courts sitting at Mobeetie had jurisdiction over twenty-six others into which were beginning to pour sheepmen, cattlemen, and rustlers. At the junction of two military roads, one a highway from Fort Elliott to Fort Concho, the other running between Fort Griffin and Fort Sumner, Old Man Singer's store was a great hangout for buffalo hunters and later for cowboys. Many an all-night game of poker has been played on the floor of his place.

The Panhandle was to become a country of immense cattle outfits. The grama and mesquite, as well as the bunch and the buffalo grasses, made excellent grazing. Cattle imported from southern Texas took on weight rapidly. Yet here too persisted the hard-dying myth of the Great American Desert. It found a place in the Census Report of 1880, with the statement that not more than seven million acres of the Llano Estacado in Texas is absolute desert. This large section classed with the Sahara evidently included most of the acreage that later became the X I T ranch. The investigator was probably deceived by the fact that the western part of the Panhandle is not so well watered as the eastern.

The first of the big outfits were already stocking the range. Goodnight formed a partnership in 1877 with Adair, an Irishman who invested $375,000 as against the Palo Duro ranch and the experience of the Texan. The new organization was known as the J A outfit. The Prairie Cattle Company, the Spurs, the Matadors, were all buying up great quantities of land and pouring in longhorns. Soon the X I T, owned by the Capitol Syndicate, the greatest ranch in America in its time, was to pull off its big deal to build a state capitol in exchange for three million acres. Land was still cheap. It had been acquired by script and was for sale at bargain rates. About this time a well watered tract along the Canadian could be bought for fifty cents an acre. Goodnight acquired a block of 265 square miles for twenty cents an acre, even as late as the early '80's.

The Texas Panhandle is a country of level plain and rolling land covered with native grass rich for forage. For hundreds of miles not a tree could be found. By reason of which fact the first man hanged there—convicted promptly by fellow punchers of killing the boss—had to be suspended from the propped-up tongue of a wagon.

With the honest cowman came, of course, the riffraff and the rustler. It was a country where a thief could hole up easily and do a lucrative business in other men's cattle. Henry Fleming, a saloon keeper and gambler, was elected sheriff. He had nerve of a high quality, and during the years of his incumbency arrested scores of desperate men without killing or being killed.

But the thieves grew bolder. A meeting of cattlemen was called at Mobeetie, and the Panhandle Stock Association was organized with Goodnight as president.

Fleming was succeeded by Cape Willingham, who was willing to humor cowboys on a bender but found it necessary to let his sawed-off shotgun roar occasionally. It was soon after he took office that the episode of Mrs. Turner's ducks occurred. Fred Leigh and a group of trail men rode into Tascosa to get roostered. They were already well organized. Mrs. Turner, who ran a restaurant, was in her yard feeding some ducks. It is likely that Leigh did not see her. He boasted that he could shoot the ducks through the head, and he made good his promise. He did not observe that Mrs. Turner keeled over in a faint.

Tascosa would not have stood that sort of thing, even if Mrs. Turner and her daughter Victoria had not been popular. No man on earth could terrorize a woman in the cow country.

Sheriff Willingham found Leigh in Jack Ryan's saloon and told him he was under arrest. Leigh was not in a condition to understand why. He asked no questions but reached for the .44 in his belt. The sheriff's work was faster, and Leigh dropped with a load of buckshot in his heart.

He was buried next day, one of the first men to find a resting place in the town's Boot Hill. The funeral of Bob Russell, bumped off by Jule Howard, had dedicated the cemetery. In the years that followed it was used frequently as a burial place for those who checked out with their boots on. The Tascosa that was has vanished and is no more, but those who once lived there point with pride to the fact that not more than thirty of its unlucky gunmen were laid to rest on the morning after. The Panhandle could not have been wild, since its most roaring town had such a meager record for its Boot Hill.

In Haley's *The X I T Ranch of Texas* he quotes a recommendation from an old trail driver, J. E. May, to the effect that of all the frontier towns from the Pecos to the Canadian line Tascosa was the best. A man was never robbed. He could get as drunk as he pleased, pass out with a pocket full of money, and find the same amount there when he awakened. The town was "wide open but not mean."

Two factors combined to make Tascosa a lusty young offspring of the Panhandle. One of them was the fact that it was on the Northern trail, the other that half a dozen big outfits were running cattle within riding distance. When the cowboys jingled in after the spring round-up Rome howled.

Jim East, who had helped Garrett capture Billy the Kid, became in due time sheriff of Oldham County. During his incumbency the town had its wildest night. Some killings were casual. They arose out of a moment's savage impulse. But this one had its origin in an anger that had been growing for some time.

Among the L S men were Fred Chilton, Frank Valley, and Ed King. They had been hired, it was claimed, to ride the range with rifles on the lookout for rustlers. In the course of time they fell afoul of a group of hard-eyed men which included Charles Emory, Lem Woodruff, and one known as the Catfish Kid.

It is said that King came to town looking for those of the other faction. With him were Chilton and Valley. The men separated. If King was on the hunt for trouble he certainly found it. Out of a peaceful quiet the night woke to a roar of guns, Messrs. Woodruff and Emory in the center of the stage. King fell, mortally wounded, but the iron of the frontier was in his blood. He half raised his body from the ground, took aim at Woodruff, and wounded him severely. As Emory ran forward, a bullet stopped him in his stride. He stumbled and fell, badly hurt.

"Fair enough," gasped King hardily. "I'll teach those sons of wolves to bushwhack me."

With which comment he ceased forever to take interest in mundane affairs.

The word was carried to Chilton and Valley. They came a-smokin'. Jess Sheets indiscreetly ventured out to learn the cause of the shooting. Promptly the two newcomers killed him.

Woodruff had taken refuge in a cabin near. The two gunmen sent bullet after bullet crashing through the door. Woodruff returned the fire. Unknown friends rallied to the support of the besieged man. From a little hillside not far away spits of fire flashed in the darkness. Chilton and Valley were both shot down. Neither of them lived out the night.

About this time Sheriff East, aroused from sleep, put in an appearance. He came on the run, in time to see from a distance the last of the battle. The men on the hillside vanished into the night. Woodruff surrendered.

The sheriff found Emory, much the worse for a very serious wound. Some years earlier the two had been on the man-hunt which netted Bowdre, O'Folliard, Billy the Kid, and some others. One of the men on the hill had also been with them on that occasion. Now the old comrades were on different sides of the fence.

"You played hell, the whole caboodle of you," the sheriff told Emory.

The wounded man grinned. "I'm claimin' self-defense," he said.

There were two funerals next day when the four victims were buried. The innocent bystander who had been the victim of his own curiosity was taken to the cemetery where went those who died in their beds. A scant dozen were in attendance, for at the same time the three L S men were being planted at Boot Hill. Tascosa preferred the more dramatic ceremony. A dozen armed men, some attached to one party and some to the other, stood grimly at wary attention beside the graves. There was always a chance that someone might decide to renew the feud and drag out a gun.

Mr. Emory's claim of self-defense went before a jury. He and his friends were acquitted.

Clarendon had from the first made up its mind to be a good home town. A saloon keeper at Mobeetie sent wagons loaded up with liquor, women, and gambling apparatus to open up a frontier dive. Goodnight had just come in from the round-up and rode down to the wagons of sin. He told the man in charge to hitch up and get out. The other gamblers gathered around. The law was with them, and they resented this dictation. They wanted to know why a dance hall could not be opened.

"Because the people of Clarendon don't want one," the cattleman said.

"We'll find that out after we open," the leader of the gamblers said curtly.

"You'll take my word for it," Goodnight said quietly.

He did not care to have such a place so conveniently accessible to his riders.

The trigger fingers of the gamblers itched, but this man was one out of ten thousand. The fact that he had a nerve steady as tested steel would not alone have saved the situation. That was almost a matter of course on the frontier of Texas. But to back courage he had a forceful personality. Charles Goodnight was a born leader. The gamblers argued and cursed and threatened, but they folded their tents and departed.

On one occasion Dudley Pannell and Charley Siringo were members of a posse led by Bill Moore, an excellent cowman but a man with a reputation as a hard character. They followed eight Mexican thieves for days, caught up with them, and demanded surrender. The Mexicans forted up behind their wagons and held the cowboys off with their long-range buffalo guns. An armistice was arranged. Later the cowboys disarmed the men. It was proposed to hang the Mexicans. Pannell and Siringo demurred, not because they had any tenderness for the outlaws but because of the pledge made. Moore reluctantly gave way. Some time later, let it be mentioned incidentally, Pannell was killed at Tascosa.

In the Dodge City *Times*, April 6, 1878, may be read a news item not quite so innocent of sinister significance as it seems. Mr. Jesse Evans, it appears, was leaving Dodge with fifty riders to gather from the Pecos Valley range twenty thousand cattle that had been bought by Hunter and Evans from John S. Chisum. The paper failed to mention that the fifty riders were gunmen and that they expected trouble before they got back with the cattle they were buying.

Chisum had left behind him in Texas before moving to the Pecos some outlawed notes it had not been convenient to pay. Hunter bought these up for about ten cents on the dollar. After the deal had been made for the cattle Hunter rode in with Chisum to the nearest town and paid him with his own notes. Before the cattleman of New Mexico could gather his riders in numbers enough to stop the little army from Dodge the forces of Evans were across the line and in the Panhandle. This was the kind of a joke that Texans could appreciate. Thousands of their stock were being run off by rustlers into New Mexico, and even a respectable cattleman from that territory was fair game. But it is said that Chisum did not find the transaction amusing.

The first humble ranch headquarters in the Panhandle, either dugouts or adobe, gave way to commodious frame houses. Fences began to appear. For barbed wire had come to Texas in 1875. The end of the open range, of the free grass days, was in sight for the cattlemen.

In the early '80's the Capitol Syndicate Company began to build the statehouse at Austin in exchange for a vast tract of land in the Panhandle. This acreage bordered on New Mexico and lay in the tier of counties which ran down along the western edge of the state, Dallam, Hartley, Oldham, Deaf Smith, Castro, Lamb, Hockley, Cochran, Parmer, and Bailey. It had never been surveyed but was more than two hundred miles in length. Within two or three years the Syndicate had put up eight hundred miles of fence. After the ranch was better established, cross fences increased this mileage to fifteen hundred. At first mustangs, buffalo, and other wild game were inclosed within the barbed wire. The outer fence alone cost more than a hundred and seventy-five thousand dollars to build.

The construction of the statehouse, which is one of the largest in the country, cost more than three million dollars. This was financed by a holding company in Great Britain which owned bonds on the Panhandle investment. Such well known men as the Earl of Aberdeen and the Marquis of Tweeddale were on the board. But the ranch was the property of the American promoters of the enterprise, Taylor, Babcock, and the Farwell brothers.

The first cattle put upon the range of the Capitol Syndicate ranch were brought to Buffalo Springs from

Tom Green County in 1884 by Ab Blocker. They had been bought by the syndicate from John R. Blocker. The general manager of the ranch, Barbecue Campbell, had not decided on what brand to use. Blocker suggested the X I T. It was easily made. It could be read at sight. It could not be readily blotted out. And finally it stood for Ten In Texas, the number of counties in the ranch. Barbecue accepted the suggestion, and Ab Blocker branded the first cow that carried this legend.

By this time the bonanza cattle days were at hand all over the West. Anyone could make a fortune in cows. No gold mine could be as profitable. One could get a 90 per cent calf increase. Money rolled in by a law of natural growth. It cost a dollar to drive a Texas steer to the North and its value was increased four dollars by the change in location. A man could sit at ease in Cheyenne or Denver and imagine himself in process of becoming a millionaire. The result of this misconception of the situation was that most of the big companies were managed very slackly both in the South and in the North. The period of inflation was of course followed by a smash that was epic in proportion. But during the magnificent days when the boom was at its height the cattleman sat on the top of the world.

He prospered, at least on paper, in spite of an enormous amount of thieving. There was a lot of fence cutting. Cattle were driven out of the immense pastures as easily as they could be from the open range. The foremen and even the managers of some of the big outfits were stealing from their employers without scruple. It is charged that at one time most of the men working for the X I T, from the boss down, were rustlers and crooks. The caprock ran through the property, and in this rough country calves could be held and hidden until the rustlers found it convenient to drive them away.

One foreman of the L X ranch was a killer and a suspected cow thief. While working for the Panhandle outfit he was stealing calves for himself and sending them to a place he owned at Coldwater Springs in No Man's Land. Several of the cowboys were operating with him. Siringo, one of the company riders, was asked to join the thieves and refused.

Hair branding was an effective method of acquiring ownership without the cost of purchase. Sometimes this was done at the round-up, with the connivance of the wagon boss. The man with the iron put it on the calf so lightly that the hair sizzled off without the skin being marked. More often the rustler did his hair branding in the chaparral. He chose a calf that had been overlooked in the round-up and cut the earmarks of the mother. With knife held against the thumb he plucked the hair from the skin so that the brand could be plainly seen by any cowboy riding the range. The calf became a "sleeper." The thief watched it. If the animal got by at the next round-up without arousing suspicion he finished the job with a hot iron and a deft change in the earmarking. Usually the yearling passed muster now as the property of the hair brander, but sometimes a wideawake boss discovered the fraud and rebranded, maybe with the guilty man sitting his horse not ten feet away.

The range rider and the cow thief matched wits: the one to get evidence of guilt and the other to escape proof. Sometimes the honest waddy cut a small slit in the skin of a calf and slipped inside a marked dime or quarter. The cut was then sewed up. This did not usually get the owner of the coin very far. He rarely ever saw the silver again. On one occasion a company went into court with this evidence, and the jury set the hair brander free. With amusing hardihood the man demanded the quarter and was given it by the judge. A few years later this cool customer had stolen himself into respectability and joined the live-stock association to protect himself against robbers.

Martin Monroe was one of the most remarkable of the rustlers. He was at the head of a band of desperate outlaws that operated for ten years, during which period they stole not less than twenty thousand cattle and ran them across the line into Mexico. The leader of this outfit became a popular hero because he was faithful to his associates and preyed chiefly on the brands of syndicates. Like most of his kind, he was a pitcher that went to the well once too often. An El Paso officer shot him while resisting arrest.

Reckless of the rights of others though they were, many of the rustlers could appreciate courage which expressed itself audaciously. Against the advice of wise men, "Sug" Robertson, aged twenty-four, bought a herd of three thousand graded cattle in Tom Green County, Texas. This bunch of cows had suffered very much from the depredations of thieves. Armed with a rifle, the new owner rode alone to the camp of the marauders. Without a word they watched him dismount and stride up to the fire. He sat down cross-legged and "talked turkey" to them. There was not going to be any more mavericking of calves belonging to his brand. Anybody who cared to try it would "go to hell on a shutter" very soon. That was his message, and he got it across in two sentences. The leader of the outlaws laughed. This was a man after his own heart. He invited Robertson to stay all night as a guest. "Sug" stayed, ate beef from one of his own four-year-olds (it was a point of honor with professional rustlers never to eat meat that belonged to them), and in the morning departed. He carried with him a pledge, never broken, that his herd would be as safe as though guarded day and night.

In his authentic book, *The X I T Ranch of Texas*, J. Evetts Haley tells scores of stories of the fight made by the big syndicate ranch against the pestiferous rustler. There was the Rogers gang, for instance, bold and audacious in its methods.

Ira Aten, manager of the Escarbada, had been a Texas Ranger and sheriff of Castro County. He was a strong, resolute man, and he made life a terror to outlaws. With some cowmen from New Mexico he rounded up some of the Rogers outfit, but the rustlers would not be warned. They thought they were strong enough to defy the owners of the stock they stole. Again the New Mexican cowmen met and rode out to clean up the gang. The Rogers band fell into a trap at Mesa Redonda, south of Tucumcari, and three of them were shot from their horses.

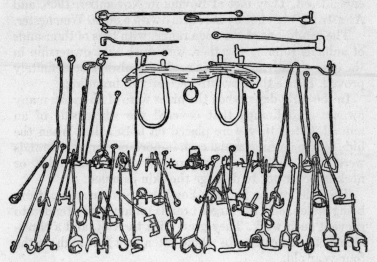

THE CATTLEMAN'S COAT OF ARMS

The collection of branding irons and other articles reflecting different phases of Southwestern history owned by W. C. Holden of Abilene, Texas.

On one occasion Colonel A. G. Boyce, general manager of the X I T, was invited from the ranch house to talk with a gang of rustlers headed by one of his own wagon bosses. Boyce guessed they had come to shoot him down. He was a fearless, indomitable man, and he went out alone to meet them. His gaze ranged coolly over the outlaws before he began to curse them for a set of scoundrels. Hardily he asked them why they did not cut loose and promised that he would kill their leader if one of them lifted a finger. Knowing he would keep his word, none dared to start hostilities.

John Armstrong followed Aten as manager of the Bovina and Escarbada properties of the X I T. He accused J. W. Williams of rustling. Williams denied this. The men attacked each other by legal procedure, and ill feeling was engendered. They met at Bovina in November, 1908, and Armstrong was shot by his enemy with a 30-30 Winchester.

The conditions of the open range, with tens of thousands of animals running together, were such that ownership in the case of individual calves could not always be definitely proved. Hence the absolute necessity of branding.

In the early days, when the hides were of no value, many owners used brands that covered the whole side of an animal. Often they were placed on both sides. When the hide took on a substantial cash importance, smaller brands were used, and they were stamped on hip, shoulder, or neck in order not to damage the skin as much.

The chief reason for branding is to keep the animal from being stolen, and the larger brands undoubtedly tended to prevent such work. They grew with the calf, and a three-inch iron on a calf's ribs would often be a foot high on the four-year-old.

In an effort to find brands that could not be "worked over" or "run out," range men showed much ingenuity. The rustlers seeking for methods to change or run out brands developed equally clever ideas.

In many range states the use of "running irons" (that is, pothooks, rings, or horseshoes for branding an animal) were and still are forbidden by law. Only a regular "stamp" iron made in the exact shape of the brand may be used. It soon became unlawful to brand on the range except during the round-up and in the presence of the round-up crews or in the owner's own corrals.

There is a distinct nomenclature of range brands. This character — placed above or below a letter or design is called a "bar." Thus X̲ is read "X bar" or ō̄ "bar O."

This design ∧ is known as a "rafter" or half diamond, and when used thus ⤳ becomes the "rafter S" or sometimes the "half diamond S." Again, the quarter circle ⌒ is used in the same way. ⤳ is "quarter circle E." ⊕ is known on the range as "circle H."

There are many quaint and odd names given brands; ℧ is the "moustache" or "flying O." ⩊ is known as the "flying W." ∆ made thus is known as the "diamond A," ⊥ is the "lazy H," ⌣ the "lazy J," ⊬ the "cross A," ∧ the "open A," ♀ the "buckle."

Since about 1545 the Mexicans have always used brands for identifying their animals. Some of the present-day marks have been in active use for more than two hundred years. One especially worthy of mention is that of the well known De Baca family, which traced its lineage back to the famous Spanish explorer and conquistador who visited New Mexico as early as 1536, Cabeza de Vaca or de Baca.

The name translated literally means "head of a cow." The family has used the brand ♡ for more than two centuries, and it is on the New Mexico state brand book of to-day. Many owners worked their initials into their brands, thus ♋ for Bob Jones in northern Arizona, D I K for Dick Greer. Old Ace Jenkins put A on the left shoulder, C on the ribs, and E on the hip. Sometimes the owner's name suggested his brand. Frank Starr naturally used the ⅍ brand. Pete Coffin smeared the left side of the cows belonging to him with ▣. Old Jack Barber claimed his cows by this, ⴵ. Mr. Fish recorded ⟿ , Robert Bell took a bell (◮) for his, Henry Spear naturally used ⟶, which ran across the whole side of his cattle. The brand ⵔ belonged to the Frying Pan Cattle Company.

In southern New Mexico there was a genial Austrian by the name of Bujac, which his "longhorn" neighbors would pronounce "bootjack." He met them more than halfway by using as his brand the design ⊏⋜ . Another well known New Mexican, Bill Slaughter, had four fine daughters. When they were born he branded out fifty heifer calves for each young lady, placing their first names May, Sue, Ana, Jen on the ribs and the family brand S on the hip. If anybody's calves were kept well branded up, it was those belonging to the Slaughter girls.

It was in planning designs that could be registered legally and yet used to "work" over some well known brand that the greatest skill and ingenuity were displayed by men eager to become cattle kings with the least expense. There are few brands which cannot be burned over so as almost totally to obliterate the original iron.

In his way the professional rustler was an artist. He liked to do a good job. The touching up of old brands was often done skillfully, by the use of a piece of telegraph wire adroitly applied. Goodnight's J A ($\mathcal{A}$) became a D A ($\mathcal{A}$), a 3C was transformed into a B O B by the addition of two strokes and another letter, and an S Bar ($\underline{S}$) read after a little deft work Box S ($\blacksquare$). Cowboys sitting around the camp fire often exercised their ingenuity in devising new brands that could be made from old ones. These they would draw on the ground with sticks. The Flying U ($\mathbf{U}$) would make a very good Seven Up ($\mathbf{U}$) or a pup ($\mathbf{U}$). Out of a simple V would emerge an X. Occasionally the rustler turned to more elaborate artistry, as when he turned a Pickle Bar ($\supset$) into a Walking Peanut ($\mathcal{S}$). A $\bigcirc$ on the left ribs easily graduated into the Terrapin ($\mathbb{Q}$) and an E into the Pitchfork ($\longleftarrow$ E). A brand recorded in Arizona as I C was worked over into I C U. In this case the lawful owner of the stock took a leaf from the book of his neighbor and recorded a brand $\frac{ICU}{2}$ and rebranded the very calves that had originally belonged to him. One large Wyoming outfit used the Eleven Quarter Circle ($\underline{\mathbf{\mathsf{u}}}$). Its cattle ranged over a wide territory, much of it rough country of rolling hills and timber pockets. There began to appear upon the range the Rocking Chair ($\mathbf{\Pi}$).

To prove crooked work it was often necessary to kill an animal and examine the scars on the inner side of the hide.

The brand on a young calf is written plainly inside the skin, but one burned on later is less definite inside and sometimes not visible at all. Courts recognized the validity of the testimony of experienced range men concerning the markings on a dried hide.

This question of the relative rights of the big outfits and the small cattlemen was a controversial one in Texas, Arizona, and New Mexico, as in Wyoming and the North. In addition to other ways by which the big owner harried the nester, he fenced illegally land which had previously been the range of the homesteader. No honest man could make a living near those monopolizing the country. So the small man claimed. There was probably blame on both sides. The result was bad feeling which resulted in fence cutting, a too free use of the running iron, occasional sniping from ambush, and other amenities of the kind.

Old-timers in the Panhandle will tell you to-day that it never was a bad country, that its citizens held a high average of character. This is beyond question true. The incidental lawlessness was much less than that which obtained at the same time in the neighboring territory of New Mexico. What was characteristic of the Panhandle as to its long struggle for the rights of property in live stock applied also to most of that part of the state from the water shed of the Brazos west.

A horse thief was one degree worse than an illicit dealer in calves. This conviction was born of the frontier conditions. A cow was property, but in the Indian days a man's horse might be his life. To set a rider afoot in the wilderness was at times equivalent to pronouncing a death sentence upon him. Therefore one's right to his mustang became sacrosanct. A captured horse thief expected little mercy.

The amazing story of the Marlows shows the depth and fury of this feeling. The drama centers at Graham, Young County, Texas. There were five Marlow brothers. According to their story, the big cattlemen "ran" on them because they stood up for their rights. The other side said bluntly that they were horse thieves and bad men.

The Marlows were of a restless temperament and shifted headquarters freely. They spent a good deal of time in the Indian Territory, then a resort for the wildest and most lawless characters, moving to and fro in the Chickasaw Nation and the territory adjoining it which had been the hunting ground of the Comanches and Kiowas. This was a convenient terrain for those "on the dodge." It was wild and rough, and the Texas Ranger could not interfere with the habits of the night riders. Close to it was the big Dan Wagner cow outfit. If a man had a fancy for calves rather than for broncos he could indulge it discreetly. But horses were on the whole a better bet. They could be moved rapidly from the scene, and one did not have to remain to meet searching questions.

The Marlows were married. Sometimes their families moved with them. Sometimes they followed the men more leisurely to new fields. From Wilbarger County, Texas, they trekked to Las Animas, Colorado. One of the brothers, Boone, had been too handy with a six-shooter, and James Holdson had as a result been buried. The family held to a strong clan feeling. Their covered wagons followed Boone north.

Whether they were honest men as they claimed or thieves as their enemies charged, the Marlows were unlucky. They left Trinidad under a cloud. From Doc Burns, sheriff of Las Animas County, a wire went to Ed W. Johnson, a deputy United States marshal of Texas. The telegram advised him to look out for five Marlow brothers trying to get away with forty head of horses stolen in the vicinity. It is only fair to the Marlows to say that they were never proved guilty of rustling horses, though they were arrested time and again.

Johnson, a big rawboned Westerner, acted with energy. He guessed that the Marlows would make for "the Nation" to trade the herd of broncs to the Indians. He wrote letters, received answers, headed north, found and arrested the Marlows, took them to Graham. The mother of the five boys gave bond, and they were released until the time of trial.

A capias came from Wilbarger County for the arrest of Boone for the murder of Holdson. Sheriff Wallace and a deputy rode out to the place where the Marlows were renting. Boone killed the sheriff. Once more he slapped a saddle on a horse and rode into the chaparral. A reward of $1,700 was offered for his arrest, dead or alive.

His brothers were flung into prison. Wallace had been a popular officer and public opinion was inflamed. The Marlows had few friends at Graham. They believed that Johnson had been appointed to represent the larger cattle interests, that the new sheriff and the lawful authorities of the county were against them. A lynching seemed to them probable. They broke jail but were recaptured. The authorities shackled them in pairs.

A mob stormed the jail, with the connivance of the county officers, the Marlows charged. But the prisoners, unarmed though they were, presented so resolute a front that the would-be lynchers had not the nerve to go through with what they had started.

United States Marshal Cabell telegraphed Johnson to move his prisoners to Weatherford for safe keeping. When the Marlows saw the guard selected to accompany them they protested, saying openly that this was a plot to murder them.

At Dry Creek an attack was made upon the convoy. What followed seems as impossible as the dime-novel exploits of Nick Carter. Though chained together and unarmed, the Marlows won the day. Charley and Alf rolled out of the hack, hobbled to the surrey where their guards sat, and wrested weapons from the men. Upon one of the mob who indiscreetly rushed forward George and Epp Marlow fell like a ton of bricks. They took his rifle and six-shooter. In the mêlée which ensued one of the guards

and two of the attackers were killed, several others seriously wounded. Alf and Epp Marlow were riddled with
bullets; the other two brothers were both wounded, one
badly. Johnson, a one-armed man, was hit in the hand.

The mob fled, and with them the officers. What part
the latter played in the fight is a moot question. The prisoners claimed they were allies of the attackers. It is probable that they took little share in the battle.

The condition of the surviving Marlows was desperate.
Bleeding from half a dozen wounds, Charley could hardly
stand. Both he and George were still chained to the bodies
of their brothers. With a knife found in the pocket of a
guard, they disjointed the ankles of their dead relatives.
George gathered such weapons as had been left on the
field, helped his brother into a hack, and drove to the
farm where their families were living. Here they held off
the officers for two days until a United States deputy
marshal arrived with a promise of protection against mob
violence.

The cases against the Marlows and their enemies
dragged on for years. Young County was torn by a divided
sentiment. Good citizens demanded conviction of the men
who had put themselves above the law. There were indictments and trials on both sides. In the end the matter was
dropped. It is to be noted that the tragic affair of the
Marlows came to a climax not in the early '70's but as late
as 1889.

Some time after the attack of the mob three men drove
into Graham. With them they had the body of Boone
Marlow. They had come for the reward. They had killed
him, they said, in the Chickasaw Nation. The reward was
paid them, but later they were indicted for having poisoned the man they dared not face while he was alive.

"It is a curious fact," the Graham *Leader* made comment, "that everybody who has anything to do with the
Marlows has more or less trouble with them."

The editor might have extended his comment to say

that in early days anyone who had anything to do with cattle in a rough and brushy country sooner or later had trouble. Laws were of necessity laxly enforced. Ownership in property on the hoof could be maintained only by unceasing vigilance and by ruthless reprisal. Even then there was a percentage of loss. There were too many bold, unscrupulous men on the make to permit a cattleman to get a 100-per-cent return on his calf crop, to let him feel confident that some of his remuda on the range would not change hands overnight. Rustlers were suspected even when definite proof was not forthcoming. Their brand blotting could be proved when a court conviction was not possible. The cattle owner had been brought up in as hard a school as the thief. If the law could not or would not protect his property he knew how to do that himself. He did not intend to wait patiently until the lank brown waddies whom he met on his range had robbed him blind. Instead, he slammed a heavy fist down on the table at the home ranch and said grimly to his cowboys, "War." And war it was. From this condition came trouble that ended often in tragedy. Young County was the scene of other feuds than the Marlow one, and Young County was one of many such battlefields which dot the map all the way from the Gulf to Canada.

The trouble with the rustler was, however, only an incident in the life of the community. Children went to the little red schoolhouse and learned reading, writing, and arithmetic. Young men rode twenty miles to "go gallin'," attended dances, slipped into rear seats at church to see the maidens of their dreams, and in due time asked the fatal question. Girls sat before cheap mirrors, put ribbons in their hair, giggled together, and watched furtively the awkward lads who hung together for support to prop up their courage against an oppressive shyness. Young brides and grooms started housekeeping in simple fashion, begat children, made sacrifices for them, even as to-day. Churches prospered. Sinners came into the fold, stirred to

contrition at hectic revivals. Men met at the market-
place and talked of the price of beef and the need of rain.
All the ordinary aspects of existence moved on undisturbed
by the occasional lawlessness.

The people of the cow country were in the main a
sturdy, kindly folk, neighborly and often deeply religious.
They had the Nordic love of order. They were ready to
fight if necessary for a quiet and peaceful life. Law they
believed in profoundly, even though they sometimes had
to shape its enactments to meet their personal and communal needs, as it were. Even when they stepped outside
the ordinary channels of legal procedure, there was often
a sober and impersonal behavior much more like the
ancient Teuton gathering of freemen in the forests of the
Old World than the savage call of revolutionaries for the
blood of a victim. When they hanged without process of
law the men preying on the property of settlers, they did
it with stern reluctance. Not always, but usually, they were
trying to bring to the frontier the stability that makes for
a safe and ordered routine. What they had to do was done
with the same thoroughness and with as much legal sanction as that invested in the Cromwellian court which cut
off the head of a king. Right or wrong, they were sons of
those old Commonwealth men who decided that for the
communal good Charles I could not be permitted longer
to live. Sometimes rustlers could be run out of the country.
Sometimes they laughed at threats and warnings. When
there was no other way to stop them, Cattleland exterminated the cow thief and the horse thief as it would have
put an end to a trapped wolf.

4

Up till Panhandle days the biggest outfits had been in
southern Texas. Some of these had developed to the point
of beginning to breed up the stock and of fencing large
pastures. Since this was before the day of barbed wire the

lumber required for these inclosures made them expensive luxuries.

While it is true that every fundamental feature of the cattle-range business had its origin in Texas, one striking characteristic of it was the swiftness with which those engaged in running, trailing, or feeding cows had to be prepared to meet new conditions. The changes came so rapidly as to swamp financially those not long-sighted.

In early trail days, before fencing made segregation possible, the dogie was better adapted to survive in the chaparral than what came to be called American cattle as distinguished from the longhorn. The long-legged, pot-bellied "sea lion" could travel farther for water, could cover a wider range of feed territory, could stand up to hardship better than stock graded up by imported bulls. The Texas steer was a product of his environment and fitted it. Even his tendency to become panic-stricken at nothing, his sullen savagery, and irascible temper were protective assets.

But as stockmen got land under fence they began to build up their herds. Goodnight brought Herefords to the Adair ranch and improved a selected bunch of stock. This herd was cut off from the dogies and received the J J brand. For years this was generally regarded as the best bred brand in the Panhandle. Other range men brought in Galloway, Hereford, Shorthorn, and Angus bulls. A cross of a Hereford with a longhorn cow would show a weight of three hundred pounds more than one with a scrub bull.

As early as 1871 the firm of Coggins and Park had graded up a herd of thirty thousand. The Comanches swooped down over the range and ran off seven thousand head in one raid. The major-domo pushed the rest of the stock to a safer feeding ground, but on Christmas Day a second raid through Concho and Tom Green counties swept away ten thousand cows and many horses. Of these five thousand belonged to the Coggins and Park outfit. This was the biggest single drive of stolen stock the plains tribes ever pulled off. Many of the longhorns were sold to unprincipled dealers in the Northern country. A little thing like this misadventure could not stop a Texas frontiersman. Ten years later Sam Coggins was importing a carload of registered bulls from Kentucky. During that decade the cowman saw the Indians driven to reservation life and ways of peace, the buffalo exterminated, the unfenced range of vast extent covered with cattle, the end of free grass and the coming of barbed wire, and the establishment of scores of great brands that in a few years would be driven out of existence by small farmers.

Until the '80's had well begun there was no great change in the general appearance of the Texas steer. It took time to work over the outward characteristics of the dogie as a mass. One bull was required for twenty-five cows, and the expense of importing pure-bred animals could be met only gradually. But as stock increased in value, both on account of quality and market demands, fencing became profitable. Barbed wire inclosed the grass lands rapidly. At first much of the acreage was leased, but later the bigger outfits owned the range upon which their cattle fed. In Texas much of this territory was acquired by means of scrip obtained from old soldiers who had acquired it as a bonus for military service.

The leasing of the range and later the ownership of it in large quantities by big cattle companies worked a hardship on the smaller cowman. It had been the habit of cattlemen to claim everything in sight as range rights. They resented the approach of neighbors on the ground that this interfered with their priority claim. As the country settled new men crowded the feeding ground, just as they did in the old Biblical days of Abraham and Lot.

When the fences of the cattle barons inclosed what had been free grass their smaller neighbors complained bitterly. In many cases this meant ruin to them. The range rights upon which they had counted because of priority of occupation, always a figment of fancy without real legal status, were wiped out ruthlessly. Their cattle were cut off, not only from accustomed feeding grounds, but from the more important essential of water.

The owners of the small outfits were driven to desperate expedients. They had to get out, allow the longhorns to die, or use their wire cutters to let the animals through. There was war on the plains. For once the honest "little fellow" was on the side of the rustler. A loose organization of rebels developed. Night riders moved through the chaparral and nipped away strands of wire. Houses were burned, men ambushed and shot down. Public sympathy was at first with the disinherited fence cutters.

Some of the big companies bought land completely surrounding the holdings of nesters and refused to give them ingress or exit. They had to sell at the price offered. Hundreds of horses and cows, trying to reach their usual watering place, ran into the barbed wire and tore wounds in their flesh. These became infected with screw worms. Deadly feuds arose, flashed to red tragedy, and died down.

But the fence cutter was trying to put back the clock. Free grass had had its day. "Bob" wire had come into the Western grazing lads to stay. Here and there irrigating ditches ran. Alfalfa fields were segregated. The haystack became an integral part of ranch life.

The dogie was doomed. It did not pay to feed hay to longhorns, and after pastures were inclosed the stockman bred his cattle up more rapidly. The raising of cows had become more of a scientific business and less of a haphazard adventure.

This crowding of the range and the subsequent fencing went on all over Cattleland. There had been a time when a drift rider felt almost as though he were in a city if he met two men in as many days. As elbow room grew less the cowman left the Brazos for newer pasturage. He went to New Mexico or the Panhandle or Wyoming or Oklahoma. Sometimes he leased railroad land and fenced it, forgetting that only each alternate section belonged to the company. A good many cowmen from Texas moved to the Indian Territory and leased from the Nations or from the government.

But always the push of settlement followed at the heels of the stockman. Even the Indian Territory was no safe refuge for him. The granger wanted the land, and though the big outfits there fought to hold possession, their efforts failed. In 1885 President Cleveland ordered cattle to move out of a range country as large as the state of Ohio. It was a disastrous time for a drive. All over the West the ranges had been overstocked in consequence of the great boom. The cowmen moved their outfits, lock, stock, and barrel. But the carcasses of a hundred thousand starved cattle marked the trail of their departure.

5

Since the earliest records of history the question of water for stock has been a prime consideration. The Old Testament is full of references to this fundamental need. Of Uzziah, King of Judah, we read:

Also he built towers in the desert, and digged many wells: for he had much cattle, both in the low country, and in the plains: . . .

When the Children of Israel were moving their cattle because of drought Edom, King of Kadish, refused to give or sell water to the tribes. On another occasion Isaac with his many flocks and herds went into the Valley of Gerar to dwell.

And Isaac's servants digged in the valley, and found there a well of springing water.

And the herdmen of Gerar did strive with Isaac's herdmen, saying, The water is ours: . . .

And they digged another well, and strove for that also: . . .

And he removed from thence, and digged another well; and for that they strove not: . . .

These old Biblical accounts verify to a remarkable degree the saying that history repeats itself. In the arid West the streams and the desert water holes meant the difference between life and death. More conflict arose over them than over any other factor of range activity except that of rustling. Water was developed at certain strategic points through the digging of deep wells and was sold to stockmen driving cattle or sheep through the region.

In the years between 1885 and 1895 thousands of cattle and a good many sheep were trailed from northern and eastern Arizona across the Datil Mountains of New Mexico to the nearest shipping point, Magdalena, New Mexico. There was an eighty-mile stretch across this region, known as the San Augustin Plains, where the only water to be had was well water pumped by burro and horse power out of deep wells. Drivers were forced to pay ten cents per head for every animal, big and little, in the herd, and in order to water they had to cut the cattle into one-hundred head lots, the troughs being only large enough to water that many at a time. It usually took all day to water a trail herd of fifteen hundred steers.

In 1879, at Maricopa Wells, Arizona, there was a very deep well on the road between Yuma and Tucson, traveled by the old stage line. The motive power for raising the water was a yoke of small Mexican oxen driven by a Mexican boy. The machinery consisted of a forty-gallon wooden barrel, a three-hundred-foot rope, and a wooden pulley. The barrel was filled by means of a valve in the bottom. The oxen, belabored by the boy who kept yelling, "*Andele . . . andele*" ("Go on . . . go on"), walked slowly to the end of the rope. As they neared the end of their walk they always began slowing down, sometimes stopping with the barrel just at the mouth of the well. Then the old Mexican at the well mouth would sound an agonized shriek: "*Poco mas, muchacho—poco mas!*" ("A little more, boy—a little more!")

The charge at Maricopa Wells was twenty-five cents a

head for horses and cattle. As there was a heavy travel over the road of prospectors, emigrants, and stockmen, the place was a regular mint.

There were many fights between stockmen over possession of water holes. Sometimes men would refuse to pay for the water, and bloodshed would follow.

In the Far West the stock-watering question has always been one that dominated the use of the arid ranges. Originally the settlers located along the streams and upon springs; then they went back to the ranges and took up water holes, such as lakes and ponds, some fed by springs and others supplied by the drainage from the surrounding country. The lakes were full or empty according to the amount of rain or snowfall on the watershed. As these watering places were protected by claims, the late comers were forced to go farther back into the desert and dig wells to water their stock.

In the early days of the Western range business cattle went long distances to water. Along the Little Colorado River in Arizona, the Platte in Nebraska, the Arkansas in Colorado and western Kansas, as the grass adjacent to the streams was cropped down the animals worked farther back, until it was no unusual thing for them to travel as much as fifteen miles out from water in search of feed, watering but every third day.

On the ranges in the valley of the Little Colorado in the early '90's, one could often count a hundred cattle in a single long string, plodding wearily but steadily down the deeply worn trails that concentrated at the general watering places.

Water development, especially in the Southwest, thus became a necessity. Wells from which the water was raised by power of various kinds were dug to great depths. In some cases these wells were sunk in regions where in early days travelers and explorers suffered and even died of thirst.

Often Western stockmen handling cattle or sheep in large numbers on the round-up found it difficult to water their animals. It was sometimes necessary to cut the day herd of perhaps twelve hundred or fifteen hundred mixed cattle into small bunches so that each animal could get a drink. At times those coming last found the water so disturbed and fouled by animals wading through it that they would not drink.

In the Petrified Forest region of northern Arizona, where surface water was extremely scarce and cattle were numerous, on one occasion years ago the Hashknife round-up day herd contained fully fifteen hundred cattle of all ages. The first day it was not watered at all. The second, the wagon boss told the man in charge to work it down to the Rio Puerco, distant about seven miles. The latter had observed a day or two before that the river was as dry as a smoked herring, but he knew enough about the wagon boss to realize that what he said went. He and his fellow day herders drifted the cattle down the range toward the long streak of white sand that was a river in the rainy season. The thirsty cows needed no "boosting" from the rear. It required four men in front to check the leaders, and even then, by the time the first steers reached the river bank the drags were three miles back on the range.

The boss knew his business. He had sent the horse wrangler with an extra man to drive the remuda to the river. "When you get there, throw them hosses onto the river bed and chouse 'em up and down the sandy bed for half a mile," he gave orders. "Go at it easy-like, for that creek's almighty quicksandy along there, an' if you don't keep 'em moving you're likely to get a lot of 'em bogged down."

The wrangler and his assistant beat the day herd by two hours. They pushed the horses carefully upon the yielding sand, which swayed and bent under the hoofs like soft ice under a heavy weight. Dry as a bone at first, the tramping of one hundred fifty horses gradually hardened the sand until it became as firm and solid as a road. Water began to show on top of the sand. The horses were kept moving. By the time the herd leaders came in sight there was about a half mile of clear running water on a solid safe bed of sand.

Twenty-four hours later the water had disappeared, and so far as surface indications went there was no moisture for miles. Moses, striking the rock in the desert with his rod, did not have a thing on that Hashknife wagon boss when it came to producing water in a dry and thirsty land.

As the early range men began to appreciate the value of better blood in their herds, many carloads of expensive bulls were purchased from the East. Heavy and slow moving, they were far more comfortable in an Eastern farm lot where feed and water were under their noses all the time than in their new environment on the open range where they had to hustle for their daily bread and walk many weary miles for grass and water.

In many parts of the Southwest, especially in the "malpais" lava bed formation, the imported bulls became so sore footed that they hung around the water holes and in some instances starved to death rather than tramp over the rough country looking for food.

Some observing cowman conceived the idea of shoeing these animals. He had seen shod oxen pulling freight wagons across the plains, and he saw no reason why the plan would not work with blooded bulls. He and his men spent a week gathering up the bulls and by the aid of a home-made shoeing stall the blue-ribbon bulls were equipped with iron shoes.

There was considerable sarcastic comment over the idea, but the laughter died down when the lumbering, heavy-footed creatures were seen tramping serenely over the roughest parts of the ranges. The increased calf crop next year returned a good profit on the operation.

Since that time the shoeing of bulls on rough ranges has become a not uncommon practice in the Far West.

6

The Texas trail drivers, searching for pastures new, looked with hungry eyes on that corner of southeastern Arizona where the Apache raided.

It was good cow country. There was plenty of grass in the valleys and enough of forage in the hills. The winters were the balmiest in the world, with sometimes just a scatter of snow in the uplands to give zest to the clear dry atmosphere. Though the summers were hot, the torrid sun robbed the atmosphere of any prostrating humidity.

But cows came late there except those held by such intrepid pioneers as Pete Kitchen and Billy Fourr (the latter still living at Dragoon), men who forted up their ranch houses and never moved abroad without rifles in their hands. There could be no general occupancy of land while the menace of Cochise, and later of Victorio and Geronimo, was always present. No man could tell when the blood-chilling yell of the Apache would be heard.

In the early trail days herds had passed through Arizona on the way to California. Damon Slater in 1868 took one from Llano, Texas, by way of Apache Pass, Tucson, and Yuma, and, finding it profitable, threw in with the Moss brothers next year and drove fourteen hundred "sea lions" (another local name for the longhorn) to Los Angeles. Even before this, in the early '50's, drives had been made to the Pacific Coast. In the more protected parts of the territory cowmen had started herds. But in general it may be said that the cow business was off to a late start in Arizona.

The discovery by Edward Schieffelin of the rich ore deposits at Tombstone brought a swift rush of settlers and made that town for a time the largest in the territory. Pell-mell they came, good and bad, in wagons, on horseback, with freight outfits, on stages, all eager to get rich in the scramble, merchants, miners, mule skinners, laborers, prospectors, saloonkeepers, gamblers, and the usual scum of the border.

It chanced that about this time other states were house cleaning. Missouri was closing in on the James gang, New Mexico on Billy the Kid and his followers. Kansas was emerging into respectability from the wild days of the trail towns. Out of Texas the Rangers were sweeping the riffraff of the frontier. With remarkable unanimity these undesirables migrated to that corner of Arizona which later was to become Cochise County. Side by side with them came also thousands of law-abiding citizens hoping to better their condition in life.

The Texans were not interested in town life, except for recreational purposes. They settled in and about the valleys which parallel one another as they run north from the border, the San Simon, the Sulphur Springs, and the San Pedro. Some honest cattlemen drifted in and began to run stock. So did a good many not so honest cowboys. Most of them had outworn any welcome there might once have been for them in their home state.

Cochise County was a paradise for the rustler. The country was full of canyons, arroyos, and hill pockets where one of a predatory turn could hole up with stolen stock. All that was necessary was to squat on the land and build a corral within convenient distance of water. In these corrals lifted herds could be rebranded and worked before starting them on a drive to a market.

These cows came from Mexico. The Texans had been brought up to hate "greasers," and the wild hill nesters had no scruples about robbing them. It was at first easy to ride across the line, sweep down upon some sleepy hacienda, gather up a bunch of longhorns, and hustle the raided stock into the Animas Valley and over the Peloncillo Mountains by way of Skeleton Cañon into the San Simon. Rustlers thrived. They spread to the neighboring valleys. In their chosen habitat they had the whip hand. Tombstone was too large for them to dominate, and not close enough to the scene of their operations. Moreover, its principal interest was mines and not cows. So the brand-blotting fraternity gathered as a headquarters at Galeyville, a small mining camp on the eastern slope of the Chiricahuas, just above the San Simon. One might have found them at Soldier Holes, at the Clanton ranch on the San Pedro River, at the McLaury place in the Sulphur Spring Valley, or in any one of a score of wooded canyons in the hills. Groups of them rode down to Charleston, about ten miles from Tombstone, and "turned loose their wolves" there, spending the money they had obtained from the sale of rustled cows.

There were probably nearly a hundred of these rustlers nesting in the hills of Cochise County and riding in and out of the chaparral. As many as forty or fifty of them could sometimes be found at one time in Galeyville, their cow ponies waiting patiently with drooping heads at hitch racks for their roistering masters.

The rustlers had a loose organization or at least an understanding among themselves. Their leaders were John Ringo and "Curly Bill," whose real name was William Brocius. It was understood that the Clantons had a kind of supervision of the stock on the San Pedro, and the McLaurys of that in the Sulphur Spring Valley, though any small group of waddies could play a lone hand if they preferred. Among the rustlers were groups of outlaws who varied their cattle activities by hold-ups and stage robberies, such men as Zwing Hunt, Billy Grounds, Pete Spence, Frank Stilwell, Billy Leonard, Harry Head, and Jim Crane. Incidentally it may be mentioned that all of these named, with the possible exceptions of Pete Spence and Curly Bill, came to violent deaths within a few years. Ringo committed suicide. The Apaches accounted for Hunt and the Mexicans for Crane. The red vengeance of the Earps rubbed out Stilwell. Head and

Leonard were killed by head hunters for a reward. Break-enridge shot down Grounds while he was resisting arrest.

The situation in Cochise was unique. Most of the cattlemen made no protest against the rustlers. The ranchmen were new arrivals, and some of them bought "wet" horses and cows to help stock their ranges, paying, of course, a fractional part of the real value. As long as the thieves confined their attention to Mexican stock nobody but those south of the line were greatly interested in the depredations.

The big Sonora ranches made at first attractive hunting ground for the Cochise rustlers. The cattle were on the open range, practically unguarded, and the cowboys could pick up a bunch without reprisal and head for Skeleton Cañon. If a vaquero had the misfortune to cross the line of retreat his comrades found the body a few days later.

Some of the Mexicans did a little in lawlessness themselves. Smugglers were active on the border. There was an export duty on silver and a tariff on goods. What could be more profitable, then, than to take adobe dollars north to Arizona and exchange them for merchandise, thus making a profit going and coming? The border was scarcely guarded at all, so that there was little danger of official interference. Tucson became a Mecca for smugglers—until the rustlers moved into the Chiricahuas.

In July, 1881, a pack train of Mexicans was ambushed in Skeleton Cañon, near the spot where Geronimo surrendered to General Miles, and the party of nineteen murdered almost to a man. Curly Bill and "Old Man" Clanton were given the discredit of leading the foray.

Mexicans are long-suffering, but anger blazed in Sonora when the news came of the Skeleton Cañon massacre. A score of vaqueros took the trail after the men engaged in the next cattle raid. At San Luis Pass Curly Bill turned on his pursuers savagely and killed a dozen of them.

Old Man Clanton bought the stock secured on this expedition and after rebranding headed for a market. He was ambushed by Mexicans in Guadalupe Cañon and killed with four of his men.

Other rustlers rode into *mañana* land to raid the herds and failed to return. Somewhere they had been trapped and had paid the price. It became safer to steal from the cattlemen in Cochise. This was the beginning of the end of the rustlers' paradise. The stockmen who had protected thieves, or at least had acquiesced in their operations, became active enemies of the night riders and joined with the officers of the law to suppress them. As sheriff of Cochise John Slaughter issued an ultimatum, "Rustler, get out or be killed." He was one of those indomitable little men who did not know fear. The rustler got out or was buried. For Slaughter considered himself the law and waited for no judge or jury.

But before Slaughter's term, for a roistering year or two the cow thief ruled the hill country. Tombstone was the county seat, and the sheriff had about all he could do to handle the immediate vicinity. Johnny Behan was the name of that official. It occurred to him that the hill men ought to help pay the taxes, which as yet they had not done. He could not stop their rustling, except occasionally when they stole horses in or near Tombstone, but it was only fair that they should support the local government to a certain extent.

A young deputy named Billy Breakenridge was sent to collect the taxes. It was an assignment most men would have declined, one apparently hopeless and also dangerous. But Breakenridge said he would take a whirl at it. He rode alone to Galeyville and hunted up Curly Bill, a black-headed athlete of uncertain disposition. Breakenridge told the leader of the rustlers why he had come and invited him to ride with him through the cattle country as his deputy. Curly Bill always enjoyed a joke, even when it was on him. He looked Breakenridge over and liked him.

"Damfidon't," he said with a laugh.

So Curly Bill became for a few days an officer of the law and explained to his cohorts that they had to support the government as good American citizens. Bill in his new rôle was a success. He told the cowboys and the cattlemen they had to dig up—and they dug. Breakenridge took back with him to Tombstone a thousand dollars of tax money.

Those were wild days in Cochise. Galeyville and Tombstone witnessed several killings, Charleston a good many more. For Charleston was a hangout not only for the cowboys but for the rough characters from Fort Huachuca, Bisbee, Tombstone, and various points in New Mexico. It was a small town but a ripsnorter. Nobody went there as a rest cure for jangled nerves. Jerry Barton was constable, Jim Burnett justice of the peace. Both were exponents of a wide-open town. A few killings were to be expected. Difficulties punctuated by the six-shooter were subjects of gossip but hardly misdemeanors.

Billy Claibourne killed Jim Hickey, but Jim was a tough nut nobody missed. . . . Dick Lloyd interrupted a poker game by riding into O'Neil's saloon with a rifle in his hands. After Mr. Lloyd by unanimous consent had been pumped full of holes, Curly Bill asked Ringo whose deal it was. . . . John Ringo looked upon the wine when it was red and held up a game one night but returned the enforced loan when he was sober. . . . Jim Wallace shot Curly Bill in the cheek and said good-bye to Arizona from the back of a vanishing horse. (This was the same Wallace who was once stopped by an officer and asked where he had got the horse he was riding. Wallace drew a gun and shot a hole in the ground. "If you want this horse more than I do, take him," he said. The officer didn't want the horse.)

So life moved breezily along at Charleston.

To return to Justice Burnett. If the impulse moved him he collected fines, usually when he or Barton was in low funds. Jerry ran a saloon and was his own bouncer. He was so strong physically that he bragged he could kill a man with a blow of his fist. This boast later sent him to the penitentiary after he had demonstrated by crashing the skull of a cowboy.

Jerry was a character. He stuttered when he spoke, but his trigger did not. The man had a lot of notches on his revolver handle. When asked once how many men he had killed, he wanted to know, after a moment's reflection, "Do you c-c-count Mexicans?" A salty story illustrative of his callousness comes down out of a hundred which grew around his name. Two Mexicans made the mistake of stealing horses from him. Jerry took the trail. A week later he returned with the horses and the thieves. The latter were dead, drilled through by bullets. Someone asked Jerry why he had not brought his prisoners in alive. "They p-p-packed better this way," he explained.

A parallel anecdote is reported of Pete Kitchen. He came up with and captured a Mexican heading for Sonora with Kitchen broncos. From behind a gun Pete persuaded the rustler to right-about face. They traveled for hours. The day was a broiler. The heat danced in front of the two men as they rode. They came to some cottonwoods by a water hole. Kitchen decided that what he needed was a siesta. But he could not sleep while the Mexican slanted what the movies call baleful eyes at him. It would be a little too hazardous. Mr. Kitchen had a happy thought. He tied his prisoner's hands behind him and mounted him on his pony. Around the man's neck he put a rope. The other end of the rope he attached to the limb of a tree three feet above the head of the vaquero. Then Pete slept peacefully. He awoke refreshed and saw that the sizzling sun was setting behind the horizon hills. Also he observed that the horse thief was no longer in the saddle. He was hanging by his neck to the branch of the cottonwood. "That ornery bronc of his had wandered down the gulch to graze," Mr. Kitchen later reported.

Burnett was an autocrat. He cared nothing for the letter of the law. When one litigant threatened to appeal he informed the "low-down son of a Mexican" that there was no higher law, and if he didn't light out pronto he would remind him of it with a sawed-off gun. Burnett was shot down some time later at the O K corral in Tombstone by W. C. Greene, one of the most famous cattlemen in Arizona. He was a little too slow on the draw.

The career of Greene reads like a soldier of fortune romance. He had a remarkable individuality. An old Indian fighter, he had been wounded by them five times. On one occasion he killed two in a long-distance duel. Strong and fearless, he proved time and again his audacious courage. His amazing energy is evidenced by the fact that within a few years he acquired six million acres of land, a great cattle outfit, one of the big copper properties of the world with the railroads and equipment necessary to run it, and built a city of twenty thousand inhabitants at Cananea, Mexico.

Zwing Hunt and Billy Grounds, known to be cattle thieves, varied their occupation by holding up the Tombstone Mining Company at Charleston and shooting through the heart a young man named Peel. This was an entirely different matter from the casual bumping off of a cowboy. Billy Breakenridge took the trail with a posse. There was a desperate battle in which every member of the pursuing party was either killed or wounded except Breakenridge himself. Billy wasted no time and no bullets. He killed Grounds and shot Hunt through a lung, after which he piled the casualties into two wagons and took them to Tombstone.

While the cowboys, which word in that section was then recognized as a synonym for rustlers, ruled the outlying districts of Cochise, Wyatt Earp was attempting to impose himself upon Tombstone as overlord. He had come from Dodge with a group of relatives and followers. There were five of the Earp brothers, all of them stalwart fighting men. Among Wyatt's other retainers the chief was Doc Holliday, a consumptive gambler of a quarrelsome temperament, already notorious as a killer.

A saloon keeper or a professional gambler was not by reason of that fact an undesirable citizen. The business he engaged in was considered by the public as respectable as selling hardware or groceries. He supported churches and schools generously. Crooked games in Tombstone were probably rare. The legitimate percentage of the house was enough to make the owner wealthy.

In such a town as this there were at first no social distinctions. The faro dealer at the Crystal Palace and the Reverend Endicott Peabody, the girls from the hurdy-gurdy houses and the principal of the school, the judge of the district court and the rustler in from the hills, put their feet beneath the same table at the Can Can restaurant.

There was at first no quarrel between the Earp group at Tombstone and the rustlers in the hills. "Live and let live" seemed a reasonable motto. But gradually a bitter feeling developed. The Sandy Bob stage was held up and two men killed. There was a persistent rumor, backed by evidence, that Doc Holliday had ridden out from Tombstone and taken part in the stage robbery, that he had while drunk actually done the shooting. The hill outlaws believed the Earps were protecting him at the expense of his three cowboy companions. The Tombstone–Bisbee stage was robbed. Wyatt Earp took the suspected road agents into custody after Dave Nagle and Billy Breakenridge had arrested them. The rustlers were incensed at this.

There was a secret conference between Ike Clanton of the cowboy faction and Wyatt Earp of the gambler contingent. Someone blabbed, and both parties were afraid of what the other might tell.

Young Billy Clanton and the McLaury boys rode to Tombstone and were joined by Ike. At the O K corral they ciashed with three of the Earps and Doc Holliday. Ike Clanton was unarmed and escaped, but his three companions were killed.

There was much bitterness in the hills. Ringo took the matter hard. Billy Clanton was only nineteen and a protégé of his. He had liked the McLaury boys. Something ought to be done about the matter at once.

John Ringo, be it said, stood out among all the rustlers of Cochise because of his personality. He was an educated man, a great reader, fond of the classics. Somewhere back in "the States" he had left relatives who were respected and looked up to in their community. The man had sad brooding eyes, the prophecy of tragedy in them.

Ringo took none of his adherents into his confidence. He rode to Tombstone and left his horse at a hitch rack, then walked up Allen Street to the Bob Hatch saloon. The Earps were standing there in a group, Wyatt, Virgil, and Morgan, stalwart men all, gun fighters of repute. With them was their little shadow, Doc Holliday.

Ringo strode up to them and said his piece. "Let's end this row here and now, Wyatt, before a lot more good men are killed. I'll fight it out in the middle of the street with any one of you. Whichever one of us wins, that will be the end of the feud. What say?"

Earp's cold eyes met those of the hill man. He was game enough, but he could see no profit in such a duel. "What's the sense of talking hurrah stuff like that, John? I'm out."

The chief of the rustlers turned to Holliday. "They say you're quite a gunman, Doc," he sneered. "I've heard you can shoot a man right from the top of a stage even when you're masked. Like any of my game? I'm making the same proposition to you I did to Earp."

"And he's giving you the same answer I did, John," cut in Wyatt. "We're law officers. We don't engage in street brawls."

Ringo laughed bitterly. "So you're law officers, eh?

Well, run along with your little badges. Maybe sometime you'll find some more cowboys in town without their guns."

He turned on his heel and left them.

A few weeks later Virgil Earp was wounded by some party unknown. Morgan Earp was assassinated in the Bob Hatch saloon. In reprisal the Earps killed Frank Stilwell and Indian Charley, after which they left Arizona for Colorado.

Times were changing in Cochise. The little red schoolhouse was coming into the hills. Occasionally an itinerant circuit rider drifted out into the Chiricahuas and preached the Gospel. Women were tired of the old rip-roaring days. Moreover, law had pushed out to the cactus country. Rustling stock was not so good any more.

Meanwhile, a stream of longhorns was pouring in from Texas. Big cattle outfits were being built up in Arizona and in New Mexico. There was in the latter territory the Diamond A (A) owned by the California millionaires Haggin and Hearst, who had one fenced pasture near Engle that included eight hundred thousand acres. There were the Denver-owned Red River Cattle Company, the Bar W of Governor McDonald, and the N A N. By 1888 the Aztec Land and Cattle Company, known as the Hashknife (⊥) outfit, was running more than sixty thousand head of cattle on its northern Arizona ranges near Holbrook and Flagstaff. Some of the herds of southern Arizona were as large. These included the Chiricahua Cattle Company (generally called the Cherry Cow), the Vail brothers' Empire ranch, the Babocomari Company, the San Simon, and Bill Greene's holdings on both sides of the border. None of these concerns ran less than twenty thousand cows and some of them more than sixty thousand. Most of them did not know exactly how many they owned. When the county assessors wanted to know, the best the ranch foremen could do was to make a guess.

With the coming of the big companies rustling again

became active, so much so that some of the cattle outfits thought of going out of business. Mormons, Gentiles, and Mexicans engaged in thieving, for a time with impunity. The headwaters of the San Francisco and the Salt rivers were almost inaccessible wilds where murderers and bandits could hole up after their depredations. To remedy this the Arizona territorial legislature authorized the appointment of a body of Rangers. Such a force was needed. The raids of the outlaws · had become intolerable. They would sweep down from the hills, round up a small herd, and be safe in the mountain fastnesses before a posse could reach them. There were a dozen bands of miscreants engaged in stealing horses and cows, at the head of them such men as Bill Smith and the notorious Augustine Chacon.

As has been pointed out, the rustler did not wear horns and hoofs. He was often a pleasant companion and a loyal friend. Billy Claibourne saved the life of his employer John Slaughter by bulldogging a vicious steer at much risk. Billy Clanton was a nice boy with a charming smile, who would go through with you to the limit. Often the stock thief treated his own delinquencies with sardonic wit. Colonel Breakenridge tells a story of one who came to Tombstone to sell a horse. A prospective customer looked the animal over at the O K corral and asked how good the title was. "Well," the young rustler drawled with a grin, "it's perfectly good if you travel west, but not so good if you go east."

Burton C. Mossman, previously range foreman of the Hashknife outfit, was the first captain of Rangers. He had under his command a sergeant and twelve privates. The Rangers were recruited from old cowboys, most of whom had served with Roosevelt in Cuba. They had to know how to follow a cold trail for a month at a time in all kinds of weather, how to rope and ride anything on four legs, how to shoot straight and fast but not until they had first been fired upon. Their knowledge of frontier conditions had to be supplemented by patient audacity and by brains. So effective was the work of this force that within a year the territory had been largely cleared of the bad characters who had infested the mountains and lurked along the border.

Chacon had been for years a thorn in the side of honest men on both sides of the border. From the Sierra Madre Mountains in Old Mexico he rode to the raids that terrorized settlers. He was a many times murderer of the most brutal kind. On one occasion John Slaughter just missed kiling him at Tombstone.

Near Morenci, Arizona, in 1896, Chacon robbed a store and cut the throat of the merchant. Riding for his getaway, he turned on a sheriff's posse and killed Pablo Salcido under pretense that he was ready to surrender. Later he was wounded, captured, tried, and sentenced to be hanged. He broke jail and once more resumed his ferocious career.

Mossman determined to capture this desperado. With the help of Burt Alvord, who had been in turn cowboy, scout, Ranger, rustler, and train robber, Mossman located and met Chacon near Greene's pasture in Mexico. The Ranger captain pretended to be a fugitive from "the States," ready for any deviltry. Chacon was suspicious, prepared at the least excuse to fling bullets into this stranger. The impulse was not at any moment quite strong enough. He waited for developments.

Captain Mossman was a jaunty, devil-may-care young fellow in those days, a cool and hardy rider of the plains, handy with his gun and speaking faultless Spanish, but it may be conceived that his nerves were taut. Of Burt Alvord and the fourth member of the party (Billy Stiles, one of the Southern Pacific train robbers in the gang with Alvord) he was not at all sure. They might plot with Chacon to destroy him. All night he lay by the camp fire, apparently sound asleep but warily watchful. Morning found Chacon very doubtful of him. They discussed stealing horses from the Greene pasture, but the heart of none of the men was in it. At last Chacon announced flatly that he was through. He wasn't going to help rustle horses. Mossman shrugged his shoulders and drew out the makings for a cigarette. Deliberately he rolled the tobacco and picked up with his left hand a glowing branch of juniper from the fire. He lit the cigarette, then transferred the lighter to his right hand. Casually he dropped the stick, his arm falling to his side. As he raised his hand a revolver came up with it. Chacon was covered.

Mossman ordered Stiles to disarm and handcuff the man. The ex train robber did so. The Ranger took his prisoner across the line without extradition papers and turned him over to the authorities at Solomonville. In due time Chacon was hanged, a game and hardy ruffian to the last.

Not all the exploits of the Rangers terminated as successfully as this. Four Rangers pursued the Smith gang of horse thieves into the mountains in the dead of winter. For three weeks they stayed on the trail, weeks of incredible hardship, in deep snow, with many storms and insufficient provisions. The Rangers separated one day, to meet in the evening. Bill Maxwell and Carlos Tefio came on the thieves suddenly, themselves unseen. To capture the outlaws it was necessary to cross an open place fifty yards wide. The two did not hesitate an instant but took the chance of being seen. Bill Smith looked up and ordered the intrepid men to surrender. They refused. The robbers were behind cover, their hunters in the open. Tefio and Maxwell were killed in the fight that followed.

There was grim tragedy enough on the frontier, but in the life of the cowpuncher was always the saving grace of humor. He laughed at hardship, grinned hardily if the cards went against him. When five of the members of the Heath gang were hanged on the same gallows at Tombstone they made a jest of death and hoped the sheriff would not hang the attending parson by mistake. It was a part of the code to keep a stiff upper lip no matter what happened.

They were primitive days, of elemental simplicity. The story is told of a storekeeper at Ehrenberg who could neither read nor write. His system of bookkeeping was unique. He kept his accounts on a whitewashed wall of the store. A customer came in to pay a bill and found himself charged with a cheese.

"Guess again," the cowman said. "I don't eat cheese."

"Well, you got a cheese, an' it weighed eight pounds, an' I reckon you got to pay for it."

The customer demurred. They argued the matter for a time. The storekeeper was obstinate about it. He took the ranchman in to see the account on the wall. This was what he saw:

"Three pounds of coffee, eight pounds of bacon, three cans of tomatoes, four horseshoes, and a cheese," the storekeeper elucidated. Light came to the customer. "Didn't I get it when I got the horseshoes? It wasn't a cheese. It was a grindstone."

"Well, I'll be doggoned. Reckon you're right. I done forgot to put the square hole in the middle. Less go get a drink. It's sure on me."

After the cattle-boom crash in 1885 cowmen faced a series of lean years. The value of stock steadily declined. Many a small owner found the railroad companies life-savers as purchasers. In Arkansas, Texas, Arizona, Colorado, New Mexico, and Wyoming—in fact, at every locality to which the railroad had penetrated—the transportation companies were involuntary buyers. The tracks had not yet been fenced, and cattle straying upon them were frequently killed. It developed later that such stock was very valuable, quite unusual animals compared to the run of the herd. This was the view of the owner. The railroad claim agent looked at the matter from another angle. He explained how cheap cows were. The range was so overstocked, he thought, that the killing of a few cows was really a favor to the ranchman. After the matter had been adjusted by compromise he would suggest as a pleasantry that it might help if the cowman would quit salting the right of way.

Even the big companies running cattle did not object to being the beneficiaries of such accidents. When W. D. Duke was manager of the Diamond A outfit a great number of its cattle were run over by the Southern Pacific trains during the year 1896, a very dry one in the Southwest. On behalf of the railroad Colonel W. M. Breakenridge called upon Duke to find out if his cattle ever ranged anywhere except on the S. P. track. Duke said his riders tried to keep the Diamond A stuff in the Animas and Playas valleys, but the best market he had for animals too weak to ship was the Southern Pacific. He accompanied this with a grin that said the remark need not be taken too literally.

With the market in such a condition buyers from the North to stock the fine range of the Little Missouri country were eagerly welcomed. Henry S. Boice was an outstanding figure among these. Beginning in 1891, for ten years he came down early each spring and bought from twenty thousand to twenty-five thousand steers for feeders. He bought at Holbrook, Arizona, and shipped to the Berry-Boice ranch in South Dakota, by way of Cheyenne and Orrin Junction, trailing from the latter point to the journey's end.

When the bartender of the Bucket of Blood saloon at Holbrook passed the word that there was a stranger in town who wanted to buy cattle the news was too good to be true. Cattlemen drifted in to the bar to take a look at Santa Claus. He was a quiet, well dressed man, low voiced, pleasant of manner, with hands as soft as those of a schoolgirl. Yes, he wanted two-year-olds, June delivery, good stuff, full age—all cripples, runts, swaybacks, and big-jaws to be cut out.

In his room at the Apache Hotel Boice received the cowmen and signed contracts, paying down five dollars a head to bind the bargain. After which he departed, leaving more real money in the hands of these Arizona cowmen than they had seen for six years.

Boice was on hand the day of delivery. Having looked at him once, the Arizonans agreed that he was a bird to be plucked. A man with hands like his could not possibly know a yearling from a two-year-old. Mr. Boice, still in low shoes, colored socks, and little felt hat, rode through the first herd offered him. In the twenty-five hundred offered there were at least five hundred yearlings. Very leisurely he examined the bunch, then rode up to the sellers who had stacked the cards on him.

"Ain't going to cut a critter!" one man whispered to another.

It looked that way. Mr. Boice dismounted, and he said his little piece.

"When you get a few hundred yearlings, and about forty cripples, runts, stags, and big-jaws out of the herd, send me word to the hotel and I'll come look at what you've got."

With which he climbed into a livery rig and drove back to town.

Never had a group of cowmen been more humiliated and chastened. They re-read their contracts and got busy. They cut the herd thoroughly. Not a doubtful animal remained. When Boice saw the herd next it was as clean as a hound's tooth. Never again did a cowman in Arizona try to "run anything" on him.

The experience of Boice subsequent to this time is fairly typical of that of many big operators. The man with the hoe so hemmed him in that at last he had to abandon his South Dakota range on the Little Missouri River. He located on Beaver Creek, Oklahoma, and was again driven out by the forward rolling covered wagon. He bought the C C C (the Chiricahua Cattle Company) outfit in southern Arizona, one of the big range herds in the West, running almost entirely on the Apache Indian reservation. At the time of his death he was by far the largest individual cattle owner in the country. Boice and Theodore Roosevelt were close friends. They used to range their stock in the same district in the Dakotas. Henry Boice, the son, to-day runs the C C C herds on the same range as did his father.

Long before cattle came in any quantity to the great plains east of the Rockies, stock was grazing in sunny California on great ranchos owned by Mexican and Spanish dons. It was an outlying province of Mexico, and the soldiers who had come with Portola from the South were encouraged to take grants as colonists. They were offered large grazing tracts for cattle and sheep, and it was with difficulty the men were induced to accept them.

Life was easy, and in that well favored land cattle throve. Cut off as they were from the great plains of Texas by the desert, and from the country farther North by the Rocky Mountains, the cattle of California make a story largely independent of the epic swing northward of the Texas herds. The latter, in their march, founded the backbone of the American cattle industry, which has been called the greatest pastoral movement in history. The California tale is self-contained, for the Spanish dons, living in feudal splendor with their herds and their vaqueros, neither needed nor sought markets. The unrest and the economic consequences of the Civil War touched them in a different way. But the gold rush of '49, with the growth of San Francisco, did have its own effect, quite independent of the sweep of the mighty river of cattle east of the Rockies.

One of the first grants given was to Manuel Nieto. His land was in what is now Los Angeles County, and it included all the territory between the San Gabriel and the

Santa Ana rivers from the hills to the sea. Out of this
other grants were later carved. To Jose Verdugo went
140,000 acres. It included country now covered by a
dozen towns, among them Glendale and Garvanza. Don
Christobel Dominguez received the San Pedro Rancho,
part of which was later leased to the Bixby family of
Long Beach. The Yorbas and the Peraltas were also
grantees of large estates.

Cattle ranged at will over the San Joaquin and Sacramento plains. They had so little value that anyone might
kill for food as he needed provided he left the hide where
it could be found by the owner. Land was of even less
account. Bancroft tells the story of how George Yount
went to Salvador Vallejo's rancho looking for work.

"What can you do?" the don asked him.

"I could shingle your house."

"Tchingle? Tchingle? What is that?"

Yount explained what a shingle is and its use. Not in
all California was there a shingled house, so Vallejo decided
to be progressive and have the first. After Yount had
done the work he came for his pay.

"What do you want?" the don questioned.

"A half a league of land."

Now, land lay unoccupied for a thousand miles to the
north and five hundred miles to the south and east.

The puzzled Vallejo looked at him. "What do you
want with half a league? You may have four leagues."

The civilization was not of the aggressive American
type. There was always to-morrow, so why hurry? They
were a gay and laughter-loving group, these grandees and
their dependents. They lived an indolent and care-free
existence. Hospitality, friendliness, and ease were of the
essence of their lives. Much of the time the dons spent
on horseback riding over their estates, hunting, roping
wild mustangs for pleasure, visiting their neighbors.
These visits were state occasions. Not only the don and
donna went, but a troop of servants suitable to their

degree in life. They danced, twanged guitars, made love, drank wine, and left to posterity large and healthy families.

While San Francisco was still Yerba Buena, the country round about was filled with the estates of these early Californians. Don Mariano Guadalupe Vallejo had 10,000 cattle at Petaluma. In Napa Valley Don Salvador Vallejo had stock on a hundred hills. The Rancho Pinole was owned by Don Ygnacio Martinez and it pastured 8,000 cows, 3,000 horses, and a great number of sheep. Where Oakland and Alameda now stand was the Rancho San Antonio, the property of Don Luis Peralta. There were a score of other fine holdings, ruled over by gentlemen most courteous, kindly, and honorable. It was their pride to be just and fair, to be good masters, to scorn a petty meanness.

The padres at the missions watched with a jealous eye the growth of the lay grant holders. To begin with the missions had been dominant. Few of the settlers were independent. The native Indians worked under direction of the Fathers. Weekly each mission had a round-up and killed twenty or thirty oxen for meat to feed its dependents. The Church was supreme.

The collapse of its power came fast. In 1834 the twenty-one missions supported 31,500 Indians and owned 396,400 cattle. Eight years later the number of Indians had been reduced to 4,450 and of cattle to 29,000.

But the Spanish-Mexican grantees continued to flourish. They had little money, but they did not need it. A rawhide would roof a wagon, patch a saddle, or make a pair of shoes. Would one be happier if he had much money like some of the gringoes? These young Californians were the most dexterous ropers in the country. They rode like centaurs, gracefully and with the utmost daring. The round-ups were festive occasions. The families of the grandees came, danced fandangoes, listened to serenades, and watched the gayly dressed young gallants ride races and play athletic games. Bull and bear fights were in vogue.

The cattle of California were valuable only for the tallow and the hides. There was no market for meat, except from a few trading vessels putting in at the Pacific ports. The stock was slaughtered in the summer. In large pots brought by American whalers the tallow was rendered. Afterward it was put into hides sewn together closely. The hide and its contents was called a "beta." In his *Seventy-Five Years in California* William H. Davis makes an estimate of the exports from 1826 to 1848, tabulated by the records of the ships taking the freight. There were 1,048,000 hides, according to his check (which was not complete), and 62,501,000 pounds of tallow.

But with the conquest of California by the Americans and the subsequent discovery of gold this peaceful existence was shattered. The smiling don, in velvet trimmed with gold and silver lace, was out of step with this generation on a mad hunt for gold. He could not join the scramble, nor would it let him ignore it. The taint of money lust was in the air.

For example, Salvador Vallejo. His rancho covered 146,000 acres, though he could only guess at the size of it by leagues, never having had it surveyed. Three hundred vaqueros and near-peons called him chief. Their women and naked children flashed warm smiles of welcome at him. When Chiles and Baldridge found a good mill site on the Napa River in the don's rancho and wanted to buy or lease, Salvador shook his head. A flour mill would frighten the cattle. As for the money, what could it buy him that he did not have? Could one purchase more health or friendship with it?

The civilization of the aggressive gringo was disturbing. The dons might try to withdraw from it, but the poorer people could not escape contacts. They did not like the

Americanos, especially in the rôle of the dominant race. Young Mexicans took to banditry, finding inclination and patriotism hand in hand when they preyed upon the enemy. Chief of these outlaws was Joaquin Murieta. He was of good family, and before he met Americans had been a gay and attractive youth, no better and no worse than many of his fellows. He ran away from home with his sweetheart, Rosita Feliz, and came to California. Some ruffians jumped his mining claim, violated Rosita, and drove him away. Later he was accused of stealing a horse. His brother was hanged, and he was whipped until the blood ran down his back. Young Murieta was now nineteen years of age. He gathered together a band of Mexicans and renegade Americans. They swore eternal vengeance on the gringo. The leader paid especial attention to the villains who had committed the outrages upon him and his family. One died by the revolver, another by the swift thrust of a knife. Friends found the bodies of two more lying face down in the chaparral. A prospector came upon a fifth spreadeagled to a live oak, with a neat hole bored through the forehead. So the tale of vengeance went on, till fear rode the heart of each man who had taken part in the amusement of torturing three helpless Mexicans. No matter what precautions the terror-stricken victims took, Murieta's mocking *"Buenos noches, señor"* came at last to their ears, just a moment before the blow fell.

He gathered a choice assortment of villains to help him rob treasure trains, stagecoaches, and ranches. Many of them already had evil reputations more notorious than the boy Murieta. There was Joaquin Valenzuela, twenty years his senior, who had been cutting throats when Murieta was in the cradle. There was Manuel Garcia, Three-Fingered Jack, a gorilla man dreaded for his savage cruelty. There were Claudio and Gonzales, one a sly and wily spy, the other a horse thief known for hundreds of miles. All of these had been leaders of bands, but within a short time they hailed Murieta chief. For Murieta had the

genius of a born cavalry leader. He was here to-day raiding a mining camp. To-morrow he was far down in the
plains rounding up a bunch of cows from a rancho owned
by some American.

Men moved against him at their peril. He killed a deputy sheriff named Clark at San Jose for arresting two of
his men. He ambushed Sheriff Buchanan while the
officer was hunting him, desperately wounded him, and
shot down several of the posse. The audacity of the youth
was amazing. He rode into towns placarded with reward
offers and played monte in gambling halls filled with men.
One young officer named Wilson gathered a group of
determined citizens to rid the country of this pest. Before
they got started a swarthy lad, gayly dressed from sombrero to spur, rode into Los Angeles, called Wilson from a
building, shot him dead, and galloped away. General
Josh Bean organized militia companies to pursue the
desperado. Murieta and Garcia waylaid him, threw a
rope, dragged him from his horse, and stabbed him to
death.

Man hunters found small profit in the chase of Joaquin
Murieta. But there are always men on the frontier ready
to fight for law and order. Harry Love was one of them, a
bronzed Texan who had fought the Comanche on the
border of the Lone Star State. He had been a Ranger and
a captain in the Mexican War. Love took the trail and
never left it till his job was done. He killed Gonzales and
captured Murieta's brother-in-law Reyes Feliz, who was
later hanged in Los Angeles. In a desperate battle he slew
a dozen of the robber band, including Claudio. Twist which
way Murieta would, he found this cold avenger always
crowding close. But the boy had plunged his hands in
blood. He could not turn back. Still he raided mining
camps, and on one occasion a schooner loaded with
treasure. Wherever he and his band went they killed.

In the end Captain Love got him, crept up on the camp
where the outlaws were resting. Murieta was sponging

off his fine horse, one bandit was cooking breakfast, others were smoking and chatting. Out of the chaparral came the clump of galloping men.

Joaquin Murieta was caught without a weapon. He moved toward a rifle and was warned back. Instantly he made his decision. Vaulting to the back of his horse, he dug his heels in and whispered a word to his mount. They were off like the wind. But it was rough going. There was a precipice ahead. The gallant horse took the cliff without hesitation but crashed down among the rocks below. Murieta sprang up, ran dodging down a ravine. Four or five rifles sent bullets after him. He staggered, stumbled, steadied himself, and turned. "Enough," he cried, and sank to the ground a dead man.

So passed Joaquin Murieta, a boy not yet twenty-two, the most renowned thief and murderer in the history of California.

Hard on the heels of Murieta came Tiburcio Vazquez, Tom Bell, and Jim Irvin, another trio of desperadoes who infested southern California with their bands. During 1853 there were more murders in California than in all the other states of the Union, and more in Los Angeles than in all the rest of California.

From mining, many Americans drifted into farming and into cattle ranching. William Dunphy, a pioneer of '49, was one of the earliest. He ranged twenty thousand cows, most of them in Nevada. Miller & Lux was another outfit which had ranches from southern California to Oregon and into Nevada. Warner's property was of feudal extent and character. His major-domo said that if it were necessary he could put three hundred fighting men in the field for the boss.

Like cattlemen all over the Western country, ranchers arrived in California and Oregon from the East before the law was established. When it caught up with them they interpreted it to suit themselves as did those on the other side of the Rockies. They picked out good land with plenty of water and had their cowboys homestead, later paying the punchers a nominal sum to relinquish in their favor. Those who bought from the owners of land grants were of course not obliged to obtain possession in this manner.

In southern California the cattleman was always in dread of a drought. During the days of Mexican supremacy there had been several severe ones, but the end of cattle running as a range proposition came in 1864. There were by this time three million of the cow kind in the state. The lack of rainfall continued for years. As a result stock perished to the number of several hundreds of thousands. At Santa Barbara in that year fifty thousand cattle were sold for thirty-seven and a half cents a head. Ten thousand were driven over the bluffs into the sea to save the pasturage for sheep on the chance that the latter might survive.

The cattle industry never fully recovered. In the South sheep supplanted cows until general farming and fruit came to occupy much of the land. Between 1870 and 1875 most of the large holdings were broken up and sold to the granger, who even before that time had been creeping up to the very edge of the grants.

DURING the late '70's and early '80's various causes combined to bring about an extension of the open-range grazing of cattle. The country was recovering from the panic of '73, and business in general was good. The resumption of gold payments in the United States in 1879 had created a great boom. England was looking for an investment outlet. America offered the best field for this. Money flowed westward across the Atlantic, drawn by the opportunities offered in a rich undeveloped land.

The prosperity was reflected in an increased sale of steaks and soup bones to the consumer. The packing houses had developed improved methods of canning and dressing their product. Prior to this time there had been much complaint in England about the American cattle sent over for slaughtering, and prejudice existed against beef from the States, owing to the furore about Texas fever and pleuro-pneumonia. But now that refrigeration had come into its own, prime beef could be delivered at Liverpool in as good condition as it could be laid down in New York, and there was a strong British market.

These conditions showed a favorable reaction in the

price of cattle. In the summer of 1878 Chicago quotations were about $4 a hundred for Northwestern range steers and about $3.50 for Texans. Naturally this stimulated breeding.

Many of those who had suffered most from the panic were still looking westward for a chance to better their condition. Farmers from Wisconsin, Iowa, Illinois, and Missouri moved out in their covered wagons to cheap land in Nebraska, Kansas, and South Dakota. The resumption of work on the Northern Pacific Railroad brought in thousands of settlers. These pushed the cattlemen into the high plains and the hills.

On March 10, 1879, a young fellow named Kendrick started from southern Texas with a herd of mixed cattle bound for the range near the present town of Lusk, Wyoming. His count the morning they pulled out showed more than 3,150 head of animals old and young, big and little.

The trail boss brags to-day that they arrived at their destination with a full number despite several leakages and wastes along the way. "In all the fifteen hundred or more miles driven," the present United States Senator from Wyoming, John B. Kendrick, says, "not a single fence or other artificial barrier was met except for the few small towns we touched here and there, and they were rather welcome sights to us all."

This was one of the earliest herds of Southern cattle to reach that range. "We made three dugouts in the side of a hill right behind the town of Lusk," Senator Kendrick states, "and there we holed up during the long winter of 1879–80. The next spring we rode about five hundred miles back on our trail to find the leaders of the drift that had started back to Texas before the winter storms."

The slow-moving but resistless river of cattle now swept into the rich grazing country of the Northwest. Dammed up to this time by various economic factors, it at last broke through all barriers and poured into the new lands open to settlement. It was possible now for the Texas steer to nose its long narrow head into the vast country of the Sioux, and their kinsmen the Shoshones, Blackfeet, Piegans, and Gros Ventres. For at last, after a fierce struggle in which the whites had been held at bay by the valor of the Northern tribes, the Sioux and the Cheyenne were subjugated. The discovery of gold in the Black hills and elsewhere, the forward march of the railroads which had wiped out the protective isolation of the tribes, the need for more range land, had all contributed to this effect. The defeat of Custer had been the last defiant gesture of the red man, and this had turned out a Pyrrhic victory. The result of it had been to create a resentment in the West that stirred Washington to put forces in the field that could not be successfully met.

The tide of cattle swept forward on the very heels of the troops. A hundred thousand Texas cows were driven into the valleys of Montana during the summer of '79. The buffalo had not yet gone, but during this and the succeeding years the hide hunters were busy exterminating the last of the great buffalo herds. The pour of cattle into this territory continued until by 1883 more than six hundred thousand "cow critters" were grazing in Montana. Many of these had been driven north from Colorado, where as early as 1879 the range was in many places overstocked. During this time, and even until the crash in 1885, the demand for stock cattle in the Northwest was so great that it could not be fully supplied. Most of the herds were contracted for before they left Texas. Longhorns from the Lone Star State had been reinforced by thousands from the farms of the Middle West. One railroad alone carried one hundred thousand barnyard animals westward in 1883. A considerable number of these were pure-bred bulls.

These "pilgrims," as the farm cattle were called, were far less hardy than the shaggy longhorns which had come up the trail. They did not know how to rustle for a living when the temperature was below zero and the ground covered with snow. They lacked the independence of the Texas steer and hung around corrals waiting to be fed from non-existent haystacks. Since they were more valuable, the loss when they failed to rough through the winter was greater. Moreover, there was always the chance that they would bring with them from the farm the disease of pleuro-pneumonia which had been ravaging the East but had not spread to the West.

Most of the cattle used in stocking the Northern range were prodded up the trail from Texas. The single firm of which Captain John T. Lytle was the chief partner sent four hundred and fifty thousand longhorns north. The Slaughters and Shanghai Pierce and Seth Mabry and Doc Burnett had a score of herds plodding up the road of destiny each year. Ike T. Pryor and George W. Saunders, and Dan Waggoner and John Blocker, all of whom may be seen to-day around the headquarters of the Trail Drivers' Association, were active for a dozen years in supplying the Northern trade.

The farmer trekking westward in his covered wagon and later by rail had made it more and more difficult for the trail driver to get through with his herds. He had fenced and plowed everywhere. In 1884 a big convention of cattlemen memorialized Congress to establish a national livestock trail from the Red River to the Northern boundary of the United States, a stretch of ground from five to fifty miles wide (the trail drivers differed as to how broad it should be) to be set aside in perpetuity for the moving of stock. This was to be fenced and bridges built over all the streams to avoid the necessity of swimming.

The memorial was ten years too late. Not only did representatives of farming districts oppose it, but the new railroads added their influence to defeat the project. The Fort Worth & Denver and the Missouri, Kansas & Texas, as well as other lines, tapped the cattle country of the South. There was no longer a vital need for a trail.

The northbound movement of swarms of cattle on the hoof was a declining one. In 1886 the total drive from Texas was about two hundred and twenty-five thousand. Many of these went to the Northern ranges of Panhandle outfits such as the X I T, the Matador, and the L S, which had breeding ranges at home and fattening ones in the North. After this year no such number ever took the trail. The difficulty of getting through was too great. Nesters had fenced up near the trail towns and built irrigation ditches. Drivers were harassed by charges for crossing No Man's Land and various points north. Water was no longer free from Texas to the Canadian line. Nor did a cordial feeling exist between the drivers and the farmers. The battle lines were drawn, and at times the hostility culminated in bloodshed.

The Northern trail now ran from the Panhandle to Lamar, Colorado, from Lamar to Brush, from Brush to Lusk, Wyoming, and from Lusk to Miles City, Montana. In spite of the difficulty in getting through, driving was still cheaper than shipping by rail, and cattle frequently arrived at the journey's end in better condition than those sent by train. As late as 1896 some herds took the trail, including several of the X I T. Probably the last herd driven up on the hoof was one in charge of John McCanles. The drive was one continual row from start to finish, but the boss delivered his charges.

The last of the great Texas cattle trails had been closed. The paths they followed had been plowed up by the farmers who settled the frontier. The long slow trudge of millions of feet, chiseled into the soil for a thousand miles, had been obliterated. Only in the character of the West they did so much to make does the imprint of these trails remain.

But before they were at last closed, the great cattle boom had swept the West and left desolation in its wake.

Chicago, St. Louis, and Kansas City were the chief shipping centers. Prices received increased month by month. In 1879 cattle sold in Texas at about $8 per head to supply the new territory. Two years later the price was $12. Except in the Northwest the range was already overstocked by 1880. But the grass was still good, and this year and the next were profitable ones for the cowman.

The cow business had become fashionable. The boom by this time was well under way. Wild prophecies were accepted as sober fact. Predictions of promoters and the figures prepared by them were given wide circulation. As the center of the Northern cattle country, Cheyenne was marked by destiny to be as great a city as Denver. Lusk was to become a metropolis. Other towns were affected by delusions of grandeur. Legislatures, railroads, chambers of commerce, and newspapers propagated impossible fairy tales about the amount of money to be made in cattle. Books were published to spread the story, most of them written in perfectly good faith. Baron Richthofen and Sir Charles Dilke, the British statesman, were responsible for two of these, General Brisbin for another, *The Beef Bonanza*. The grazing resources of the West were said to be illimitable. Boundless and inexhaustible were words frequently used to apply to the range. It could feed all the cattle of the world for all time.

Under the spur of this advertising the price of range cows jumped to $20. Instead of selling, experienced cattlemen who should have known better bought until their ranges were greatly overstocked. Money was pouring in, and they wanted to make all of it they could while the boom lasted. There was feverish buying in Arizona, New Mexico, Colorado, and Texas, as well as in Wyoming, South Dakota, and Montana.

Market prices continued to rise. Thirty dollars a head was paid for range stock. In the summer of 1882 a shipment of beef sold at the Chicago market for $9.35 a hundred, according to Osgood in *The Day of the Cattleman*. Naturally, four-year-olds in the Panhandle kept corresponding pace. They were taken by feeders at what seemed the prohibitive price of $40 and even $50 each.

From the East and from Great Britain money was arriving to form vast cattle syndicates. Investors were lured by tales of the immense profits of the earlier companies, one of which was to announce (so the story went) a 40 per cent dividend. There was so much money to be picked up in cattle that the representatives of investors bought the holdings of cattlemen at fancy prices with no investigation of what they were buying. A great deal was made of range rights, which had no basis whatever in law. Instead of checking the number of cattle by a careful round-up the buyers accepted range delivery and a tally-book count. Even when the seller was honest, the numbers written in the tally book were deceptive, because no account was taken of losses in roughing through the winters or in the calf crop. This loose method of purchasing lasted for a year or two. The agents of syndicates appeared to be afraid that if they did not buy sight unseen the unparalleled opportunity might vanish overnight. The old ranchmen capitalized this impatience, unless they too were blinded by the golden mirage.

John Clay tells a story that was circulated around Cheyenne, accompanied by many a cynical chuckle. There was a blizzard, and some of the cowmen at Luke Murrin's saloon were bemoaning the probable effect of it upon their cattle and wondering how great the loss would be.

"Cheer up, boys, the books won't freeze," Luke told them genially as he set out glasses and a bottle.

Wise old-timers accepted the amazing profit within reach and sold out. Others held on and plunged wildly, as did the newcomers, deceived by the glittering rainbow of easy fortunes. Men speculated in cows as they did during the 1929 boom in stocks. They bought outfits they had never seen, including hundreds of cattle that did not exist, and sold them on a rising market to someone who turned them over to another purchaser.

Men with money descended from every stage and train

in the cow country to make investments. They came from all over America and Europe to the new El Dorado. Great Britain sent scions of wealthy families. Young Germans joined the pilgrimage. A few drifted over from Australia. Some of these bought individual holdings, and others were the local representatives of great syndicates that had been formed abroad. The canny Scot was an especially willing victim. Millions were raised in Edinburgh to garner the overseas treasure.

The thing was a contagion. Everybody talked about it. The conservative Briton was worked up to such a fever of excitement that any company organized could be sure of selling its stock. Aristocratic families outfitted their younger sons, who arrived with pockets overflowing to pick up the easy money that waited for them on the plains. The swindler flourished. Many companies without an acre of land or a single longhorn steer sold stock to unwary buyers.

The holdings of some of the foreign companies were immense. The Prairie Land & Cattle Company, organized in 1881 and dissolved in 1915, had three main ranches. The first of these, covering 3,500 square miles, from the Arkansas to the Cimarron, was an extension of the J. J. outfit, formerly owned by the Jones brothers. A second one in New Mexico and Oklahoma included more than 4,000 square miles. The third property was the L I T ranch in the Panhandle, near Tascosa, and it covered 400 square miles. The three big outfits of this company ran nearly 140,000 cattle, and the total value of the property was more than $4,500,000.

The Swan Land & Cattle Company, operating in Wyoming, was bought from the American founders by British capital. Its stock ranged over 500,000 acres of land, and its property was estimated to be worth $3,000,000. The Matador, the Texas, and the Pastoral companies each controlled between 500,000 and 700,000 acres. The X I T had holdings six or seven times as large.

Most of these big companies went out of business during the decade ending with 1920.

There were scores of other syndicates, some large and some small, many of them wholly irresponsible. Even the reputable concerns felt almost at once the evil results of overstocking. The prices held throughout 1883, but in order to pay a dividend of 20 per cent that year the Prairie Company had to sell more than 21,000 head of stock. The newer companies could not, of course, show any such profit. Even during the boom, when the new outfits were competing for cows and calves with which to stock the range, a shrewd observer could have foreseen the result. Already the prices for beef cattle were slowly dropping.

It had been impressed upon the foreign investor that after a stocked range had been bought all one had to do was to sit down and wait for the dividends to roll in. Priority of occupation would take care of the range rights. Returns were bound to come from the law of natural increase. The results did not justify such optimism. Free grass had been one of the lures that had drawn capital, but this was turning out to be a delusion. New outfits crowded in, and the older ones could not keep the cattle of these from the public domain except as that could be done by the fencing of private property accessible to water.

The local handling of the foreign companies, with some notable exceptions, was at first very wasteful. The British managers put in charge of some of these properties knew nothing of range conditions and were generally slow to learn. They were often younger sons of good families, sometimes in exile because they were embarrassments at home. Not many of the young Englishmen made any permanent contribution to the welfare of the country. America was alien to them and continued to be so. They called Britain home. They continued to read the London society papers. It was from England that their monthly or quarterly remittances came. They had a keen interest in big-game hunting and acquitted themselves creditably in drinking and gambling. For many of them real work was not in the scheme of things as they read their horoscopes. Incidentally, they wanted to pick up a fortune without effort. They were usually good fellows, likable and picturesque excrescences in the plains country which they adorned. Some were more adaptable. A number were wealthy in their own right, men like the late Lord Dunraven, who bought Estes Park for a hunting preserve.

A hundred stories have been told about these young Britishers who arrived with "postage stamp" saddles and blooded horses. One of them, who has recently inherited a title in England, was invited to a Christmas dinner at a ranch house thirty miles away. He went in a dress suit, through a howling blizzard, and had to be lifted from his horse frozen to the eyebrows. This was in Montana, where one traveled in winter clad only in the warmest clothing.

In those days England was the financial center of the world. Black times had not come upon her landed aristocracy. There was plenty of money. She had become through her trade the greatest creditor nation. It is curious and interesting that one finds in American newspapers and speeches of those days the prediction that this country was fast being mortgaged to Britain and that the War of Independence had been fought in vain, since England would eventually own everything worth having here. Oddly enough, the same plaint has been heard from Europe about us in recent years.

It is only fair to say that some of the resident managers, especially those coming from Scotland, were men of character and first-class ability. Nowhere in the Western country have there been better examples of the genus cattleman than John Clay and Murdo Mackenzie. They learned every angle of the business and applied their shrewd native sense to the solution of the problems confronting them.

Cheyenne was the capital of the Northern cattle country. Here were all sorts and conditions of men, cattle kings, railroaders, bullwhackers, stockmen, cowboys, gamblers, tradesmen, and idlers, such an aggregation as can never again be gathered. For a brief year or two vice flourished. Cheyenne had its lynchings and its difficulties which resulted in killings, but it was never a bad town as compared with Dodge and Abilene. The scarlet woman beckoned, of course. The town was wide open. You tossed a dollar into a barrel at McDaniel's Theater as an entrance fee. A quarter was the smallest coin used. The lavishness reminds one of the early days at Cripple Creek, when a certain broker, upon leaving for lunch, left a sign in the window, "Shove the money under the door."

For those with means the Cheyenne Club was the center of Wyoming. It was unique, never has been duplicated, and never will be. During the floodtime of the cattle boom in 1883 and 1884 its gay abandon became nationally known. The faded blue eyes of many an old cattleman will sparkle to-day when you mention to him the Cheyenne Club. It brings back to him the glories of his youth. Its frequenters had fine traps, four-in-hands, tallyhos, and thoroughbred horses. They kept racers, and the old track had as much color as Ascot. Harvard and Oxford lads rubbed shoulders with cow hands from Lampasas on equal terms. British peers were almost a drug on the social market. One might be offered champagne at the Cheyenne Club for breakfast, luncheon, or dinner. One could get into a big game any time. It is characteristic of the West that the old home of the club is now occupied by the Chamber of Commerce. Rotarians meet and discuss freight rates where wild young hellions used to dance the cotillion till ten o'clock in the morning. Paul Potter's bull, which occupied the place of honor in the lounge, through which John Coble shot a hole one night when on a spree, has probably found a dusty refuge in a garret.

BRANDING CALVES ON THE RANGE

Brand	Owner	Brand	Owner
M ∞	Geo. P. Rodreick, New Castle, Garfield Co.	MC ∞	William T. Moore, Las Animas, Bent Co.
Ʌ ∞	W. P. Noble, Nathrop, Chaffee Co.	M/◦ ∞	W. M. Wells, Hooper, Alamosa Co.
M∀ ∞	F. E. Gilder, Moffat, Saguache Co.	Ʒ ∞	Anna Herlick, Rouse, Huerfano Co.
M/∀ ∞	Mandigo & Roderick, Salina, Boulder Co.	MD –∞	Michael Dwyer, Firstview, Cheyenne Co.
ⱻ ∞	John H. Allen, Livermore, Larimer Co.	M) ∞	G. C. Atwood, R.#2, Cedaredge, Delta Co.
Ʒ∀ ∞	Ralph B. Harding, Grover, Weld Co.	M/3 ∞∞	J. P. Snider, White Park, Pueblo Co.
MɅI ∞	William Chavez, Manassa, Conejos Co.	M/ᴍ ∞	John Contoleon, Durango, La Plata Co.
MɅS ∞	W. H. Aughe, Box 98, Eckley, Yuma Co.	Ⱬ ∞	J. A. Green & Sons, Swallows, Pueblo Co.
MA ∞	C. J. Hunter, Arapahoe, Cheyenne Co.	M/ᴄ ∞	Mrs. S. G. Johnston, R. F. D.#2, Ft. Lupton, Weld Co.
MɅ– ∞	J. Frank Mayhew, & G. Stewart Taylor, Howbert, Park Co.	Mᴛ ∞	M. Jeannette McPherson, Masters, Weld Co.
ɅɅ Q∞	Armand Marriott, La Jara, Conejos Co.	Ʒᴦ ∞	Ralph D. & Myrtle C. Werden, Trinidad, Las Animas Co
MɅ/ ∞	Antonio B. Montoya, Troy, Las Animas Co.	MF ∞	George E. Wales, Olathe, Montrose Co.
MɅ) ∞	B. W. Lauterman, Simpson, Adams Co.	MG ∞	Henry Reuker, Westcliffe, Custer Co.
MႸ ∞∞	Catherine Heister, Salida, Chaffee Co.	M/G ∞	Hudson & Krist, Julesburg, Sedgwick Co.
M/B –∞	E. L. Seay, Tobe, Las Animas Co.	MƏ ∞∞	M. G. Meek, Breen, La Plata Co.
ƷB ∞	Walter Sterling, Grover, Weld Co.	M/Ɔ ∞	George Reiswig, Sugar City, Crowley Co.
ƷƠ ∞	W. E. Lewis, Campo, Baca Co.	M/H ∞	Lucy, Beverly & Robert Platt, Aetna, Kansa, Rge-Fluec, Las Animas Co
MB ∞	L. D. Bleauvelt, & B. H. Moon, Granby, Grand Co.	M_H ∞	Morgan Ryan, Keenesburg, Weld Co.
M/C ∞	C. E. McNutt, Simpson, Adams Co.	Mꜧ ∞	Albert Denny, Bristol, Prowers Co.
MC ∞	J.E.& G.W.McDaniel, Montrose, Montrose Co.	ᴍ/Ⱶ ∞	Honesimo Medina, Swallows, Pueblo Co.
MU ∞	Richard McNamara, Tarryall, Park Co.	Ǝᴛ ∞	Charles Hawley, Rule, Bent Co.
M/Ɔ ∞∞	U. G. McKinley, Dillon, Summit Co.	MꜦL ∞	William Victor Mitchel, Burlington, Kit Carson Co.
MƠ ∞	W. J. Cowhick, 222 W. 4th St., Pueblo, Pueblo Co.	MH ∞	Manila Ranch Co.%P.H. Chartrand,108 S.Lincoln Denver.Rge: Jefferson Co

A PAGE FROM THE COLORADO STATE BRAND BOOK

The evils of overstocking were very greatly increased by the boom, though even before this was under full headway there had been observed a notable deterioration of the feeding capacity of the range.

This overstocking has continued year after year, through good seasons and bad, until it is the opinion of some of the most experienced cowmen of central Texas that the injury has gone almost past the point where redemption is possible [one observer comments]. The ranges have been almost ruined, and if not renewed will soon be past all hope of permanent improvement.

One factor in decreasing the pasturage value of the prairiers of southern Texas was the need of keeping out prairie fires to preserve the winter feed. In the old days these fires swept across the plains and burned up the brush and young trees, so that grass covered every foot of the country. The seedlings were killed. But with the elimination of fires by the stockman to preserve hay, fences, and improvements, prickly pear and mesquite gradually pushed out the grass, the thicket becoming so dense that a rider could with difficulty force his way through the chaparral. From the prolific seeds of the mesquite, planted by birds and cattle wherever they wandered, sprang millions of young trees to blot out the prairies.

The same condition applied to other sections, notably in northern Arizona, where large stretches of treeless range were planted to dense thicket by grazing sheep.

The overstocking of the range was probably worse in Texas during the boom than in any other state, but it applied to the whole grass country of the West—to Colorado, New Mexico, Arizona, and even to the Northwest. Cattle—cattle—more cattle was the cry. The old cowman, with a lifetime of experience behind him, was as bad an offender as the foreign syndicate, the manager of which had to show profits and must produce as large a calf crop as possible regardless of the ultimate effect upon the pasturage. He crowded cows on his range far beyond its feeding power. He watched them crop down the spring feed so closely that there was a scarcity of summer grass, in consequence of which stock were, from underfeeding, not prepared to rough through the winter.

The greatest percentage of loss fell upon the barnyard cattle brought in from the farms of the Middle West. The owners had no hay with which to feed and could only watch the cattle slowly starve to death.

Yet in spite of the signs of coming trouble, more cattle were brought up the trail in 1884 than in any year of the drives with the exception of 1871. Texas stuff to the number of 420,000 hoofed it north during that spring and summer. All the old-time drivers could have been seen putting up herds. Captain Lytle had 91,000 cattle on the trail this banner year. Fant & Ellison, Seth Mabry, Pryor, and Saunders were all prodding herds along to sell for stockers. Murphy, Driskill, Dickey, and several of the Texas syndicates were pushing trail herds north to supply their own feeding grounds. There appears to have been no general recognition even then that there had been both overgrazing and overexpansion. Will Rogers says that John Blocker sent 82,000 cattle up from Texas in 1885.

The longhorn on his native heath suffered during the winter of 1884–1885. There had been little grass on the depleted range, and a large die resulted during the winter. Hundreds of thousands of cattle drifted south. The country was strewn with carcasses. Spring and summer fell very dry. After the round-up the remnant was driven back home through a hot desert, where the drag perished by thousands. One Texan running stock on the Brazos had 25,000 cows with a range of 100,000 acres. This was far too many for the grass. Winter found the stock poor and thin. The owner rounded up 10,000 living skeletons in the spring.

Some years before the boom a section of good grazing land in southern Texas might feed 150 cattle. But after the grass had been injured by too heavy a stocking, it took ten acres to pasture one animal.

2

The evils that accompanied absentee ownership could not be ignored. The resentment against these big cattle companies owned in Great Britain extended even to the honest citizens of the communities where they had their holdings. In the early days of cattle ranging the loyalty of the cowboy to his employer was almost axiomatic. Even though he might be a wastrel and a profligate, he was true to the hand that fed him. He fought through blizzards, endured exhausting fatigue, ran stampedes, and swam racing rivers for the brand that paid him $15 a month. There was a bond between the cowman and his vaqueros that did not always depend upon personal attachment but had its roots in the traditions of Cattleland. It soon became apparent that this universal loyalty did not carry over to the big outfits. The cowpuncher was essentially rural in his outlook. He belonged to the neighborhood where he lived. The very name syndicate was an abstraction. How could a Texan or an Arizonan feel any warmth of feeling for a corporation with a board of port-drinking directors sitting in London or Edinburgh?

Unwittingly the stockgrowers' associations in various states contributed to the alienation between employer and employed. They had it enacted into law that any maverick on the range belonged to the association and not to an individual, that it must be sold and the sum received put into the treasury to meet expenses. A bonus was paid to the riders of the various outfits for every maverick branded with the mark of the association. The waddy often had a few cattle bearing his own brand, for his ambition was to be a cowman himself some day. If he was not too scrupulous he would brand the calf with his own iron instead of that of the association. To defeat this chance, the cattle associations made a ruling that none of their members should employ a rider who had cattle of his own.

The habit of stealing cattle, once acquired, was one not easily broken. To graduate from an amateur rustler into a professional one was an easy step. In the days of the neighborhood cow hunts a rustler was looked down upon by his neighbors as a thief, but there was a changed public attitude toward those who mavericked calves of such a company as the Prairie Land & Cattle Company or as the Swan Company. Smaller ranchers and the citizens of the county seat held no brief for the big fellows. Let them look after their own stock. They were considered high-handed, arbitrary, and none too scrupulous. Some of them were in local politics, to get their taxes cut down. The small owner feared that he was going to be squeezed out. If his herd increased he was looked upon with suspicion. The association, he claimed, was being used by the large companies to dominate the range.

The hostility between the small cowmen and the big concerns grew. Some of the little men were undoubtedly picking up stray calves to add to their herds. Even those who were honest themselves were aware of the rustling and would do nothing to stop it. Moreover, a good many farmers were drifting in to homestead along the creeks, especially in Nebraska and Colorado. Most of them were poor foreigners just one jump ahead of starvation. They killed cattle to feed themselves and their families. They killed because the stock wandered upon their corn patches. Occasionally they shot down animals from mere wantonness because of animosity toward the syndicates.

So rustling increased, became more prevalent than it had ever been before. From Texas to Montana the calf thief went after the "slick ears," as maverick calves were called. Never before or since has there been as much cattle thieving as in the days of the big companies. Often the work was wholesale. Such was the case of the notorious Al Cochran, who later served a term in the Colorado penitentiary for murdering a settler and driving his entire herd into Nebraska to rebrand and sell.

It was almost impossible to secure convictions, no matter how good the evidence. Members of the jury were either tarred with the same stick as the defendant or else were strongly prejudiced against the big cattle company. Most of the rustlers posed as poor and honest ranchers trying to get along. Some of them were not bad citizens, but a great many others were determined ruffians, unsafe for their neighbors to oppose.

A former sheriff and stock inspector of Weld County, Colorado, arrested a man for having seven calves in his barn that belonged to the Pony Cattle Company. Several witnesses swore in behalf of the accused that it was quite common for calves to leave their mothers and break into a barn. The man was acquitted. The sheriff, A. J. Elliott, after the trial, said in the lobby of a hotel that no other result could be expected when a cow thief was tried by a cow-thief jury and a cow-thief judge. Word of this comment got back to the judge, who fined Elliott $25 for contempt of court.

During the first days of cattle running there were no organizations of live-stock growers. The necessity for them developed with the extension of the range and the increase in population. What the cowman wanted was to be let alone, not to be crowded. The less he had to do with others in the same line the better, except for social purposes. He was fundamentally friendly, but he played a lone hand on the range. He was an individualist. The periodical cow hunts were the chief occasions for meeting his neighbors.

But problems arose which could not be met except by coöperation. These had to do with the settlement of grazing rights, with the securing of equitable freight rates, with opposing the packers' trust by a united front. There was a need for the passage of laws favorable to stockmen, such as that obtained very early by the Colorado Stock Growers' Association prohibiting the running on the range of any Texas bulls except in certain counties inhabited chiefly by Mexicans. Ticks and quarantine and Spanish fever were more than individual problems. And the rustler was both an individual and a universal one among cattlemen.

Nearly always the rustler was the most potent factor in bringing livestock associations into being. During the '70's these organizations arose in every state and territory where cattle ate free grass. In 1871 the Wyoming Stock Grazers' Association was formed at Cheyenne. Shortly afterward the Colorado cattlemen organized. In Graham County, Texas, the live-stock men came together in 1874, as they did the same year in Montana at Virginia City.

These associations became active in all the affairs that had to do with cattle. They regulated round-ups and passed upon disputes between neighbors. They laid down a system for working stock. They determined difficulties as to ownership where the brand was in doubt. Many of their rules they incorporated into state laws. The range cowman, from the very nature of his business, had to have protection, even though such protection had always to be reinforced by his own vigilant and sometimes illegal coöperation. In a cow country pure and simple, the community at large supported the association, and it was dominant. This was not so true where mining or farming engaged a part of the population. Neither in Colorado nor in Montana was the stockman ever in as great ascendancy as in Wyoming, where the cow was queen, although one Montana legislature was composed of members a majority of whom were in cattle. The conflict of interests was greater in the states with diverse industries. But in Wyoming the association was given legal right to enforce its rules upon live-stock growers. For years the cattlemen controlled the state, except locally.

Through the association range detectives and cattle inspectors were appointed. The detectives rode the range and secured evidence for the conviction of thieves. The inspectors watched feed and butcher pens. They checked herds on the trail at strategic points. They examined shipments by train. They passed upon slicks and calves rebranded by men in the chaparral. No rustler knew at what moment a detective would step out of the brush and challenge his right to brand or drive or hold in a corral the stock he claimed.

The practice of driving stolen longhorns north was engaged in by unscrupulous men from the first. The great majority of the drovers were men of character who took clean herds, but such men had to be protected from those of more easy morals. As early as 1872 the Cattle Raisers' Association of Texas had a law passed requiring drovers to keep a record of the number, brand, name of seller, and date of purchase of all cattle. The bill of sale had to be signed by the vendor.

An expert inspector such as Sam Dunn knew every brand in his district and hundreds outside of it. He might be stationed at Amarillo one day and be on the train headed for Denver the next. Not only was he able to read ownership, to know absolutely whether a brand had been tampered with and changed, but he had information enough about all the range men within a hundred miles to give him a shrewd idea as to whether they were adding to their herds unlawfully. Sometimes an inspector had to shear the hair away to examine closely the brand on an animal. Occasionally it was necessary to shoot one, skin the steer, and examine the inside of the hide. On the flesh side the mark where the new brand is joined to the old one shows plainly.

Always the inspector kept on the track of the cow thief,

on the range or the trail, around town slaughter houses, at points from which cattle were shipped or where they were received. He was the inexorable enemy of the cow thief. He recovered more stolen stock and secured evidence against more thieves than all the other law officers of the West.

But he had hundreds of miles of territory to cover. No matter how competent he was, the brand blotter could always be busy at the place where the detective was not. In spite of this check on stealing, the trade in other men's cattle continued merrily.

Driven to it by desperation, the cattlemen went outside the law. They were just as much sons of the frontier as were the rustlers. Their methods were as harsh and as ruthless. Some of them fenced land that did not belong to them. They drove out nesters without legal right. Often they consolidated their position by methods that seemed arbitrary both to the other party involved and to outsiders. Under the plague of maverickers which devoured their profits they did not fold up their tents and flit. They appealed to the courts—and they found no justice there. County officials were responsive to the public opinion which had elected them. There were more votes among the little fellows than the big ones. Moreover, the little fellows were their neighbors, and in a good many cases the big ones were overseas landlords.

Through their associations the cowmen banded together. They warned proved rustlers and suspected ones to get out of the country. Sometimes this was effective. But most of the men living in cabins in out-of-the-way gulches were hardy cowboys who would not be daunted by warnings. They continued their depredations. Some of them were shot, some hanged. In one campaign, which extended through Wyoming to Nebraska and Dakota on the east, and to Montana on the west, seventy-five cow thieves were disposed of by these vigilance committees of the cattlemen. From one railroad bridge thirteen were hanged. So says J. W. Thomas in his book, *Prose and Poetry of the Live Stock Industry*, printed in 1905 under the authority of the National Live Stock Historical Association. In the decade from '76 to '86 more men were killed by those working in the cattle interests than a dozen states have legally executed in fifty years.

In his book, *My Life on the Range*, John Clay sums up in a paragraph the defense of the cattleman. What would any man do, he asks, if a burglar broke into his house repeatedly and stole property, regardless of remonstrance, and the courts laughed at complaints made against the thief? He would do what the cattlemen did, if he had a spark of manhood in him.

In spite of overgrazing, overproduction, and the loss from rustling, most of the companies, by juggling figures, could show paper profits in 1884. But any manager who was not blind could see stormy weather ahead. One alluring prospectus had shown that by natural increase a herd of 100 cows would in ten years number 1,428 cows and as many steers. The owner of these cows must inevitably soon become a Crœsus. But the statistics somehow were not being translated into reality. Too many adverse factors had been left out of account by the writer of the advertisement. Lack of grass, a failure to propagate, hard winters, calf thieves, and disease all played a part in the problem as it actually worked out.

Conditions had changed so swiftly that the cowman had not yet realized fully the fact that he was in the midst of a transition period. The epoch of free grass had ended, or was about to end. Cattleland had grown up. It was passing out of its adventurous youth into sedate and responsible manhood. Modern methods were to take the place of the slipshod ones hitherto in vogue.

This inflated prosperity could not endure. In 1885 the crash came. It was nothing less than a catastrophe. The depreciation of values was amazing. Everybody wanted to sell and nobody wanted to buy. One man who had refused $1,500,000 for his holdings in 1883 sold after the deflation for $245,000, all of which went for indebtedness incurred. Hundreds of stockmen were wiped out, caught in a declining market. Everything they had went to satisfy creditors. The belted earls, as the English blue-bloods were called, headed for home, their remittances having been cut off. Their packs of hounds vanished, and the coyotes had a long rest. Dozens of cowmen went to work for other people as managers.

Prices went down so low that the choicest beef sold in Chicago for $2.40 a hundredweight, out of which had to be deducted freight, commission, and yard charges. There was, however, no marked reduction in the cost of retail meat to the consumer. Cattle ranching was in a slump. There had been too much beef for the market, too many head of stock for the grass. For about ten years cattle values continued to depreciate. In 1884 Colonel Ike T. Pryor offered to buy a herd for $25 a head. He bought the same herd in 1893, loaded on the cars at Uvalde, no calves counted, for $6 a head.

Cattlemen had passed through more than one disastrous winter. One long blizzard in '71–'72 wiped out several hundred thousand head of cattle in Kansas and Colorado. The mortality percentage in Dakota and Montana ran from 30 per cent. to 40 per cent. in the winter of '79–'80. But the most calamitous ever experienced was the winter of '86–'87. Storms swept the whole West. There were repeated blizzards, heavy snows, great cold, and many chill rains. About one half the cattle in the Northern country succumbed, owing in part to under-nourishment during the summer previous. Stock crowded into empty dugouts and corrals. They hung around ranch houses, bellowing pitifully for food. They drifted before blizzards and lay down by hundreds at the fences which barred their way. The situation was almost as bad on the Southern range, the pasturage of which had been injured more severely than in Wyoming and Montana.

Herman Hagedorn, in his *Roosevelt in the Bad Lands*, describes that winter as it affected the Dakotas.

The first blizzard came early in November and was the worst within the memory of the settlers. One blizzard followed another for three months, and the plains were drifted deep with snow. The cattle recently brought in, largely yearlings, succumbed first. The older stock kept going a while on sagebrush and the branches of young cottonwood trees. They wandered into the towns, eating the tar paper off the shacks. There was no fodder or any chance of help, nothing to do but watch them die. They died by the tens of thousands.

Under such conditions the calves succumb first, then the cows carrying calves. After these the bulls give up. Cows not in calf and full-grown steers endure the longest.

The owners could do nothing to help the perishing stock. They had no hay and could only suffer impotently as they saw the great die increasing month by month.

This was the turning point of the live-stock industry.

The cattlemen themselves were shocked at the inhumanity that necessarily accompanied the old ways of the open range, free grass, and no winter feeding. There had to be a change.

It was apparent that the happy-go-lucky conditions which had dominated the production end could no longer endure. Readjustment along radical lines was needed. The loose, extravagant methods of operating the big concerns must be overhauled and management made efficient. Rigid economy had to be introduced. It would not do any longer to keep a calf tally on the back of an envelope and lose the envelope. The most vital questions were those of feed and protection. By breeding it up stock had become too valuable to let rough through the winter without hay and shelter. Pasturage must be protected from overfeeding, and the only way an owner could have any assurance of this was to fence. He must forget about free grass and own or lease the range his cattle used. Winter feeding involved the raising of hay, which in turn called for irrigating ditches to water alfalfa fields. Since scrub stock were not worth carrying under such conditions, the up-to-date cowman had to breed up his herd still further.

THE great tide of longhorns which swept across the wilderness on the heels of the vanishing buffalo met one gentle but persistent obstacle in Mary's little lamb. In Montana, in Wyoming, in Arizona, in Colorado, wherever the flood of cattle poured, the docile ewe penetrated to the range and often succeeded in driving back the longhorn. The nature of the woolly is such that he could lose every battle and yet win the war.

From the earliest records of the open range there come stories of difficulties between sheep and cattle owners. When the sheep came bleating across the hill slope where cows ranged, trouble was in the offing.

Even in the time of Joseph, the son of Jacob, sheepmen were in bad odor. His brothers came to him for help to escape the drought in Canaan. Joseph took them to King Pharaoh, but he warned them not to mention that they dealt in sheep. "For," he said, "every shepherd is an abomination unto the Egyptians."

The prophet Ezekiel put his finger on one of the great causes of feud between sheepmen and others who wanted to use the land. "Woe be to the shepherds of Israel. . . .

"Seemeth it a small thing unto you to have eaten up the good pasture, but ye must tread down with your feet the residue of your pastures? . . . "

The belief was general that sheep and cattle could not get along on the same range. The basis for this impression was experience. The fundamental trouble was that sheep are destructive to an overstocked range. They eat a country bare when grass is scant, cropping it down to the ground. It used to be a common saying that they kill more than they eat. John Muir dubbed them hooved locusts because they feed in compact masses, and their sharp chisel feet, driven by a hundredweight of solid bone and flesh, cut out even the roots of the grass. Vegetation may be killed for years to come. In the arid lands every bit of green stuff serves to conserve moisture. Fallen leaves are a mulch no less than growing twigs. Without vegetable life rain is not absorbed but runs off the ground, forming arroyos and ravines. Many a good range has been destroyed by overfeeding, and sheep are more destructive to an overstocked area than cattle.

Local conflicts between rival sheep and cattle owners occurred in every state and territory of the West where stock ranged. There were attacks and reprisals. Sheepmen, mostly nomads, banded together and drove their flocks upon a cattle range to inevitable trouble.

The Forest Service has since established the fact that sheep and cattle, when properly handled, can graze on the same ranges without injury to either grass or stock. But in the early days of the West this organization had not yet been created. Sheep and cattle began to crowd together, and there was war.

It inevitably followed on the encroachments of sheep that the cattlemen defended what they believed to be their rights. By priority of occupation they held the range, and from their viewpoint the advent of sheep was an interference with existing vested rights. Since they could not appeal to the law to protect them, the riders of the plains became a law to themselves. They drew deadlines beyond which sheepmen were not to bring their flocks. They scattered saltpeter near the watering places of the sheep. It was harmless to cattle, but the woollies tasting it died. The sheepmen refused to recognize the existence of the deadlines and moved their flocks across them into the territory claimed by the stockmen.

It was not to be expected that the reckless cowpunchers would tolerate submissively this defiance of their orders, for they understood that if the sheep were to remain their occupation would soon be gone. In many cases they fell on the flocks and drove them out of the country. The herders returned with reinforcements and met force with force. Then followed raid and counter raid. Here and there over the grazing lands of the West—in Colorado, New Mexico, Texas, Arizona, Nevada, Idaho, Wyoming, and Montana—fierce and bloody conflicts were waged. The result was a strange one. Defeated in nine battles out of ten, the sheepmen usually came out victor in the end. Everywhere, by reason of the law of the survival of the fittest, they encroached upon the grazing lands of their foes. Along the line of the Santa Fe, for instance, through northern Arizona, the sheepmen came to control most of the territory. They had the advantage of being able to carry their flocks for long periods without water when the grass was green; or they could buy tank water hauled in by the railroad to convenient sidings along the track, a plan not feasible for the watering of cattle on account of the quantity needed.

The sheepmen were usually defeated in the individual battles because they were fewer in numbers than their opponents. A couple of herders with dogs can care for thousands of sheep, and the well armed, swift-riding cowpunchers, swooping suddenly down on them, took them at such disadvantage that often they were obliged to stand aside helplessly and watch the slaughter of their charges.

As early as 1884 on the Little Colorado River ranges in

Arizona a party of cattlemen raided a sheep camp in which two outfits were located. The herders, surprised, were tied to trees while the four thousand or more sheep were driven in one great mass into the river, which was boggy and full of quicksands. Hundreds of sheep mired down and died like flies on sticky flypaper; the rest scattered all over the country. The raiders rode back to the camp, wrecked it completely, killed all the burros and pack animals, and turned the herders loose to make their way to safety on foot.

A favorite evening amusement was to ride out from some cow camp after dark and shoot up a solitary sheep camp, using the "Dutch ovens," camp kettles, and coffee pots on the fire for targets, "just to liven things up a little for the lonely sheepherder," as one cowboy put it.

There was a year or two on the Arizona ranges when a sheepherder would take a shot at any horseman wearing chaps who came too close. One of the authors rode with a friend out of a cedar brake into an open glade in which three sheepherders were making camp. All three jumped for their Winchesters. The horsemen tore into the thicket for cover, shots ringing in their ears. Nor did they stop in their mad drive to get out of that vicinity until they had put a good long mile between themselves and the camp. A hasty council of war resulted in a unanimous vote of two not to return. There was nothing in that sheep camp they had the least desire to investigate.

A former superintendent of the Hashknife outfit, so called from the shape of the company's brand, detailed to one of the writers how his punchers had on one occasion raided a sheep camp and forced the herders, who were cooking breakfast at the moment of the raid, to break camp at the point of their rifles. The playful vaqueros shouted with glee as they turned over pots and kettles and dumped the food out on the ground, leaving the herders to go breakfastless.

A thousand stories could be told of the conflict between

SHEEP ARE GREAT WEED EATERS. THEY DEVOUR FORAGE THAT OTHER STOCK WILL NOT TOUCH

THE SHEEP MUST ALL BE DIPPED

COMING INTO THE BED GROUND AT SUNSET

sheepmen and cattlemen. The owners of some large flocks amounting to about one hundred thousand head moved their entire herd across the deadline drawn by cattlemen of western Wyoming. At once the cowmen attacked them, disarmed the herders, destroyed wagons and sheep to the value of twenty thousand dollars, and warned the sheepmen to leave the country immediately on penalty of death. That night all was peace in the shadow of the Tetons, for cattle held the range alone, while thousands of jaded sheep were plodding back to safety across the deadline.

A few weeks after this occurrence nearly twelve thousand sheep were slaughtered near Rock Springs in Wyoming. Many of these were shot and clubbed to death, and the rest were driven over a precipice. The Associated Press dispatches announced briefly from time to time fatalities among herds of sheep caused by their eating blue vitriol which had been scattered over their grazing ground. One Sheridan owner had his flock destroyed by dynamite thrown among the animals while they were feeding. Owners at Laramie and Cheyenne were annoyed greatly by sudden attacks from cowboys, who drove the flocks into foothills to be devoured by coyotes and mountain lions. Griff Edwards was one of several sheep owners who fought back, but his enemies captured him, tied him to a tree, and killed his flocks before his eyes. In one season he is said to have lost more than fourteen thousand sheep.

The sheepmen retaliated in kind. A cattle herder riding the range would see through his field glasses a motionless mass in the distance, and riding up to investigate would find a fine cow of his brand with a bullet through its forehead. Or perhaps a vaquero would disappear mysteriously, and months later a comrade would find the sun-bleached skeleton. So the silent, relentless war was carried on to the death.

In the San Francisco mountain country of Arizona one night in 1884 ten bands of sheep were camped near each other in a beautiful natural park. Coming from northern New Mexico they had moved across the state like an army of invasion, harassed by the local cattlemen every foot of the way. But with an armed force of forty or fifty men as guard, the flocks had never been seriously checked in their westward march. They were bedded down that night in peace and quiet. Breaking into the midst of this pastoral scene there rushed across the park and through the camps a hundred or more wild range horses. The cowmen had previously corraled these horses. Fifteen or twenty cowboys had worked hard and diligently for several hours throwing and hogtying a lot of them to prepare them for the ceremony. Several horses were decorated with dry rawhides tied to their long tails. Fifteen or twenty more had huge cowbells strapped about their necks—"To encourage speed," the boys said. When those horses broke out of the pine timber and into the open park with the cowboys at their heels, firing six-shooters and yelling like Apache Indians, there ensued one of the grandest mix-ups of range sheep ever known in the West.

The herders sprang to their feet and met the oncoming cyclone with shots from their rifles. But this only added to the pandemonium, for the horses tore back and forth across the park, into and out of the bands, leaving a wide swath of dead or injured sheep behind them and throwing the whole twenty-five thousand woollies into an almost inextricable, bleating, terrified mass.

The horses drifted on into the darkness, leaving some dead. But this was a small loss in those days of cheap range horses. It took the sheepherders a full week to untangle the mess and separate the various brands and marks into their respective bands.

Nor were the sheepmen at all backward about obtaining revenge so far as lay in their power. Cattle and horses were found shot down all over the range, and unoccupied cow ranches were mysteriously burned. Though the

sheepmen lost considerable in these affrays, they obtained
the grass for their sheep, stayed on the range through the
summer, and in the fall moved back to New Mexico,
knowing that their enemies would suffer far more by the
devastated ranges and the destruction of winter feed than
they themselves did from the loss of a few sheep.

The life of the cowpuncher was a much more varied and
dramatic one than that of the sheepherder. Activity and
rapid motion and the turmoil of the round-up made of him
a product something akin to an overgrown boy still full
of school-day pranks. He could be classified among the
gregarious animals. His general impression was that no
man engaged in "walking sheep" could be a reputable
citizen but must of necessity be a low-down, miserable
creature whose rights need not be respected. To him the
solitary life of the sheepherder carried with it a punishment beyond endurance. "I tended sheep once two days,"
a cowpuncher told one of the writers plaintively, "and
I'd not do it again for a thousand dollars an hour." Indeed,
few sights are more somber and impressive than the solitary figure of a herder outlined against the sky, thousands
of sheep about him and no human being or habitation in
sight. For weeks he does not see his kind, and then only
for a few minutes, perhaps, when a teamster brings a
load of chuck to keep him for another month. He grows
morbid and melancholy, and the desert comes to hold
for him a horror not far distant from madness. Possibly
this moroseness induced by their surroundings may be in a
measure responsible for the sheepmen's readiness to engage
in such a bloodthirsty war as the Graham-Tewksbury
feud—a typical instance of the trouble engendered between these adverse interests—in which twenty-six cattlemen and six sheepmen lost their lives.

This feud is generally known as the Tonto Basin or
Pleasant Valley War. A large sheep owner in the San
Francisco mountain country sent in 1887 several flocks of
sheep into Pleasant Valley, a region which until then

had been wholly given over to cattle. The Tewksbury brothers took over the care of these.

There was already bad blood between the Tewksburys and the Grahams. The two families had been friends in Texas, but had fallen out over a personal matter. The bringing of sheep into the Basin set a spark to a powder magazine. On one side were arrayed the Grahams, assisted by punchers of the Hashknife outfit; opposed to them were the Tewksburys and the sheep interests.

The sheep encroached on land upon which cattle were grazing. The herder was notified at once to withdraw. His collie dog was killed and some bullets sent flying past him as a suggestion not to linger. Other herders were sent to guard the flocks. A Navajo Indian was killed. John Tewksbury in person, with Bill Jacobs as his aid, took charge. They were ambushed and killed.

The Tewksburys had Indian blood in their veins, and they fought a wary campaign that was disastrous to the headlong cowpunchers. They trapped Jim Scott, Billy Wilson, and Jim Stott, and ruthlessly hanged them to convenient trees. They bushwhacked others.

Across the Mogollon Mountains came reinforcements for the Grahams from Holbrook, a bunch of wild cowboys connected with the Hashknife outfit. Charley Duchet, a noted gunman, was one of them.

The Tewksburys warily moved camp to a position from which none could approach without being seen. They were jerking beef one day when five Hashknife men rode up. Tom Tucker did the speaking for the riders.

"This the Tewksbury place?"

Jim Tewksbury looked at Tucker, let his eyes sweep over the group, and answered, "Five miles down the valley."

"How about getting grub here?"

"We don't run a hotel."

"Hmp! Hospitable, ain't you? Well, we can go to Vosburgh's for supper," Tucker replied.

He turned to ride away, according to the story he told later. A shot rang out. Jim Tewksbury had killed Paine, the man riding next to Tucker. Jim afterward claimed Paine was drawing a six-shooter. Bob Gillaspie, a cowboy, was killed. Tucker went down, wounded in five places, and took refuge behind his dead horse. He emptied his revolver as he lay there. One of his friends galloped up under heavy fire, dragged him to a place behind the saddle, and galloped out of range. Tucker recovered. Years later he was a law officer in New Mexico.

The cowboys started at once to wipe out the Tewksbury clan, but the sheepmen fled to the hills. They were surrounded and escaped, but not before Jim had killed one of those lying in wait for him.

The war dragged on. Young Bill Graham was killed. Middleton fell a victim. It was the bloodiest feud between white men in the history of Arizona. Nobody living in the Basin could be a neutral. He had to take one side or the other if he stayed. Several families pulled up stakes and left, sometimes hurriedly and at night. Major Frederick R. Burnham, one of the great scouts of this country, famous for his work in South Africa during the Boer, the Matabele, and the Zulu wars, was dragged in against his will, though he was only a boy. In his book, *Scouting on Two Continents*, he tells the story of his escape. Men rode only at night. Their camps were guarded. Nobody was allowed to come within rifle range until identified as a friend.

At last, of the male adult Grahams only one was alive. This was John. He gave up, left the Basin, and moved to Tempe in the Salt River country. Perhaps he might have been permitted to save his life if he had not made a mistake. Returning to the Basin, he rounded up his cattle and drove them out of the valley. Elated at his success in doing this, he boasted that the Tewksburys had been afraid to attack him. He was shot down six weeks later, close to the Cummings ranch, near the Double Buttes, as he was driving to Tempe with a load of grain. Before he died he told Duchet and others that Ed Tewksbury and John Rhodes, who had married the widow of John Tewksbury, were the murderers. Rhodes was tried first. The jury listened to conflicting evidence. Witnesses testified positively to seeing the prisoner near the Cummings ranch on the morning of the killing, companioned by another man, who wore a white sombrero decorated with a scarlet ribbon. As many swore to an alibi for him. During the trial the widow of John Graham drew a .44 caliber revolver from a handbag and tried to kill Rhodes. Her father caught her arm, and the shot went wild. Rhodes was acquitted and guarded out of town by a bevy of friends. Tewksbury, tried later, was convicted by the scarlet ribbon, but secured a new trial and was released on bail. The case against him was at last dropped. Both Rhodes and Tewksbury were men of splendid physique and were endowed with the endurance and capacity for self-protection the frontier teaches. Both were dead shots and expert trailers.

Most of the men engaged on both sides of this deadly feud, though during it they went to the most ruthless extremes, were in general good citizens in a rough way. Having once taken sides, they felt as much engaged to the cause for which they fought as soldiers do in a war on a larger scale.

Pleasant Valley lies under the foothills of the Mogollon Ridge. In 1905, after the creation of the Tonto National Forest, the region was taken possession of by the United States Forest Service.

In the Blue Mountain region of eastern Oregon range trouble broke in 1903. As soon as the snow had left the hills in the spring, thousands of cattle and countless flocks of sheep were rushed to the higher lands in Crook, Lake, Des Chutes, and Wheeler counties. The tender grass was not yet ready for grazing, and the country was crowded far beyond its carrying capacity. Most of the cattle were owned in the adjoining valleys, but the sheep came from distant territory. This particularly enraged the cowmen, for these strangers paid no local taxes and had no vested interest in the neighborhood.

The flocks of woollies swept the hills, eating the feed to the very doors of the cabins of the settlers. In self-protection the cattlemen organized. Deadlines were drawn and public warning given the sheep owners that trouble would ensue if the lines were not respected. The orders of the ranchmen were ignored and sheep poured across the line. On June 13, 1904, masked men shot and killed near Mill Creek sixty-five head of sheep belonging to Allie Jones.

An organization called the "Inland Sheep Shooters" was effected in Crook and other near-by Oregon counties, the activities of which attracted considerable attention far beyond its immediate zone of action.

An open letter from the corresponding secretary of the association, in the Portland *Oregonian* of January 10, 1905, shows the spectacular and audacious attitude taken. It is unique and is illustrative of the desperate nature of the conflict.

Sheep Shooters Headquarters,
Crook County, Oregon.

EDITOR *Oregonian:*

I am authorized by the Association [the Inland Sheep Shooters] to notify the *Oregonian* to desist from publishing matters derogatory to the reputation of the Sheep Shooters in eastern Oregon. We claim to have the banner county of Oregon on progressive lines of sheep shooting. . . . We would thank the *Oregonian* and the Governor to attend strictly to their business and not meddle with the settlement of this range question in our province. . . . Dead lines are most effective . . . and if the sheep men fail to observe these peaceable obstructions we delegate a committee to notify offenders . . . as follows:

"You are hereby notified to move this camp within twenty-four hours or take the consequences. "COMMITTEE."

These mild and peaceful means are usually effective, but in cases where they are not, our Executive Committee takes the matter in hand, and being men of high ideals, as well as good shots by moonlight, they promptly enforce the edicts of the Association. . . . Our annual report shows that we have slaughtered between eight and ten thousand head during the last shooting season, and we expect to increase the respectable showing during the next season providing the sheep hold out and the Governor and the *Oregonian* observe the customary laws of neutrality. . . . The wool growers of eastern Oregon have . . „ offered rewards for the arrest and conviction of sheep shooters, and for assaults on sheepherders. We have warned them by publication of the danger of such action, as it might result in our organization having to proceed on the lines that "dead men tell no tales."

> CORRESPONDING SECRETARY
> CROOK COUNTY SHEEP SHOOTERS ASSOCIATION
> OF EASTERN OREGON.

The humorous secretary of the Sheep Shooters Association broke into print in the Oregon papers with great regularity.

On New Year's Day, 1905, a sheepherder's camp was raided in Crook County. In the columns of the January 5th issue of the *Oregonian*, the secretary thus advises the world of the circumstances:

New Year's Day was duly observed by our association by the slaughter of five hundred sheep belonging to a gentleman who had violated our laws.

> CORRESPONDING SECRETARY
> CROOK COUNTY SHEEP SHOOTERS ASSOCIATION.

This Blue Mountain war continued for three years in spite of rewards offered for the apprehension of the raiders.

Near Christmas Lake, down on the Oregon desert in Lake County, on February 3, 1904, three thousand sheep were raided by masked men. Over twenty-five hundred sheep were put to death, the rest scattered on the range. The herders were tied hand and foot before the work began. It took five men all night to do the killing, which was done by shooting and clubbing. After it was over the herders were turned loose.

On April 29, 1904, in the same region, nine masked men raided a herd of twenty-seven hundred sheep, killing over twenty-two hundred. In each case the herder was tied up, a gunnysack pulled over his head, and later, when the job was done, turned loose with a warning not to talk on pain of death.

There were, of course, reprisals by the sheepmen, though what seemed to be reprisals may not always have been such. The Wheeler County *News* of May 27, 1904, contains the following item:

Poison was deposited on the range eight miles east of town. . . . Twelve head of fine range cows belonging to Sigfut Brothers died last week.

Naturally this was charged up to the sheepmen, but it is believed now that the deaths were due to poisonous plants on the ranges. Over and over, in recent years, have charges been made of destroying cattle and sheep by dropping poison on the range, but in every investigated case plants growing on the ranges, such as larkspur, death camas, or water hemlock, have been found to be the deadly agent.

Almost the whole mountain country over which these troubles were occurring was placed, in April, 1906, under the administration of federal forest officers, and the ranges were allotted in such a manner as to give to the owners of each class of stock sufficient range for their needs. The troubles at once ceased, nor have the two interests ever again clashed openly on the ranges in this region.

In western Colorado there is a vast section in Routt,

White River, and Rio Blanco counties where for many years a deadline has been drawn. Across this no sheepman cares to drive his flocks as he comes out of the desert ranges in southern Utah seeking the summer ranges high up in the mountains of western Colorado, where he is protected by forest rangers. Herders formerly were forced to take their flocks long distances by roundabout routes to avoid trespassing upon the forbidden area.

Occasionally the sheep could not travel over these circuitous trails, owing to a scarcity of water and feed, added to the hardship of unusually early storms and high water in the streams. In 1908 such a condition existed. In desperation the sheep owners banded together, hired more than one hundred guards, and with every herder and camp tender heavily armed, massed their herds as closely as they could without danger of mixing them, and escorted on either side by their fighting men, moved across the forbidden land like an army in the enemy's country. They were not molested, and when the last woolly was safely across the western line of the state and upon their winter feeding grounds, everybody breathed a sigh of relief. The cattlemen smiled grimly, nor did they make any attempt to stop the hegira. They were fair-minded men and realized that "their friends the enemy" were in dire straits and would take no more time for the crossing than was absolutely necessary.

This deadline, with its unwritten law, still exists in western Colorado, but never since the year mentioned have the sheepmen been forced to risk another such war-like movement. In the majority of cases they now ship their sheep by rail to the borders of the national forests. From there they move to their mountain ranges on regular stock driveways established by the Forest Service for this purpose.

With a single exception there has been no armed conflict between these warring interests on any national forest since the Forest Service took charge of the grazing of live stock on the national forest ranges. This single case occurred in 1918 on the Gunnison National Forest in Colorado.

Ever since the first settlement there the settlers had maintained a deadline against sheep. There was an immense area of high mountain ranges, far better suited to sheep than to cattle. It was known as a "weedy range," being well set with the various broad-leafed flowering plants, generally called weeds, which are considered ideal for sheep, especially young lambs. Several of the so-called weeds were of the larkspur family, harmless to sheep but very deadly to cattle. It was impossible therefore to utilize the high ranges for cattle, except very late in the fall, after the larkspur had ceased to bloom. By that time it was too near winter for the cattle to stay with safety. So the forest officers, with a heavy demand upon their few sheep ranges, decided to allot these high areas to sheep. There was a protest against the plan, but the rangers carefully explained the situation and talked the majority of cattlemen into acquiescence, assuring them that the sheep would not be allowed to trespass on a foot of cattle range.

All went well until the Fourth of July, 1917. In a little isolated hamlet a number of irresponsible men, none of them in any too good standing in the county, proceeded to celebrate the nation's birthday by a grand spree.

In the mountains above the town a band of sheep was camped, having just reached the range allotted to it. Some evil spirit prompted a raid on the sheep, and in a few minutes the men had saddled their horses and were on their way, hell-bent for mischief.

Someone in the town phoned the forest supervisor, William E. Kreutzer, of the movement. That official and a forest ranger jumped into their car and drove across the country to intercept the men before they reached the sheep. The raiders, already in an ugly mood, were furious at being interfered with and tried to ride the officers

down. They threatened to kill if an attempt was made
to arrest them. Eventually the supervisor, absolutely un-
afraid and undeterred from his duty, talked the men out
of their plans and got them to follow his car back to town.
The truce lasted that season.

In the summer of 1918 the trouble broke again. A sheep
camp owned by a man named Campbell was raided on
Oh-be-joyful Creek, the herder tied hand and foot, about
five hundred sheep driven over a cliff to their death, and
the rest scattered all over the country. The raiders terrorized the herder so thoroughly that it was impossible to get
any evidence or testimony against them, although everyone felt sure of the identity of the guilty ones.

This was the first, last, and only affair of its kind after
the Forest Service began operations in 1906.

In 1902 an outbreak occurred in Wyoming which is
known in local history as the Green River sheep war.
From the very first settlement of the valley of the Green
River the cattlemen opposed bitterly the grazing of sheep
on the fine ranges along the upper reaches of the river
north of the Union Pacific Railroad. It was an ideal
sheep country, with vast stretches of fine winter ranges
on the Red Desert along the railroad, and equally rich lush
summer feeding grounds in the mountains in which the
stream headed. By leasing alternate sections of railroad
land the sheepmen controlled the Red Desert winter
ranges, but the higher ranges lay outside of the railroad
land grant.

Over and over again some venturesome sheepowner
would work his band across the mountains from the eastern
slope where sheep were plentiful to the western slope
where only cows were acceptable to the residents. He
did not get very far, however, before he changed his mind
and went back across the mountains. Masked and heavily
armed men had a habit of dropping in on the herders at
night to advise them as to the easiest way to reach the
other side with the least possible delay. Occasionally,

when they caught the owner in camp, they used the bight of a lariat on his back to impress him with his responsibility. "We tried to settle the thing peaceably," explained one old-timer in discussing the matter. "We didn't want to kill anything, humans or sheep. All we had in mind was to impress on the world in general, and sheep owners in particular, the fact that we people in the Green River Valley didn't want our cow ranges ruined by the woollies."

Four or five sheep owners decided there would be no trouble if they went in force. About ten thousand sheep in four bands swept over the top of the Bridger Mountains to the western slope and, with a dozen armed guards to protect them, settled down for the summer. The Green River cattlemen planned a campaign to settle the matter forever.

The sheep were not molested for several days, and the sheepmen were lulled into a sense of security. They began to think that their bluff was going to stick. Meantime, the cattlemen were organizing. The little town of Pinedale was headquarters, and here scouts brought news of the location of the several camps, the number of men with each, and such details. Again the word went out that no human lives were to be taken except in self-defense. "We wanted to be perfectly law-abiding," said one cattleman. "There had been a lot of murders in Wyoming a few years before over a range war, and we all agreed to do everything we could to get results, short of taking human life."

Masked men dropped down one night on each of the sheep camps and overpowered the herders without firing a shot. After the herders had been tied up and blindfolded, the raiders put in the whole night killing sheep. The bands had been placed for the night in stout log corrals and the raiders proceeded to club the sheep to death in the most businesslike manner imaginable. "They tried shooting," said the cattleman, "but with so many to kill, decided it would take too long, and besides, they really didn't have the cartridges to spare." It was broad daylight before the last sheep was dead. About two thousand were killed at each camp. The raiders piled the camp plunder—tents, packs, and other material—around the camp wagon and burned it all. The captured sheepmen were given their riding animals and a handful of grub, instructed to travel straight across the range, and warned that the next sheep outfit that ventured into the valley would have no survivors, sheep or human.

"Did they go?" was the question.

"Did they go?" said the old-timer. "Say, they were that hurried, they just tore the Bridger peaks to pieces getting over."

This ended the Green River sheep war, and the deadline thus drawn has never been crossed to this day. The sheep bones were still there a few years ago, whitening in the sun, mute evidences of the conflict. Near at hand the steel tires and iron of a burned wagon and a miscellaneous lot of pots and kettles marked the ruins of the herders' camps.

"Why don't some of you men come up here to burn up these old corrals and bleaching bones?" was the natural query of a visitor as he sat looking over the scene. "They don't look good."

The old-timer smiled grimly. "These corrals and whitening sheep bones, and the set of wagon irons preserve the peace in the Green River Valley better than an army. They say 'Keep off the grass' in tones that reach every sheep camp and every herder's ears between the Montana line on the north and the Union Pacific Railway to the south."

Since then the peaceful wings of the Forest Service have been spread over the hills, and the deadline is but a memory, although those corrals a foot deep with sheep bones serve to keep the memory fairly green.

THE result of the collapse of the cattle boom of the '80's made clear that quality rather than quantity must be the prime consideration in live stock. Since better grades of cattle, individually more valuable, were to occupy the range, ranch owners were forced by economic necessity to guarantee food for their stock, to furnish hay and shelter in bad weather. The great die-off during the winter of 1886–1887 pointed this out so definitely that even the dullest could not miss the handwriting. The capacity of the range to carry cattle had been largely diminished, even in the North, where crowding had not been so great or so disastrous to the grass. To prevent overstocking, land had to be leased or owned. It had to be fenced.

Though it was apparent that the beginning of the end of free grass was at hand, many cattlemen by various methods attempted to ward off the inevitable. In Texas, Nebraska, and Colorado, range men could get possession legally by leasing from the state. A large part of the Western range—the greater portion of it, in fact—was still Federal land upon which any man could run his stock. The law did not, however, contain any provision for fencing such tracts to obtain sole use. Some of the cowmen took a chance and fenced government land to keep off alien cattle. Sometimes the cow outfit leased the alternate railroad sections, which had been granted as a bonus for building transcontinental lines, and fenced the entire district, enclosing Federal land in the pasture.

The theory of the stockman was that the high plains were for cattle and not for farming. How was it possible for a granger to make a living on 160 acres of land when its grass would feed no more than eight or ten cows? The government did not accept the view of the cattleman. It was always more tender toward the rights of the man with the covered wagon than toward the one with the chuck wagon. Congress had given no great study to the semi-arid lands and regarded the cow merely as the forerunner of the plow.

It was therefore by way of self-preservation that the rangeman began to fence illegally the public domain. Any further curtailment of the range or any pressure upon it from newcomers' stock would be fatal. In 1874 barbed wire had become a marketable proposition. By 1877, as shown by Osgood in *The Day of the Cattleman*, 7,000 tons of it were sold. Three years later 40,000 tons went to the ranchers. All the big cattle outfits began to fence largely, and many of the built lines included land which did not belong to the company. The United States Commissioner of Public Lands at Washington took cognizance of this disregard of the rights of others in a report issued in 1884, and he continued to do so in later ones.The Swan Land and Cattle Company he cited as having 130 miles of illegal fence. This syndicate was one of many. The offenders operated in practically every cattle state.

Laws were enacted to make swift prosecution feasible. Some prominent cattlemen went to the penitentiary by way of example. As a result of this drastic action the illegal fences were removed. The range stockman protected himself as best he could by means of the homestead and pre-

emption laws to get control of the streams, using his cowboys as entrymen. Frauds were rampant, and the grangers
complained bitterly.

Trouble followed this high-handed extension of what
the cattleman had regarded as his range rights. Smaller
owners and homesteaders protested violently. But it
must be said in behalf of the cattleman that he was faced
with conditions so adverse they bordered on the disastrous. The period was prosperous for the country at
large. There was a good demand for beef both at home and
abroad. But the producers realized none of the profits
which should have accrued. The railroad, the packer,
and the homesteader seemed to him in league to ruin
him.

At last, in 1888, the situation was so bad that a committee of five was appointed by the Senate to investigate
all questions affecting the meat product of the country.
This committee of Senators did about as much as such
committees usually do. The problem was one which had to
be worked out by patient readjustment through a period
of years.

But the cattleman was not always patient enough to
wait for such a remedy. The large companies resented
what they regarded as an infringement of their rights by
the settlers who had located along the streams and
harassed them. They refused to recognize that some of
their difficulties had been made by their own folly and
extravagance. In Wyoming this irritation culminated
in the spectacular Powder River invasion, known as the
Johnson County war.

In an attempt to weather the storm, big companies,
reversing their policy of extravagance, had cut the number
of employees down below the margin of safety. As soon as
the snows fell, managers discharged their riders and left
the cattle to look out for themselves. Economically, this
was a failure.

"The ranges were full of great big long-eared mavericks," said a veteran cowman, who went through this trouble without actually getting drawn into the fighting. "None of the big outfits kept men riding in the winter, and the temptation offered by the unguarded herds was too much for the nesters. So while the high-salaried managers hung around the club in Cheyenne and played poker for big stakes, the settlers were busy on the ranges picking up long-eared calves and putting their irons on them, taking chances on animals being separated from their mothers when the spring round-ups came along.

"The American managers of many of the big cattle companies had been carrying on their books thousands of cattle lost in the big winter die-off of 1886 rather than report the losses to the foreign owners. This tally book deception was added to the fact that more than one outfit which had bought the original herd 'range delivery' never had possession of more than 50 per cent. of the number paid for. The calf brandings proved the shortage, but the local managers looking for an 'out' in their annual reports had charged the losses to rustlers. This was used by the leaders of the 'invasion' as the excuse for their acts. I always felt the cattlemen were greatly to blame."

Undoubtedly there had been a great deal of rustling in Natrona, Converse, and Johnson counties, Wyoming. Ever since the first drives the cattle business had been accompanied by lawlessness. Now the temptation to maverick from unguarded herds was great. But the rustling was in part an excuse. The cattle owners were determined to clear the range of the small ranchers who interfered with their prosperity.

Unable to obtain convictions in court because of sympathetic law officers and jurymen, some of the cattle companies resorted to dry-gulching. A series of assassinations occurred. The guilty parties were never caught, but it is not disputed that the killings were arranged for by cattlemen.

The first killing occurred on the Sweetwater in Carbon

County, Wyoming, in early 1889. James Averill had located a farm there and opened a little store with a gin mill barroom attachment. He was also postmaster. On the next claim was a woman known as "Cattle Kate." Ella Watson was her real name. The whole country around was covered with cattle, many of them belonging to ranches hundreds of miles away, drifters before the storms. Kate began to buy from the cowboys and settlers young cattle which she branded and held in a pasture near her cabin. She was not particular as to previous ownership, bills of sale, or how fresh the last owner's brand was on the cattle she bought. Averill was believed to be a partner in the deals.

, One day ten men rode up to Averill's store and without trial or ceremony of any kind took him and Cattle Kate to the nearest cottonwood tree and hanged them both. The men were known, and their names given to the next grand jury, but they were never brought to court. The man who furnished the names and other information dropped out of sight later and was never heard of again.

Tom Waggoner had accumulated about a thousand head of first-class horses in a very short time. Waggoner was a handsome, rosy-cheeked young giant, genial and friendly, a favorite of all who knew him. He was arrested June 4, 1891, at his ranch near Newcastle, Wyoming, by three men who claimed to be deputy United States marshals and showed him papers for the arrest.

Waggoner was at his stable when caught. He asked to go to the cabin for his coat and to say good-bye to his wife and children. Probably he knew he was doomed. His request was refused. One of the men loaned him a coat. He was handcuffed and put on a horse, feet tied together under the animal's belly. His body was found ten days later hanging to a tree several miles from the cabin.

There was a story current after Waggoner's death that as the party passed a large cottonwood tree growing near a creek he nodded toward it and remarked in the most casual manner, "That there cottonwood is mighty well suited for your purpose, boys." He was taken at his word and died game.

Not long after this a body of men rode up to a cabin on the Powder River occupied by Nate Champion and Ross Gilbertson. The two were awakened from sleep by the entrance of the would-be lynchers. Champion came to the party "a-foggin'." The cabin filled with smoke, and the posse retreated. They took with them the body of a man Champion had killed.

In December, 1891, two more men, Orvill E. Jones (Ranger Jones) and J. A Tisdale, were killed by ambushed men at different places in the Powder River region.

George B. Henderson had been put in charge of the campaign against the settlers. He was generally held responsible for the death of these alleged cow thieves. In reprisal he was shot by an ambusher above the Three Crossings. His assassin was identified, convicted, and later escaped.

Rumors of an organized raid by the cattlemen against the so-called rustlers had been flying about the country for some time. Early in 1892 the organization of an "army" that was to clean up the cattle thieves was openly discussed wherever men met. All the Wyoming papers, as well as journals in Denver, San Francisco, and other cities, carried stories about the plans. Everybody knew what was going on, for the men who were engineering the adventure made no effort to conceal their plans and movements. It was announced almost openly that twenty-five men were to be hanged and a hundred others driven out of the country.

Men said to be agents of the cattle organization were known to be in Denver and in Texas, hiring men for the raid. Many of these were Texas cowboys akin to the hired killers of earlier days. They were all heavily armed. The party was equipped as for a campaign.

The Denver, Colorado, *Sun* of April 7, 1892, contained the following:

The mysterious train which left the city yesterday over the Union Pacific had a very important mission to fill, namely to get about 35 or 40 detectives to the northern part of Wyoming as rapidly as possible. The cattlemen in Buffalo, Sheridan, Bonanza, and Riverton, Wyoming, and in Red Lodge, Billings, and Fort Smith, Montana, have formed an organization with the intention of exterminating the rustlers and have called on a detective agency for assistance.

The U. P. officials here when asked about the train denied any knowledge of its having left the city.

The train evidently did leave Denver as reported, for the Cheyenne *Leader* of April 8, 1892, had several items concerning the movement.

A very mysterious expedition left here on a special train last Tuesday evening. The movement is said to be directed against Johnson County. The Denver papers brought the thrilling information that a party of at least thirty-five detectives had been whisked through this city en route to the Northern country, there to begin the work of exterminating the rustlers.

A special train left Denver with from 35 to 75 men. It arrived in Cheyenne at 5:20 P. M. Only certain individuals were allowed to go near it. The cars were kept in the eastern part of the yards. Soon after its arrival it steamed north.

It consisted of a chair car with the blinds drawn clear down, a baggage car, caboose, three stock cars loaded with horses and a flat with several wagons on it. At Casper the train stopped at the stock yards east of town and unloaded.

Rumor has it that the invading party intends to make a certain Powder River ranch headquarters and radiate from that point.

The Denver *Republican* of April 8, 1892, carried an interview with a prominent official of the Wyoming Board of Livestock Commissioners, a board created by an act of the state legislature. He was asked about the Wyoming situation which had been reported in the press dispatches as becoming somewhat serious.

He stated very frankly [said the *Republican*] that a party of about sixty well known cattlemen of that state had left Cheyenne about April 5 for the region in which the cattle rustlers had been operating, with the full intention of taking such drastic action as would put a stop to the lawlessness. He explained that the army was under the command of a well known Wyoming cattle man, was equipped for any emergencies, and carried with them a capable surgeon.

This interview and dispatches of like character, given out freely without any attempt to conceal the purpose of the movement, and including names of leaders in the affair, show the prevailing sentiment at the cattle head-quarters. It was considered a matter of law enforcement, and the men were said to be performing a real public service.

Meantime, the high-salaried general managers continued to hang around the clubs at Cheyenne, Kansas City, and other places that had more attractions than the windy Wyoming plains, and the rustlers continued to pick up mavericks or eat stolen beef in their camps. Nobody appeared to be worrying about the crisis that was approaching; not an officer of the law took steps to head off or prevent the clash that was certainly impending.

By horseback and wagon the party headed for Buffalo. Part of the baggage consisted of extra ammunition, some dynamite, and a lot of handcuffs. A member of a prominent Philadelphia family, a young surgeon out West for his health, was with the party in a professional character. Apparently nothing had been overlooked. There were at least two war correspondents along: one, Sam T. Clover, representing the Chicago *Herald*, the other the Cheyenne *Sun*. Each sent back long dispatches to his paper exactly as if the expedition were perfectly legal and proper.

North of Casper on the Powder River this army surrounded the K C ranch during the night. They had information that Nick Ray and Nate Champion were there, both of them "wanted" by the invaders. A wagon at the stable loaded with camp plunder indicated the possibility that others might be in the house. Orders were given not to shoot unless certain as to the identity of anyone leaving the house.

At daylight a man stepped from the ranch-house door and walked to the stream for a bucket of water. He was a stranger, and as he stooped to get the water he was captured and taken behind the stable where the leaders were hidden. A few minutes later another man, also a stranger, came to the stable and was captured. The strangers were two trappers named Jones and Walker. From these men the army learned that Nick Ray and Nate Champion were the only others in the cabin.

Ray came out and started to the woodpile for firewood. A volley of shots rang out. He fell, badly wounded, about ten feet from the cabin door. He crawled on all fours toward the doorstep and collapsed. Twice Champion faced the rifles of the surrounding army in an effort to drag his wounded friend into the cabin. The first time he exchanged shots with the besiegers, but being encumbered with his rifle could not handle him. A few moments later he dragged his companion inside while rifle balls splintered the logs around him. Men who were there and who were accustomed to nervy action have said it was the bravest rescue they ever saw.

The siege lasted all day. Champion took care of his dying companion, held the gunmen at bay, and in the intervals found time to write an account of the affair in a cheap memorandum book. He was as cool and brave a man as ever went to his death in any of the deadly battles that have characterized the cattle country.

The story of the burning of the K C cabin by means of a wagon rolled down against it loaded with blazing pitch-pine wood, of Champion's dash for liberty through the flames, and of his death is an epic of Western life that stirs the blood. Champion may have been a horse thief and a mavericker, but he had the superb fighting aplomb that could look death in the face for many hours without a quiver of fear. The men who killed him afterward paid tribute to his courage.

The correspondent of the Chicago *Herald* sent a number of messages to his paper describing the events. Under date of April 15, 1892, the *Herald* published the following, dated Douglas, Wyoming, April 14:

Champion was as brave as a lion. The poor devil came out with his rifle in his hand. He was in his stocking feet and jumped square into the arms of the two best shots in the whole party. He fired but one shot as he ran. The whole gang opened up on him. Their first volley broke his arm and he couldn't use his rifle. He stumbled and fell, riddled with bullets. Champion fell far enough from the house to keep his body from being burned. The men searched his body. On it, soaked with blood and with a bullet hole through it, they found a small notebook in which he had calmly set down the incidents of the fight and the last hours of his life.

The memoranda he set down are worth quoting. They evidence the quality of the man's gameness.

April 9—6 A. M.

Me and Nick was getting breakfast when the attack began. Two men were with us, Bill Jones and another man. The old man went out after water about daylight. Did not come back. His friend went out to see what was the matter and he didn't come back. Nick started out and I told him to look out, that I thought there was someone at the stable that would not let them come back. . . .

Nick is shot but not dead yet. He is awful sick. I must go and wait on him. It is now about two hours since the first shots. . . .

Nick is still alive. They are still shooting and all around the house. Boys, there is bullets coming in like hail. . . .

Them fellows is in such a shape I can't get at them. They are shooting from the stable and river and back of the house . . . .

Nick is dead. He died about nine o'clock. I see a smoke down at the stable. I don't think they intend to let me get away this time. . . .

It is now about noon. There is someone at the stable yet. They are throwing a rope out of the door and drawing it back. I guess that is to draw me out. I wish that duck would get out farther so I can get a shot at him. . . .

Boys, I don't know what they have done with them two fellows that staid here last night. . . .

Boys, I feel pretty lonesome right now. I wish there was some-one else here with me so we could watch all sides at once. They may fool around till I get in one good shot before they leave. . . .

It's about three o'clock now. There is a man in a buckboard and one on horseback just passed.[1] They fired at them as they went by. I don't know if they killed them or not. I seen a lot of men come out on horses on the other side of the river and take after them. . . .

I shot at a man in the stable just now. Don't know if I got him or not. I must go and look out again. I see 12 or 15 men. One looks like —— [name erased by party]. I don't know whether it is or not. It don't look as if there was much of a chance of my getting away. I hope they don't catch them fellows that run over the bridge toward Smith's. . . .

They are shooting at the house now. If I had a pair of glasses I would know some of those men. They are coming back and I got to look out. . . .

Well, they have just got through shelling the house again like hell. I hear them splitting wood. I guess they are going to fire the house tonight. I think I'll make a break tonight if I live. . . .

Shooting again. I think they will fire the house this time. It's not night. . . .

The house is all fired. Good-bye, boys, if I never see you again.

NATHAN D. CHAMPION.

He made his run for life and lost.

The attackers pinned a card upon the breast of the dead

---

[1]Jack Flagg of the J F and his son.

man. It read, "Cattle thieves, beware!" They might have
added, "Here lies the body of a brave man who died un-
afraid."

The army moved on toward the town of Buffalo, where
they intended to make a clean-up. Unfortunately for their
plans Flagg, with his ten-year-old stepson, had escaped
and carried the news to Buffalo. They had made their getaway by the narrowest of margins.

The sheriff immediately organized a posse to move
against the invaders, who learned that the countryside
was aroused. The army turned back, and at the T A ranch
on Crazy Woman Creek fortified themselves in the big
log ranch headquarters. At daylight on April 11, 1892,
between three and four hundred men had the ranch completely surrounded and a siege under way. More men came
galloping on steaming horses to join the besiegers. They
came, some from a distance of a hundred miles around,
cowboys, ranchmen, and citizens of Buffalo, all eager to
get at the Texans and the cattlemen who had employed
them.

Arapahoe Brown, a picturesque character afterward
killed by two of his own cowboys, commanded the Johnson
County forces. From a ridge above the ranch he kept a
constant fire on the defenders while he rigged what he called
a "go-devil." To the running gears of the captured wagons
he lashed a breastwork of logs six feet high backed up by
bales of hay. Forty men could find shelter behind the logs.
Brown intended to push this toward the cabins and set
fire to them by means of giant powder.

The cattlemen asked for no quarter. None was offered
them. For two days the fight continued. Meantime word
of the dangerous plight of the cattlemen had gone back to
Cheyenne. Governor Amos W. Barber burned up the wires
to Washington urging the President to send troops to the
scene to prevent further bloodshed. On the second afternoon of the siege, just before the fire machine was finished
and ready to use, three troops of United States Cavalry

from Fort McKinney under Colonel J. J. Van Horn rode up and took charge of affairs.

Colonel Van Horn swung his men in between the house and the posse and there held a conference with the army under a flag of truce. They surrendered to him, a record being made of every man's name and the equipment taken, horses, wagons, ammunition, etc. Under his care and escort all were taken to Fort McKinney and later to Fort D. A. Russell near Cheyenne.

When news of the affair reached the outside world it created a tremendous sensation. Denver, Chicago, Washington, and San Francisco papers ran long dispatches covering the raid and surrender. The Cheyenne *Leader* on April 13, 1892, carried the following bold headlines:

CAUGHT IN A TRAP

INVADING STOCKMEN CAUGHT IN A TRAP IN JOHNSON COUNTY

Drawing the coils slowly but surely about the devoted band. Hundreds of men flock to the scene. Consequences may be disastrous. Governor asks the President for Federal troops from Fort McKinney.

THREE RUSTLERS SHOT

One Invader Dying at the Hospital at Fort McKinney

The story of the legal proceedings that dragged along for nearly a year need not be told here. No court action was ever taken, and early in 1893 all of the fifty or more quasi-prisoners were discharged from arrest and allowed to go their several ways. In this rather ignominious manner ended the "Wyoming Invasion."

From start to finish the cattlemen had blundered. The idea was wrong in conception, and it had been badly carried out. The invasion was an attempt to set back the clock. It was many years too late. The cattleman no longer ruled the West. Civilization had closed in on him, but he had refused to recognize that the day of his supremacy was past. He had made the laws but found himself unable to execute them. The cattle associations which in many cases had arbitrarily operated against the small ranchmen had gone far beyond their legal or moral rights.

The Johnson County war proved beyond the shadow of a doubt that the cattleman's word was no longer final. The West had moved beyond him.

Yet even the failure of the Powder River Invasion failed to convince all the cattlemen of Wyoming that a new day had dawned. They recognized they could no longer publicly put themselves above the law. A few individuals, however, strong in the belief they were right, continued to do so privately.

The ranging of cattle on free grass has always been such a precarious adventure that from the days of the Civil War it has been hedged about with theft, violence, and disregard of the rights of others. The most peaceful Christian cowman has sometimes found it difficult to avoid being involved in measures which were not approved by his conscience.

There has never been a great industry in this country where those engaged in it were in large numbers such forceful individualists. This was true by reason of the conditions dominating it. The same factors produced a disregard for law among a considerable percentage of the rank and file of the cattle industry that cannot be found among farmers, miners, manufacturers, railroad men or merchants. Great financial organizations have sometimes disregarded legal restraint, but generally this has not extended below the heads of the combines except on specific orders.

Even after the beginning of the twentieth century rustling continued actively in Wyoming, though the depredators were more cunning and less bold. Tom Horn was employed as a detective to guard the range.

Horn was in some respects a remarkable character. He stood six feet, tall, arrow straight, deep chested, lean loined, and muscled like a panther. He was a strong and a hard man. In the early '80's he had gone to Arizona and worked as cowboy, government packer, and for a few months as scout under General Miles. At Globe, Arizona, on July 4, 1888, and later at Phœnix, he won roping contests from the most expert cowboys in the world. He loved to play the bad man. Always he wore a fire-red flannel shirt. He was a poseur of the first water. What a movie hero he would have made!

Like the cattlemen who employed him later in Wyoming, Horn belonged to the old West. He could not adapt himself to the new. Nor could he let whisky alone. Drunk, he was the grandest, most extravagant liar in the world. Unable to convict suspected parties of rustling, he ambushed and shot them. So it is charged.

He made a mistake and killed a fifteen-year-old boy who was wearing his father's hat and coat. To Joe LaFors, a deputy United States marshal, he confessed while drunk that he had killed Willie Nickell and several rustlers. He was tried at Cheyenne and convicted on circumstantial evidence. Efforts were made to get him to tell who had employed him. He would tell nothing. He was for months the storm center of a conflict between the old order and the new. On November 20, 1903, he was hanged at Cheyenne, game to the last. It is safe to say that a few big cattlemen heaved a long sigh of relief when Horn walked to the gallows without saying a word that could implicate them.

WHAT a world of memories the subject of the old-time cowboy brings up! Of comrades good and true who have long since "passed over the range"; of hot dust-filled days pointing trail herds, and of cold starry nights spent guarding the restless cattle on the bed grounds; of wild stampedes in which the crazed creatures tore out into the darkness, crashing blindly through the dense underbrush and falling over logs, rocks, and into deep holes; of a man lying for hours beneath a dead horse whose neck had been broken in a fall, pinning down the rider until daylight came and his comrades found him; of a blinding winter storm when the cattle, drifting before a norther, walked over the edge of a cliff and their bodies piled high on the rocks below.

The change in the character of the cowboy did not come suddenly but was a matter of evolution. The "bob" wire fence was one of the chief agents of the economic forces which modified him and made him adapt himself to his new environment. The old-timer with high-heeled boots not built for hard work on the ground, with spurs which he

---

[1]Part of this was published by the *Westward Ho* magazine, December, 1929.

hated to remove even to attend the dances in the school-house, found himself sadly hampered and really outclassed at post-hole digging, haymaking, and such "degrading" labor. His place was taken by a new type of cowboy, who, when engaged in such work, wore flat-heeled shoes instead of boots, who cast aside the chaps for blue denim overalls—"Levis," they called them, from the name of the first manufacturer, old Levi Straus, of San Francisco, a pioneer in the overall business in the Far West. The old-timers grew up on the ranges and rode from infancy. The new cowboys were recruited from among the farmer boys who, during the branding season, worked on the range and between times helped irrigate the crops and put up the hay for winter feeding.

Of the old-time type of cowboy, those who were in their prime in the years between 1870 and 1890, few are left.

It used to be a saying that when a cowboy reached the age at which he could no longer flank a calf or ride a bucker and stick to the saddle, he became either a "chamber-maid" in some livery stable or a bartender. The march of progress robbed him of both these lines of industry. When you do find one of the old-timers, he has generally exchanged the bucking bronc for a "tin Lizzie." If he had the good fortune to save his wages—and few did—he is running a motor outfit of his own. The old sign "Livery Stable, Hay and Grain for Sale" has been painted out, and the words "Garage, Gas and Oil" tell the story of the downfall of the cowboy.

"These here now present-day cow persons, they make me good an' tired," remarked an old-time New Mexico cowman not long ago. "They want all quiet hosses to ride, and I cain't git nobody to bust broncs no more. They can take the carbureter off my car and clean it, but ding bust 'em, they couldn't forefoot a bronc and saddle him in two weeks. Waugh!" How he did snort!

Texas, once the very breeding place of top waddies, has more cattle than ever, but the old ranges have been cut up into fenced pastures, and the line rider carries a couple of pounds of wire fence staples in his saddle pockets, with a pair of fence pliers and a wire stretcher tied to his saddle. He does not have to be able to rope and tie down a steer in fifty seconds—unless he wants to be a rodeo performer.

In Arizona, New Mexico, southern Utah, Nevada, Montana, and eastern Oregon there are still many good-sized range cow outfits using the public domain exclusively, and there you may find cowboys that run fairly true to type. But there are many changes. Instead of using a buckboard pulled by a couple of old cow ponies, the owner now drives out to the round-up ground in his high-powered car from which he watches the boys cut out the steers from the herd.

Roping bids fair to become a lost art, except among rodeo performers. When cows were worth about $5 each, the owners did not particularly object to having their men practise on the stock, for without constant practice no man could hope to keep up his skill. But with rising prices, and cows worth $50 and up, roping became an expensive affair for the owners. They raised serious demurrer to training expert ropers at such costs, since practice was to be had only with range stock, which meant heavy losses in broken legs, horns, ribs, and often necks.

In the old days half a dozen punchers might be riding along a road toward the headquarters ranch. Across the road a string of cattle might come trailing out from water. A high-headed steer would stop for a moment, shake his head, sniff at the men, and race madly across the flat. Fourth of July was close at hand, with roping matches in every little cow town in the country. Away went a man after him, untying his rope from the saddle horn and forming a loop as he rode. Not far behind him trailed one or two more, eager to take their turn should the first boy "waste a loop."

There were two distinct ways of throwing a steer (busting 'em). The first and most skillful was by "going over

their withers." To do this the roper lay as close as he could
crowd his pony alongside the steer on his left side. With
an overhanded reverse swing of the loop he threw it over
the steer's withers so that it hung on the right side almost
to the ground. He held fast to it until the rapidly moving
animal stepped into the loop with both front feet. With a
quick jerk it was pulled up around the front legs against
the longhorn's brisket. The pony was then swung directly
away from the steer. With the rope tied to the saddle
horn, the jerk that came when the end of the rope was
reached dragged the feet of the brute from under him. He
was turned completely over, front feet high in the air,
held fast by the rope and so stunned by the fearful bump
that there was little fight left in him. If the pony knew his
business, he held the rope taut while the rider leaped from
the saddle, ran to the steer, and with his hogging rope
quickly tied the fore feet and one hind foot closely together. The job was done. This was a clever trick and took
lots of practice.

The ordinary "sure-fire" method was to rope the steer
by the horns, give the slack of the rope a sudden flip
around the animal's rump just above the hocks, and then,
spurring the pony for a supreme effort, "go yonderly"
ahead and to the left. This pulled the steer's head away
from the rider and back against his body and jerked the
hind legs from under him. He landed all in a heap, generally
with his head under his body in such a way that it was
almost impossible for him to get up. With the two hind
feet pulled well forward toward the front feet, hog-tying
was a matter of seconds only.

But such practice was surely rough on stock and cost
the owners many a range animal.

To forbid the men their roping was out of the question.
The outfits got around the situation by getting state
legislatures to pass laws forbidding roping exhibitions.
Generally the laws were fostered by the various societies
for the prevention of cruelty to animals, which relieved the

bosses from all responsibility for starting the thing. No one ever knew such a bill to fail of passage. There was too much quiet pressure behind it from stock owners.

With the law in effect, the incentive for gaining skill was taken away, and there was, of course, far less of such work on the open ranges.

In nearly every range state the cowpunchers' wings were clipped by taking from him his ready six-shooter, the "hog leg" he had carried for years. Heavy penalties were enforced against the wearing of such ornaments in town or on the ranges. So the weapon was hidden away in the bed roll, for a genuine old-timer couldn't imagine himself without his six-gun somewhere near. His happiness was further curtailed by the passage of laws against open gambling. When the wave of prohibition swept across the range country from Canada to Mexico and the saloons were turned into ice-cream parlors and soft-drink emporiums, he had to content himself with lemonade—"sassyparilla" as he contemptuously called all soft drinks. He thought the world was coming to an end for sure.

With these waddies have gone the longhorn cattle, the maverick, and the rustler. In the place of the longhorns are great herds of range cattle with blood in their veins the equal of any in the corn-belt regions. The boys who now herd cattle frequently ride, not the bucking broncs of early times, but saddle horses whose ancestors have won Derbys. At the saddle horn, instead of the six-shooter, the riders carry a pair of fence pliers, and in the saddle pockets, instead of a pint flask of "red licker" is tucked a tobacco sack full of fence staples.

The rustler disappeared, or at least became a *rara avis*, with the breaking up of the big outfits. A thousand small ranchers, many of whom raise cattle, live on the range where one great syndicate ran its immense herds. Time was when the little fellow was friendly toward the brand blotter. He was despoiling the common enemy. But when the syndicates went out of business and left the country to the small fry, the waddy with a long loop for other men's calves found nothing but hostility. Those who had tolerated him would have none of his brand blotting now. They sicked the law on him and locked him up in a penitentiary.

The old-time cowboy was more picturesque and adventurous, but his successor is a better all-round worker and a better citizen. The longhorn too was picturesque, but his descendents on the open ranges weigh twice as much, make better feeders, and produce more high-priced meat. The open trackless range was mysterious and romantic, but the wire fence saves money for herders. It reduces losses in strays and depletion from winter storms, and it allows a much better use of the range.

The educated cowboy, so common in wild West fiction, is largely a myth. There were a few such, most of them wild, dissipated specimens far more given to excesses than the average puncher. Cowboys in general were not literate.

, Some of the best wagon bosses were Texas-born men who could neither read nor write. But they knew cows. They would ride any horse that could be saddled, and they could handle a round-up outfit of twenty-five or thirty men with ease. They were absolutely without fear of man or beast, "fighting fools" of the first water.

A trail herd from the Pecos country in western Texas would drift to the market, ten or fifteen men to the wagon, 80 per cent. of whom could endorse their names on the back of a check only with the utmost difficulty. They possessed no special qualities or characteristics that other men of the West did not have. They were the average run of the frontier of those days, no more, no less. When sober they were peaceable and quiet; drunk, they were brainless fools looking eagerly for trouble and always finding it. Theirs was a wild, free life, far from most of the restrictions that residents of towns and cities accept without question.

In their dress the cowboys were consistent. The huge

six-quart steeple-crowned hats of to-day were not found
on the ranges except in the Southwest where along the
border one occasionally saw a high, silver-bedecked Mexican sombrero. In later years many of the boys preferred
and wore the small felt "fedoras," which were light, needed
no hat string to hold them on the head, and turned down
over the eyes to protect them from the glaring sun.

Few of the old-timers had more than a hazy idea of the
value of money, except that with it they could purchase
drinks, fancy silk handkerchiefs, high-heeled boots from
Coffeyville, Stetson hats with $20 "rolls" on them, pearl-
handled six-shooters, and oceans of cartridges with which
to pepper the signal targets along the railroad on the way
out of town or devastate the glass insulators on the tele-
phone and telegraph poles.

They were hospitable to the traveler, but so was everyone in those days. Visitors were not very common at the
camps, and a newcomer dropping in to spend the night
was twice welcome, for he brought the gossip from town
or the last cow camp at which he had "hung up." Most of
the early cowboys knew little of the ways of the world. To
most of them "Fo't Wuth," Texas, was the one city of the
United States.

Occasionally some of them drifted East with a train of
steers, carrying with them every dollar they had in the
world. Nine times out of ten they lost the last cent of it
over the gambling tables of the first town in which they
lay for a day or so while the steers were unloaded, fed, and
rested. Not infrequently the boss would receive a telegram from the wanderer into strange lands, appealing to
him to wire funds with which to pay a fine for some es-
capade against the peace and dignity of the law as laid
down in the effete East.

"I'd ruther be a horny toad in the deserts of Arizony
than a millionaire in that there now Chicago," was the
frank statement of one returned traveler. He had found

his way clear back to the Chicago stock-yards, where he "mixed it" with half a dozen cops, who, after properly subduing him, loaded him into the patrol wagon and shut him up in the "hoosgow" (*Jusgado*, the prisoners' dock in a Mexican court). From this he emerged with considerable court-plaster on his countenance and several huge lumps on his skull, together with a very chastened spirit and a ticket all the way through to his Arizona stopping place. This latter was purchased and handed to him by the authorities to whom the boss back on the range had sent the money, not caring to place the coin in the hands of the wanderer lest he again fall by the wayside and need further financial aid in order to reach the home ranch.

One of the authors had in his outfit a cripple, as good a cowboy as he had ever seen. This was Charley Carter, long since gone to his last round-up. He had his right leg taken off at the knee. He wore a peg leg and was called "Pata Pala" (literally "stick foot") by the Mexicans. Once a young boy was pestering him for the particulars of the accident that lost him the leg. "See here, kid, if I tell you how I lost it will you never bother me about it again?" Pata Pala asked.

The boy promised.

"Well," said the legless one, "it was bit off."

As a matter of fact, taking a train of cattle to Kansas City he loaded up at one of the wayside stations with a supply of rot-gut whisky, and while making his way over the tops of the cars to reach one in which a steer was down, fell between them, and the wheels did the biting off.

Pata Pala always rode with his right stirrup considerably shorter than the left and tied to the other stirrup under the horse's belly by a stout strap; "hobbled" they used to call this method of riding a bucking horse. Then by sticking that peg leg through the stirrup and sitting a little to one side he obtained a grip on his horse that equalled the two legs of any rider. There wasn't a man on the range who could mount a mean horse any more easily or quickly or "stay up in the middle of a bucker" any longer than Pata Pala.

Another boy with his wagon was minus his left hand. Roping a big steer, his hand became entangled in the loops of the hard twisted rope. Around the horns of the steer at one end and tied hard and fast to the horn of his saddle at the other, when the rope tightened the boy found himself swept from his horse and hanging in the air between horse and steer. His hand was cut off at the wrist as clean as any surgeon could have done it. Yet Si Dawson of New Mexico with his reins in his teeth, the loops of his rope hanging round his left stump, would rope and tie down any steer on the range. All he asked for was a steady old pony that knew his business. Si did all the rest.

When it came to hard work the men of those days have never been equaled. Day or night, rain or shine, in winter's snow or summer's heat, they never shirked or held back. Excepting sailors, there never was a class of working men who had such long hours, suffered more real hardships, and put up with more privations than the old-time cowboys.

On the California coast the cowboys were called vaqueros (buckaroos, the Northwesterners soon translated it). They used rawhide ropes of dainty size and paid fabulous amounts for silver-mounted bridles, spurs, and bits. Their saddles were masterpieces of the saddlers' art, with great high horns on the pommels, fancy stamping all over the skirting, and solid silver plates on the corners of the skirts. Their dainty toes slipped into four-inch-wide wooden stirrups with huge "eagle bill" tapaderos, the wings of which were often ten inches long. Their saddles had but one cinch, a horsehair affair, six to eight inches wide, generally with a long fancy-colored horsehair tassle hung from its center under the horses' belly. These saddles the Texans dubbed "center fires" from the rifle and pistol cartridges just then coming into general use.

The California vaqueros were undoubtedly the most

expert horsemen and ropers the world has ever seen. Their skill with the lasso was marvelous. They worked almost entirely on horses. No unnecessary footwork for them. No bulldogging of husky steers or flanking of calves at branding time in their days. Roping was a fine art, and they were artists in their line.

To throw a two-day-old calf called for two men, both mounted, one to rope it by the neck, the other to "pick up its hind feet" with his reata. Very cleverly they did it. With the calf stretched out between the two horses, the broncos "sat back" on the ropes. A man on foot would jerk the calf on his side and do the branding with the ropes held taut. There was a maximum of horseback work with a minimum of footwork, the last done by the new men on the ranch.

Then came the Texans over the line. They overflowed the whole range country, showing new tricks in handling cattle and riding and roping that completely revolutionized the business. With them cowpunching was straight work without any fancy artistic attachments.

Along in 1883 or '84, the first double-rigged Texas saddle found its way into northern Arizona. A long keen cowboy from the Pecos country drifted along one day looking for work (a Texas ranger drifted after him a couple of months later and coaxed him to go back to the Lone Star State with him to talk over some matters with a grand jury). He rode one of those low-horned, clumsy-looking Texas saddles. It had two cinches—two, count 'em—the rear one a piece of stiff leather, the front one of horsehair. Neither was more than three inches wide. To add to Arizona's disgust, instead of the long flexible latigos of soft whang leather he merely had a heavy leather strap— "like a damned trunk strap," one old fellow put it, "with holes punched in it and a buckle instead of a ring on the cinch." Also, he used a narrow iron stirrup into which he stuck his feet clear to the heels.

On the saddle he carried a common sisal rope, not more

than thirty feet long. One end of it was tied hard and fast
to the saddle horn. His bit was the commonest of affairs,
without fancy ornamentation of any kind, and with a
"U" in the center of the bar not more than an inch high.
No long dangling chains were on the end of his reins next
the bit, and the reins, unlike the expensive fancy plaited
reins in use in Arizona and California, were merely long,
heavy, inch-wide straps, not tied together but each independent of the other, "open reins," the Texans called
them.

The Texan did not tie his mount with a hair rope, but
merely dropped the two strap reins on the ground. Instead
of heavy silver inlaid spurs with clanking chains and jingling steel ornaments, he wore a pair of steel "Petmaker"
spurs set close to the heel of his boots with a solid rowel
two inches wide, more like a circular saw than a spur—an
affair that cut the horse terribly unless used with care.
"Sure makes them git a wiggle on theirselves, though,"
said the Texan.

They were cowmen, those Texans. Their double-cinch
saddles "stayed put" once they were cinched up, and that
without cutting a poor horse half in two. When his saddle
needed tightening, he did not have to get down and work
on the latigos with their fancy loops. He simply leaned
over, grabbed his "trunk strap," pulled it up a hole or two,
caught the tongue of the buckle in the hole, and the job
was done.

When he went into a herd to rope, he "dabbed his loop"
onto the animal he was after, swung his horse round, and
started calmly for the branding fire, paying very little attention to the lively object dancing and bawling at the
end of the rope. The men on the ground were expected
to flank or bulldog anything up to an eighteen-months
"long yearling." Only in cases of larger cattle was a second
roper called in to catch the hind feet and help throw the
animal. The Texas system was rough on stock, but it delivered the goods when it came to handling cattle.

The rollicking, hard-working Texans showed the rest of Cattleland a lot of new wrinkles in working range cattle. The North and the West died hard, but eventually accepted the inevitable, tied their ropes to the saddle horn, rode "rim-fire" saddles, gave up the fancy ornaments, headstalls, hair ropes, and other beloved equipment, and got down to real work.

Texas also taught some new tricks about roping saddle horses. The Californian always swung the largest loops to rope a saddle horse. The Lone Star State man, on the contrary, would slip up to the remuda like a darkey to a chicken coop and, with his loop lying flat on the ground give it a clever underhanded throw and drop it over the neck of the horse, without stirring up the whole bunch into a rioting, milling mob as those with the huge whirling loops always did. "Ay de mi," but those Texans did knock the romance out of the cow business.

2

A midsummer afternoon in the Southwest. From a cloudless sky the sun shone down on a wide prairie, the boundaries melting easily into the distant hazy horizon.

Here and there were little islands of rugged wind-whipped cedars and junipers. Close to one of these was camped the heavy chuck wagon of a range round-up outfit. Near it a fire of cedar logs burned. On the lowered lid of the chuck box the cook was busily building pies for the men's supper. A beer bottle rolled the plastic dough into proper thickness. Having covered the filling with the overhanging dough of the lower crust, with the point of his long knife blade he carved the outfit's brand deep into the upper crust, thus: ⅂L (Seven H L), a mark worn by twice ten thousand head of cattle that grazed on the vast open ranges of northern Arizona.

Into a hole dug for the purpose he poured a shovelful of red-hot coals, patting them down evenly and gently.

Upon this he set a Dutch oven, the heavy top lid previously heated in the fire. The pie plate was inside the oven, and upon the lid had been heaped a couple of shovelfuls of coal. Two more pies followed the first into other Dutch ovens.

As the cook worked at supper, he glanced often toward a spot on the prairie from which arose a cloud of yellow dust. Occasionally a mounted figure emerged, racing madly across the range. It was the round-up, and the cook knew the men would soon be at the wagon, hungry as wolves. Like all good housewives, he had prepared his dessert first.

After the bread was made and in the oven, the "swamper" brought from the wagon a hind quarter of a yearling, from which, laid on the mess-box lid, the cook cut many thin slabs of steak, each as big as the palm of a man's hand. These he threw into the pan of flour left from his bread-making operations. Stirred into and well covered with the flour, each piece was dropped into another great iron Dutch oven, in the bottom of which was about three inches of red-hot crackling lard. Ten minutes, and one had the most delicious morsels of fried beef imaginable, each piece covered with the crisp browned batter. Generally it required two ovenfuls to meet the needs of a round-up crew of from eighteen to twenty men.

Coffee was manufactured in large three-gallon pots into which each man dipped his cup. Before doing this a second time, if the cup had rested on the ground, the puncher politely wiped the bottom on his overalls or chaps to remove any dirt that might have adhered to it. They were sure sticklers for etiquette, those boys.

Chuck has improved since the days of the old cow hunt. These three articles, bread, meat, and coffee, were the main ingredients of the meal at the average range wagon in the '80's. Three times a day they appeared on the menu, week after week and month after month. Beans came about twice a week. Boiled rice, generally called "moonshine" or "John Chinaman," liberally supplied with raisins, was frequently prepared. Kegs of mixed pickles were a staple, there being a general range law that provided severe penalties for any puncher who "picked around" to secure the choice morsels, such as small onions or cauliflower. Ordinarily the cook, to prevent such outrages against chuck-wagon etiquette, would cut a small hole about three inches square in the top of the keg, which generally held two to four gallons of pickles, drive a nail into it for a handle, and provide a long-handled fork for a spear with which to secure one's portion. Woe betide the man whom the cook caught red-handed in the act of rejecting when brought to light the piece he had speared and going back for another. "Take 'em as they come," was the order.

Dried fruit, such as apples, peaches, and prunes, were provided at least twice a day, and on every chuck-wagon lid you found a gallon can of some sort of syrup, generally good old "blackstrap" New Orleans molasses or else, in certain localities, sorghum of local manufacture.

Canned goods, dubbed "airtights," were seldom seen about a round-up wagon. Occasionally the wagon boss would let the cook lay in a few cases of corn, tomatoes, and peas, to be used on special occasions.

In the lean years between 1890 and 1895, when range cattle were almost unsalable at any price and strict economy was necessary, nearly all the big Southwestern outfits cut out sugar entirely, and "long sweetness" in the shape of molasses was served in its stead. Pickles, canned goods, and dried fruit, except of the home-made brands, were also eliminated from the bills of fare, and during those years it was straight bread, meat, and coffee for everybody.

The coffee was invariably one of two package brands— "Arbuckle's" or "XXX." An old ranch book shows that eight cents a pound was paid for either of these, bought by the case.

When all was ready the cook pulled from his box the

several drawers that held cups, spoons, knives, forks, and plates, set them side by side on the lid, and back of them cans holding salt, sugar, and pepper. Then, with a look around on his hungry crew, he yelled loud enough to wake the dead.

"Here it is. Come and get it," or "Come a-runnin', fellers," or sometimes just "Chuck away."

The men secured the necessary implements and passed from one Dutch oven to another, loading plates with a selection of everything in sight. They sat on the ground cross-legged, resting their plates on their feet, coffee cups on the ground beside them. Of conversation at such times there was very little, that little confined strictly to the business on hand.

Under the mess-box lid the cook always placed a huge dishpan, sometimes two. This was known all over the range country as the "wreck pan," and the luckless tenderfoot who did not drop his dirty dishes into it but set them in a nice little heap on the mess-box lid was in trouble. What the average round-up cook said to him was aplenty.

The question is often asked as to the health of men living on this sort of fare, probably lacking the vitamines and the variety which to-day are deemed so vital a part of human food. As a matter of fact, cowboys were by no means wholly free from bodily ills.

Open running sores, usually on the hands, were common. They were the result of injuries such as kicks of calves—their little hooves were as sharp as broken glass— flesh torn while shoeing horses, and fingers cut to the bone by "hot ropes" slipping through one's hands. These hurts were a long time healing. Proud flesh would come into them to be burned out by liberal applications of powdered alum. Outfits carried a small can of this in one of the drawers of the mess box, along with salves and ointments guaranteed to heal up such places, and several kinds of pills and powders advertised to do all sorts of things to men's interior organs. With a wagon and eighteen to twenty men out for six weeks at a time, generally from fifty to seventy-five miles from the nearest settlement, some supplies of this kind were a real necessity. Red Cross first-aid kits had not been invented at that time. Seldom was there a round-up crew that did not have a man or two suffering from carbuncles and boils. A chew of tobacco tied with a strip from one of the cook's dish towels (old flour sacks) was the usual dressing for boils. A bad cut was frequently smeared with axle grease made from heaven only knows what. The victims got well, too. Evidently their constitutions were of iron.

Cooks were paid from fifteen to twenty-five dollars a month more than riders. Long before the wagon crew was gathered for the spring work, the wagon boss had his cook hired, frequently paying him wages for a month or two before he was needed, just to hold him.

The cook was monarch of all he surveyed. Everybody paid him homage, and the wise "stray man" with the outfit, or casual drifter dropping in for a meal or two, always grabbed one of the flour-sack towels and helped him get his dirty dishes out of the way. Nor has this situation changed with the passing years. Four or five years ago, at the headquarters ranch of a big cow outfit in the Black Hills of South Dakota, the kitchen was decorated with large plainly read signs, such as:

IF YOU CAN'T WASH DISHES, DON'T EAT.
WE USE WOOD IN THE COOKSTOVE CUT 16 INCHES LONG, BUT *no longer*.
A BUSY COOK LOVES A FULL WOOD BOX.
A FULL WATER BUCKET MAKES A HAPPY COOK.
STRAY MEN ARE NOT EXEMPT FROM HELPING WASH DISHES, BRINGING WOOD OR WATER.
THE WELL IS JUST 110 STEPS FROM THE KITCHEN, MOSTLY DOWNHILL BOTH WAYS.

Just why a round-up cook had to be cranky was never clear, but all of them were more or less constructed along those lines, generally more.

With an outfit of twenty men out on a round-up which was to last for two or three months, and away from town the whole time, much depended on the cook's loyalty to his job. Consequently he was coddled in every possible way to keep him good-natured and at work. A puncher could quarrel with or "josh" the horse wrangler, or any of the men he wanted to, and the boss seldom interfered, but let him start something with the cook, and if that personage himself didn't take up the challenge forthwith the boss would quietly tell the offender either to "roll his tail for home" or let the cook alone. No wagon boss cared to have a cook quit him fifty or seventy miles from town with a crew of hungry men on his hands. Horse wranglers and punchers there were in plenty, but of good round-up cooks the supply was terribly low and the demand awfully keen.

Therefore it was always "Hats off to the cook."

3

Brrrrrrrrrrrrrrrrrrrrr. The little nickel alarm clock at the head of the cook's bed shrilled noisily in the cool night air. Four o'clock comes early under the stars.

Like most round-up cooks, Old Dad slept at some distance from the rest of the crew, but not for fear his alarm might disturb them. Oh, no! Rather it was to keep them from disturbing him during the night as they came and went every time the guards were changed around the herd bedded down half a mile from camp. "An' to make it worser, the old pagan goes and sets his clock on a milk pan turned bottom side up, as if it didn't make racket enough all by itself," the horse wrangler complained bitterly.

All around the wagon lie the boys, some sleeping double, others alone, their white canvas bed "tarps" making them look like huge snowdrifts in the darkness.

Lowering the mess-box lid Old Dad takes from one of its

compartments a piece of rich pitch pine chopped from an old pine log up in the mountains. From this he whittles a handful of shavings. With the camp shovel he scrapes away the ashes that cover the fire hole. Upon the red-hot coals thus exposed he throws the pitch shavings, together with several bits of dry wood. Using his hat for a fan he soon has a lively blaze lighting up the darkness.

From out on the prairie where the night herders are holding the cattle comes the voice of Little Joe, who is singing as he jogs around the drowsing herd:

> "Last night as I lay on the prairie
> And looked at the stars in the sky,
> I wondered if ever a cowboy
> Would drift to that sweet by and by."

Here and there the cattle begin to get to their feet. The big old wide-horned steers yawn and stretch themselves after their night's rest. Each calf is busy at the maternal font getting an early breakfast, little tail waving in the air, head butting the mother, plain evidence of supreme enjoyment.

In the distance a pack of coyotes foraging for breakfast set up a lively "yip yap yip." There are probably no more than three. From the volume of sound one would imagine there were at least fifty.

By the time the east is growing red Dad is ready for his hungry crew. Breakfast disposed of, each man mounts his night horse and rides out to the range to gather the horses hobbled out the night before. They are thrown together and driven back to the wagon, where each ropes and saddles his circle horse, turning his tired night bronc into the bunch now in charge of the wrangler. "Everybody caught?" the wagon boss asks.

He tells the cook that the cattle rounded up will be thrown together on the flat above Obed Spring. Sixteen riders jog from the camp in the chill dawn. For miles they ride, until satisfied they are outside the cattle watering at the river. The wagon boss pulls up his pony. He dismounts and resets his saddle. The others do the same. Two men are left here; the rest follow the wagon boss, dropping out now and again as directed until the boss has but one man with him. The circle of riders is now complete, and the whole line is riding back down the range. Keeping in sight of each other, turning back every cow that seeks to escape from the line of riders and get farther back on the range, the sixteen men form a moving, enveloping, sinuous line, perhaps four miles long, driving ahead of it all cattle met. Those on each end of this great arc must ride hard. They must see that no cattle work around the ends and escape.

Half an hour after the circle starts down the prong one can see for miles small bunches of cattle in motion. Some are taking it easy, but a few of the wild "cedar breakers" are on the dead run. The heavy old bulls are loafing along down the trails. Everywhere the air is full of dust from moving feet. Each man rides on a lope, drawing rein now and then only to let his horse catch his wind.

The riders shout comments to each other when near enough. "There's that old blue roan X Bar cow with a young calf," one calls to his partner. "Funny, ain't it, how she turns up every year with a blue calf right in this very draw? I bet I've hazed her and a blue baby down this prong to the round-up ground every spring for the last five years. Them old range cows sure do love to come back to the same place every spring to drop their calf."

His buddy nods. "I just seen that old pieded ["pied" from painted; generally a red and white animal] steer we lost out of the herd last fall the night before we shipped the last train. He's lookin' for a chanst to make a break and git away agin. I told Jerry to watch out or he'd waste him."

The first cattle reach the open flat above the spring. The long lines of panting animals arriving from different directions are thrown together as they drift upon the

THE OLD-TIME CHUCK WAGON
Note the two cast-iron Dutch ovens by the fire. Your great-grandmother baked the family bread in one of these.

SOME BRANDS
Left to right: Bar M Bar; Figure 2; Four E; X Bar; Seventy-Six connected; E K connected; H L; the famous Hash Knife; M O; Rafter O Bar; Bar W; Pig Pen; Quarter Circle A; M L connected.

PICKING THE HAIR FOR A REATA

*For roping animals
such a reata was with-
out equal.*

*In the old days every-
body carried a hair rope
on his saddle.*

round-up ground. When the last men of the circle are in, more than a thousand uneasy cattle are being held by the line of riders. Steers, cows, bulls, and calves—all are moving restlessly to and fro. Every cow is bawling for her calf, every calf adding to the din with a piteous wail for its mother.

Above the cattle rises a tawny cloud of alkali dust so heavy as almost to hide the whole herd at times. Half a mile out on the prairie the horse wrangler has his horses grazing. Leaving two men to hold the herd, the rest ride over to the wagon, unsaddle their tired, sweat-covered ponies, and turn them loose. Without exception each animal, rid of the heavy saddle, takes a roll on the ground, goes down to the spring and drinks long and heartily, then, with shrill nickerings, races away to join his comrades in the remuda.

There is not so much as a sage bush on the flat. Since dinner is not ready, hungry tired punchers crawl under the wagon for shelter from the fierce sun. Some are sound asleep in ten seconds.

Dinner over, the horse wrangler brings his herd close to the wagon. Each man ropes his horse for the afternoon work. The next two hours are busy ones. Experts ride into the herd, note the cow a calf is following, rope the little fellow, and with one end of the reata around the horn drag him to a fire where a dozen irons of different brands are heating.

"Bar X Y," the roper shouts, and the tally keeper checks this in his book.

The calf bawls and struggles. A man in leathers goes down the rope to the jumping calf, catches it under the flank and by the neck, gives an outward heave, and throws the youngster. Another puncher runs forward and catches a leg. The dogie is stretched taut, and a red-hot iron applied. The acrid smell of burning hair and flesh arises. Ears are slit. The calf struggles to its feet, shakes itself, and runs blatting to the mother. In a few moments the cow is

licking the wound, the unpleasant experience almost forgotten by the calf.

The calves taken care of, the beef steers being gathered
for shipment are cut out and thrown into a day herd that
is carried along with the round-up outfit, gaining in size
each day. Cattle belonging to outfits not using the immediate range are cut out of the round-up herds by the men
representing them and also thrown into the day herd.
When the "rep" or the "stray man," as these riders for
other concerns are called, believes he has reached the outside limit of the drift from his company's range, he cuts
out from the day herd the cattle so far gathered, takes his
mount of ten or twelve saddle ponies from the remuda,
packs one of them with his camp bed and personal plunder,
and, in the native lingo, "drags it for home." Several
cowboys coming from ranges close to his "throw in" with
him, and all drive back in one bunch.

With the strays cut out and the calves branded, the
round-up cattle are allowed to drift slowly out to the
range. Their faces black with dust, their ponies weary and
hungry, the boys ride out to the camp, where Dad has
driven the chuck wagon. By the time supper is eaten it is
seven o'clock. The horse herd is bunched up not far from
camp. Every man helps "hobble out."

Meanwhile the two or three men in charge of the day
herd have worked it in as close to camp as is deemed best
and by dark have ridden down the cattle into a fairly
compact bunch. If they have been well handled and
have found plenty of grass and water they soon begin
dropping down on the ground with sighs of contentment,
chewing their cuds as a herd of well filled range cattle
should.

The two riders who have the first guard move out to the
herd and send the day riders into camp. The boss and his
men call it a day's work, and rolling their camp beds out
on the ground around the wagon, turn in for the night,
except for a two-hour turn at the herd later.

"Nothing to do till to-morrow," yawns the Kid, as he pulls his boots off after returning from the night herding. He began work at 4:30 A. M. and ended at 8 P. M., not counting a couple of hours under the stars. No union hours were known on the cow ranches of the West in those days. It was hard, hard work—and the wages! Well, as the song goes:

I'm a-ridin' to-night round this damn bed ground,
　　Ridin' on a sore-backed hoss.
　　An' I don't care a cuss what happens to the cows,
For I'm gittin' forty dollars and found.

Chorus:
　　Forty a month an' chuck-wagon grub,
　　　Forty a month an' found.
　　Oh, think of the joys of a cowboy's life
　　　While you're ridin' the old bed ground.[1]

------

[1] The whole of section 3 appeared in *Westward Ho* magazine for August, 1929.

CHAPTER XIII. CONCLUSION

No MAJOR industry in the United States—not even those of the manufacture of automobiles and the making of moving pictures—has been more subject to drastic changes than that of range stock. The extension of the use of the high plains for running cattle came with amazing swiftness. Cows pressed upon the heels of the vanishing buffalo and the retreating Indian in herds that swarmed over the free-grass country. They nosed into every gulch and coulee, no matter how far and isolated.

The new railroads made this possible by putting the wilderness in touch with a growing market. A little more than a decade later the same railroads had written "Finis" over the open range by bringing thousands of grangers to dispossess the cattle barons.

The herds pushed up the trails, thousands upon thousands of them, trudging along the great roads of empire; the trails were plowed up, forgotten relics of a bygone day. The longhorn was monarch of all he surveyed; a decade later he was a despised scrub. Cattle could range anywhere from Mexico to Canada with unlimited feed; they were pressed upon and crowded until the grass was ruined. Cows roughed through winters without feed or shelter, the margin of profit being larger for the owner on that basis; all over Cattleland outfits were suddenly busy irrigating, raising alfalfa, cutting hay, taking care of stock against inclement nature. Immense syndicates covered the prairies with their holdings; they disappeared and made way for the small man. The cattle king owned the West and was applauded as the reclaimer of the Great American Desert; he was an interloper on the land, discouraged by law and public sentiment. The rustler thrived, supported often by the granger as a weapon against the common foe; the rustler was harried to the penitentiary by the men who had not long since commended his activities.

All conditions on the open range were subject to swift reversal. Yesterday the Texas steer was an adventure; to-day the Hereford is a business, the management of which has been worked out as carefully as that of any manufacturing plant. The trail, free grass, the longhorn, the unfenced round-up, the old-time cowman, have gone never to return. The cowboy of the old days has passed on with the trapper, the buffalo, the painted Indian, and the frontier.

A phase of American life, the most free and joyous ever known, has been blotted out, but it is written into the character of the high plains states. It would be hard to over-estimate the influence of the great cattle treks upon the country through which they passed and to which they moved. They gave color, action, romance, and unending battle to a history that without them would have been a dreary tale of drab pioneering. They determined the economic basis of a dozen future states, and they made traditions for the West that have profoundly affected its inhabitants and will endure long after the present generation has vanished.

Early in 1896 Western papers carried press reports to the effect that the President had designated certain areas in the West as Forest Reserves. The news created but languid interest among cattlemen. Washington was several thousand miles to the east, and the cowman had established ownership or thought he had.

Later there appeared upon the scene here and there a biped who called himself a forest ranger. He advised the stockmen that the government looked upon the grazing of live stock in the timbered mountains as injurious to the trees and the watershed, and that sheep especially were to be excluded—"and mebbeso cattle." The stockmen thought it time to laugh.

The ranger called on the owners to furnish him with a report of the number of sheep or cattle they had been grazing in the mountains, how long they had used these ranges, how much land they owned, and various other information. To all of these inquiries the cowman was inclined to reply that it was none of his blankety-blank business. Some did make such reply in loud coarse voices and with ill-concealed disrespect for the ranger's authority. In those days a forest ranger was certainly *persona non grata* to the majority of stockmen in the Western range states. The pioneer spirit of the ranchman boiled over at the idea of any effete Easterner telling what he could or could not do with the ranges. He demanded to be shown—and eventually was.

There followed a year or two of wrangling over the removal of the stock. Those fellows back in Washington seemed really to mean what they said. In 1897 came orders that each grazer must procure a permit covering every head of stock he was grazing on these sacred areas. What the Western stockman said about the proposition was lurid, but the permits were secured in due time.

The final blow-up came in 1905 with the announcement that the government was going to charge for the live stock using the forest areas. A plan for hanging all forest officers, regardless of their personal charm, seemed the most satisfactory means of settling the controversy, and the method was talked over very freely wherever a few ranchers got together.

In 1905 an act of Congress took the Forestry Bureau from the General Land Office in the Interior Department and placed it in the Department of Agriculture. Gifford Pinchot was put at the head of the new Forest Service, which took the place of the old Bureau of Forestry.

As they began to get better acquainted with and to learn something of the plans of the forestry men for handling the wooded areas, the more level-headed of the stockmen realized that there was more in the idea of injury to the young timber and the watersheds by heavy grazing than they had previously cared to admit.

Also they realized, although they hated to say so, that the ranges had been seriously damaged and that the grass had not been given a fair chance for its life, with the result that the carrying capacity of the ranges was steadily growing less and that they themselves were the heaviest losers. It had been obvious for some years that the stockmen could not regulate their own affairs on the range in any satisfactory manner. Hence the intervention of the government officials who had the power to lay down rules rather appealed to many who believed it was bound to have a good effect on the industry and give the stock business a stability and permanence that could be secured in no other way.

In those days forest rangers and all the "grazing men" of the Forest service were mostly cowpunchers, sheepherders, lumberjacks, and the like—well known local men. They understood the West and its people, knew the livestock business from the ground up. They had very little practical knowledge of forestry or the effects of overgrazing on watersheds, but were admirably suited in every way as pioneers in paving the way for a later class of men, educated and trained for the work, who have followed them and to a large extent taken the places of the old-timers on the ranges, in the lumber camps, in the general administration of the forests throughout the West. The first comers were able to stand an examination as to their ability in riding a bucking horse, throwing a diamond hitch, finding their way back to camp through the timber on a dark night, rounding up a bunch of wild horses, cutting cattle out of the round-ups, or handling a lambing camp. But on the technical side of their jobs the early rangers were sadly lacking.

To-day their places are being gradually filled by young fellows, graduates of the forestry schools, agricultural colleges, and like educational institutions, where they have secured a thorough knowledge of the fundamentals of forestry, including botany, a prime requisite for the grazing work to which many of them turn their attention after they enter the Forest Service. The boys now coming from the forest schools may know comparatively little about the merits of a double rig saddle, how to make sourdough bread, rope a calf, or dip sheep. On the other hand, they know all about trees, plants, and their forage values, and the effect of erosion on denuded mountain sides. What they lack of practical range experience can be secured as apprentices right on the ground under the keen eye and friendly guidance of a competent, experienced forest ranger.

The grant of National forest-grazing permits is a settlement of the overstocked range difficulty which is in harmony with the other progressive changes that have taken place in the live-stock industry. It guarantees stability, eliminates friction, and preserves the range by the application of scientific methods. Damming and directing the flow of the cattle tide, the Forestry Service has helped to change it from a turbulent flood to a placid stream, and has been a factor in transforming the cattle trade from an uncertain adventure to a business dominated by the laws of supply and demand.

IN PIONEER days the cowboy depended upon his native wit and cleverness for much of his personal equipment. Next to his horse the rope was the most necessary tool of his trade. Rawhides there were in plenty, but with no cash value. Books and papers were few. Time hung heavily on the hands of the line rider during the long nights and days in far-flung camps. So, as man has done since the beginning of time, he found both employment and recreation in supplying the wants of his calling from the materials at hand.

Thus came rawhide reatas, hair ropes, wonderfully made bridle headstalls and hackamores of thin slivers of rawhide and leather, with long reins of the same materials covered with skillfully woven knots of colored horsehair. The earliest home-made sombrero was fashioned from a selected piece of rawhide, soft and plastic. This was pressed into a hole dug in the hard ground as near the exact size of the wearer's head as possible. Then the hide was rammed home with the rounded end of a small tree trunk until it took the shape of the hole and incidentally the future wearer's head. Trimmed around with a sharp knife and adorned with a horsehair band and hat string, it made an excellent forerunner of the famous Stetsons of to-day.

Teguas, or rawhide moccasins, served for footwear. And like his near neighbor the Indian, instead of canvas for tents, the cowboy laced several rawhides together, thus forming a shelter that served the purpose admirably. The stockade corrals into which the cattle were driven for branding were nearly always bound with green rawhide strands which when dry held like iron bands, and in place of nails the overhead rafters of the rude cabins were often fastened together with the same handy materials. Incidentally, every rafter and beam in the roof of the great Mormon tabernacle at Salt Lake City was wrapped with green rawhide at the joints instead of nails, which at that time were not to be had except at impossible prices. Seventy-five years later these rawhide wrappings are still in use, as sound and firm as they were the day they were put in place. "Mexican iron" they called it in the Southwest, and surely it has justified its name.

The building of a rawhide reata was not a thing to be undertaken hastily. It took time, skill, patience, and hard work. The usual length was between sixty and seventy-five feet. For such a rope the hides of young animals were selected. Among the boys on the ranges there was a strong partiality for roan hides, the theory being that a hide of that color was more even in thickness, stronger, and worked down better than a hide of any other shade. Perhaps the choice was born of the belief that a roan horse was the toughest, longest-winded one of them all.

The number of hides required depended entirely upon the number of strands in the proposed rope. Occasionally an expert rope maker used six strands, but to do so and still keep the rope under the maximum of three eighths of an inch in diameter made it necessary to have each strand extremely thin and narrow. For this reason a four-strand rope was more usual.

A single strand used up the larger part of a hide. It took the heart out of four picked hides to make one seventy-foot rope with four strands.

As soon as the hide was off the animal it was hung up overnight to drain. The next day it was carefully cleaned of any particles of meat or fat and staked out either on the ground or on the wall of the cabin. In four or five days it was sufficiently dried out to be ready for cutting the strands.

This was started exactly in the center of the hide. With a very thin sharp knife blade a small hole was first made, and by cutting round and round this hole the strand came out in long spirals. It was a tedious job, for one had to be extremely careful not to let the blade slip and cut the strand. To keep the width even and true a small wooden gage was used. The strands for a seventy-foot rope had to be cut about ninety feet long to allow for the take-up in the plaiting. Each strand was then carefully worked down in thickness and width until it gaged exactly all its long slender length. Bits of broken glass were used to scrape off the hair and smooth off the strands.

The making and finishing of a set of reata strands alone took many hours of hard work. Sometimes a cowboy might be several months at it, working mostly stormy days or nights about the fireplace in the bunkhouse or around the camp fire in the hills.

With his strands done up in little hanks or bundles the reata-maker tied the four ends together and fastened that end to something solid. Weaving four strands is not particularly puzzling once you get started right, it being simply a case of "over one, under one" right and left. The whole secret of making a good reata is in the care with which each strand is drawn up snug and even while braiding, so there shall be no slack in any of them which throws more strain on the others to cause breaks. The weaving done, a sailor's "Matthew Walker" knot is fashioned on the *hondo* or loop end, while at the loose end each of the four strands is worked back and forth through the others in turn. This leaves a smooth end, free of a knot that might foul the rope as it slips over the saddle horn or through the hands.

Quite often the cowboy wove into this end a "cracker" of heavy buckskin. When driving cattle or horses it was quite the thing to drag thirty or forty feet of one's reata along behind the pony and with a quick forward jerk snap it with a loud crack at the heels of some animal in front, just as a bullwhacker handled his long whip. Some men could use a reata in this way with amazing dexterity, fairly lifting out of his hide some sleepy horse or lazy steer droning along in the "drags." The end of the long snakelike rope touched him on the flank like a red-hot iron.

After the rope was plaited it had to be broken in. The puncher passed the end of the reata twice over the limb of a tree and made two great loops. To the lower end of these loops he attached a heavy stone weighing perhaps a hundred pounds. After the four parts of the loop were thoroughly rubbed over with tallow a smooth pole four or five inches in diameter and eight or nine feet long was slipped about halfway through the loops. With a man at each end of this pole the stone was given a whirl which set it turning around so that the strands were twisted above and below the pole. The men then alternately pushed the pole up as far as it would go and then pulled it down, the movement of the pole twisting and untwisting the strands as it rose and fell. Every possible bit of slack was taken out by this process and the rope made perfectly round and extremely flexible. The grease was also worked into it very thoroughly, to make it waterproof. This breaking in or rubbing-down process was a tiresome one, for a careful man would spend at least two hours on each loop, often twice that if the hide was a little heavy and the rope stiff and wiry.

An easier method of breaking in was to tie a grass rope to each end of the new reata, which was wrapped three or four times about a strong post. A man on horseback then took a turn of the grass rope about his saddle horn and rode slowly out to the extreme length of the reata, while another man on the ground let its loose end slip through his hands, easing it off so as to keep it fairly taut. When the horseman came to the end he dropped the grass rope, went back and picked up the other end and repeated the process. The advantage of this system was that the horse did the hard work, a most commendable one from the point of view of the average cowboy of those days.

This done, one had a rope that was pliable and yielding under the grip and yet so firm in its handling that the loop stayed open when thrown through the air, without collapsing in a mess of figure eights just as it went over the animal's head.

The last part of the job was to make the *hondo* (Spanish "loop" or "sling") with which the knot end was decorated. This was a large rawhide affair plaited flat with eight or twelve strands. The hondo was about four inches long and one and a half inches wide, with a round hole in the end just large enough to take the reata. The loose end of the rope was then run through the large opening in the hondo. If the maker had time he rubbed more tallow or neat's-foot oil into it every day.

As an article for roping animals such a reata was without equal. Its loop stood wide open and seldom snarled. It was so slender and smooth that the wind had little effect upon it, for it cut through the air like a knife, enabling one to throw it with almost unerring aim.

The rawhide rope has its drawbacks. A rider has to keep it dry under all conditions. Moreover, it lacks the strength of ordinary manila grass or sisal rope of equal size, especially when subjected to sudden jerks. One can tie a grass rope hard and fast to the "nub" (saddle horn) and let a thousand-pound steer "go to the end" on it, with no likelihood of a break. But a reata will scarcely stand such a jerk with even a fat yearling on its end. To avoid the strain the man using a reata never tied his rope to the saddle horn, but with about half its length in his left hand took a dozen turns or "dallies" (cowpuncher Spanish for *da la vuelta*—to take the turn) around his saddle horn and then let it slowly slip as the strain came, thus easing the effect of the jerk. Many a saddle horn has smoked from the friction as the roper let his reata slip in this way with a big steer dancing all sorts of didoes on the "yonderly" end of it. From its small diameter and stiffness the rawhide reata is a difficult thing to handle on foot. It slides through one's hands as a piece of wire would, and without the aid of the horn one can hardly hold a two-months-old calf with it.

Reata is a Spanish word really meaning "a rope for leading a string of pack mules." This has been corrupted to "lariat" from the Spanish *la* (the) *reata* (rope). *Lazo* (lasso), a slipknot or loop, is really the proper word for the article here described.

In the old days on the range almost every rider carried on his saddle a hair rope or *mecate* (generally called "mecarty" by the boys). They were used as reins in handling young horses with a hackamore—a bridlelike affair without a bit, the pressure and control over the horse being entirely due to the close-fitting nosepiece (*bousal*), so placed, low on the animal's nose, as to almost shut off his wind if necessary. They also made handy tie ropes for use at a "snorting post." Hair ropes were larger than reatas, generally about an inch in diameter, and, being somewhat loosely twisted, were soft and pliable, easy to grasp, and not so likely to slip through one's hands.

On the round-ups, during off afternoons, or in winter camps, someone would dig up a gunnysack full of horsehair. Another would produce a set of hair spinners from his bed roll, and soon the outfit was hard at work making hair ropes.

By selecting hair of various colors—white, black, and red—one could get very handsome effects. When ready to spin a black and white rope, two separate piles of hair, one white and the other black, were prepared. The little wooden spinners were called "doll babies" and were whittled out of pieces of hardwood.

A man slipped a loop of hair over the head of the spinner, drawing it from a roll held loosely under his arm. A second man began to whirl the spinner to the right, which, of course, twisted the hairs into a tight string. Keeping it fairly taut, he walked slowly backward, while the other man fed out the hair with both hands.

About fifty feet away a wooden peg was driven into the ground. When the man with the spinner reached this he stooped down and deftly slipped the loop of hair from around the neck of the "doll baby" over the top of the peg. The other man then detached the strand or cord of hair from the bundle under his arm and, drawing it as tight as seemed proper, tied it securely around another peg at his feet.

If it was to be a "pepper-and-salt" rope, he alternated white and black strands. If it was to be a regular four-strand black and white, he made one strand of white and one of black. If an eight-strand rope was wanted, he made four strands of alternating colors. When the long strands were finished, one man went to the middle of the strands and tied round them a bit of whang leather. From this point the strands were doubled back on themselves.

The next and most critical step in the process was to allow the natural twist in the strands to wind them tightly about each other. Many a *mecate* was spoiled at this point. The man holding the leather string eased up slightly, turning his wrists with the twist of the rope and passing the string from one hand to the other, so that the four or eight strands began to wind themselves closely around each other. He continued to ease up as the twist came. The twisting process in a fifty-foot strand took up four or five feet, so that the finished rope from fifty-foot single strands was about twenty feet in length. The bit of whang leather was plaited up nicely, and with a "Matthew Walker" knot in the other end the rope was finished.

These hair ropes were useless for roping, since they were too light to throw well and offered too much surface to the wind. Nor were they particularly strong, though there was a lot of spring to a good one which saved it from breaking when a sudden strain was put on it.

Quirt making was also an art among the old-timers. While spurs were absolutely necessary, the quirt was a much better implement with which to get quick action from a slow-moving or tired horse.

The tools for quirt-making were a keen knife, a long slender steel marlin spike, not larger at the big end than a lead pencil, and a little wooden gage such as was used to cut strings for reatas, but much smaller.

The foundation was generally a piece of rawhide sewed when wet around an iron rod and carried down about ten inches in a tight roll as a core for the quirt below the rod. The whole thing had considerable taper to it. Then the maker decided as to the character of his work. Generally the first plaiting was done with rawhide strands, either four or eight.

A very intricate overlay of leather strings was worked around and through this rawhide plaiting. The maker began at the upper end and plaited from six to twenty-four strands of very carefully cut leather strings, sometimes completely covering the rawhide and again working the strands through it so as to get a very effective black-and-white combination. With a large "turk's head" at either end of the handle and one or two below it, two leather tails about a foot long, and a stout piece of whang leather through the hole for a loop, the quirt was complete. In the hands of a skillful operator these quirts were made into works of art and represented an immense amount of patient, careful labor. One of the commonest amusements about a round-up outfit was stealing quirts. When off his horse the rider always hung his quirt over the saddle horn by the leather loop or snapped it into a spring snap fastened on the pommel of the saddle. Thus it was easily lifted by some stray man leaving the outfit.

F OUR-LEGGED enemies take heavy toll from the flocks and
herds of range outfits. The sheepman is the hardest hit, for his
are the most defenseless of all exposed live stock. It is not possible
to determine the losses, but judging by the estimated number of
predatory animals the cost to American stockmen is probably
between fifteen and twenty million dollars a year.

All the Western range states used to pay bounties on predatory
animals. Up to about 1916 these totaled annually more than
$500,000. In spite of this the ravages seemed to be as heavy as
ever.

In 1913 the state of Idaho paid more than $70,000 in bounties
on 30,088 coyotes, 2,564 wildcats, and 135 wolves. The number
destroyed in adjoining states was quite as large. And this went
on year after year. There seemed to be a regular and dependable
annual crop of these animals and apparently an undiminished
one.

Fifteen years ago government officials announced their opposition to the payment of bounties on the ground that hunters
and trappers were "nursing" the animals as an industry and
really protecting instead of exterminating them. They claimed
also that there was a certain economic balance to be maintained
in all such matters, which the unlicensed trappers wholly ignored. In place of the bounty system, hunters employed by the

federal government and stockmen were substituted. These men are paid a regular salary. They keep their jobs if they get results. This means that no animals are spared. Females as well as males are killed, and the pups are brought in instead of being allowed to escape for future bounties.

In 1929 the paid hunters of the Biological Survey of the Department of Agriculture took and scalped 1,410 wolves, 40,254 coyotes, 252 mountain lions, 5,463 wildcats and lynxes, and 280 stock-killing bears. The state and privately employed hunters probably got as many more. In addition the Department estimated that poisoning operations did away with over 54,000 additional coyotes, the bodies of which were not found.

Old Jim Barker, riding one day over his range in New Mexico, found a yearling steer dead. The carcass was still warm. Jim easily recognized the work of wolves. The steer had been hamstrung; that is, a piece had been torn out of one hind leg just above the hock joint in such a way as to sever the large tendon. This is the wolf's favorite method of attack. And there is no doubt that many such killings are made in sheer wantonness or vicious play, and not solely to obtain food.

Naturally Barker was interested in the dead yearling, for while he owned 3,000 head of first-class range cattle, he still hated mightily to furnish even one of them for wolf meat, with yearling steers worth $35 a head. He had suffered no losses on account of wolves for two or three years, and the trail of the dead steer and its pursuers was carefully studied. Following the spoor, Barker easily read the signs, and half a mile from the first yearling he ran across another, killed in the same way but hamstrung in both hind legs instead of one. Two wolves had made this kill.

Here the raiders had stopped to feast. Huge pieces had been torn from the steer's flanks and hindquarters. Again the stockman noted the signs about the spot, which were to him an open book. The great footprints of the wolves indicated both to be adults. Since one had here turned back the man guessed them to be male and female. The latter had returned to her den where her pups were doubtless whining for their breakfast, while the male, unhampered by family cares, kept on his way, seeking more amusement.

Foot by foot the rancher followed the female's track until

finally it led into a canyon that opened out to the prairie from the mountain behind. Here, in the smooth sand of the canyon bed, the tracks of the wolf were plain enough to follow on horseback. Feeling sure that they led straight to the den where the pair had made their home, the man rode back to his ranch for help.

Barker returned with another man. They followed the tracks up the canyon until, halfway up the walls of the gulch, they saw a sandstone ledge in which the den might be located. Heeding the direction of the wind, they worked their way up the side of the canyon until they reached a place from which they could scan with a pair of field glasses the face of the ledge. Soon they located two or three caves.

For hours they watched that cliff. As the evening shadows began to creep up the ravine the long, mournful howl of a wolf came floating up to them from below. With nerves tingling they waited for her coming, for they felt sure it was the female. Soon she came trotting unsuspectingly around a bend in the gulch. Through the glasses the men noted that as she neared the opening to one of the caves a couple of dark brown spots began floundering about in front of it. The pups had heard her voice and were ready for their supper. Stopping an instant to smell her offspring the she-wolf slipped out of sight into the cave.

Certain she could not now escape them, the men watched the cave until dark, hoping to get a shot at the male as he returned to his family. That wily outlaw, however, either scenting danger or else having gone too far afield, did not make his appearance.

In Barker's cabin that night the two men sat until late, planning the destruction of the wolf family. There was a state bounty of $20 for each adult wolf and $10 for every pup, which with the hides would more than repay the loss of the yearlings.

A couple of heavy steel traps were smoked in the fireplace to remove all "man odor," and a pair of buckskin gloves likewise treated. From a shelf above the fireplace they took a small bottle of strychnine and a box of gelatine capsules. In each of a dozen of the capsules they placed as much of the poison as would lie on the point of a pocketknife blade. They cut up some fat bacon into small cubes about an inch square and into a small slit in each tucked one of the capsules. Each cube was stuck on the end of a sharp stick and dipped into a pot of melted tallow, then turned over and over until heavily coated with the grease.

Thus the poison was sealed up in such a way that no trace of the bitter taste might reach the tongue of any wolf tempted to swallow it. The bait was handled with two sticks for tongs so as to eliminate all possibility of taint from human touch.

One of the men took a dozen cigarette papers and placed in the center of each a dose of strychnine. Each paper was folded to make a very small package, to which about six inches of fine silk thread was attached. These tiny packages were handled with the smoked gloves.

Long before daylight the next morning the two men were on their way to the spot where the yearlings had been killed. One led a mother burro at whose side trotted a little one about a month old. Of all animal food the wolf prefers burro meat. Every Western stockman knows this, and often a bunch of burros is kept about a ranch for nothing else than wolf bait.

Arriving near the place where the second yearling had been killed, one of the men leaned from the saddle and knocked the mother burro on the head with an ax brought for that purpose. Barker dropped on the ground a piece of dry rawhide about three feet square upon which he stepped from his saddle. Standing on this hide and wearing smoked gloves, he cut from the dead burro's leg several pieces of flesh and out of one fashioned a dozen cubes about an inch square. To each of these he attached one of the cigarette-paper packets in such a way that the tiny bundle swung from the meat and a wolf could swallow it without getting the taste of the strychnine as the package slipped down his throat. In the stomach the paper would quickly dissolve and the poison probably not be ejected by the animal, as it often is when other methods are used.

These baits and also the tallow cubes were dropped about the dead burro and upon her body, in the hope that they might attract attention and be eaten. After setting two traps Barker mounted his horse from the piece of hide and, leaning down, picked it up. The two then rode away. They had been careful not to spit or smoke or leave any sign about the place, for of all wild animals none is keener to scent human presence than the big gray wolf.

The baby burro followed the men for a short distance, braying at the top of his small voice, then suddenly turned and raced back to the spot where his mother lay. As far as the men could hear, his voice was raised in loud, far-reaching wails. This the men had known would happen, and they expected it to attract the attention of the keen animal whose death they were so carefully plotting.

The sun was just peeping over the mountain tops to the east next morning when the men rode into the canyon where the den was located. Leaving their horses, they worked their way carefully toward the spot. An hour's watching through the glasses was unrewarded by any signs of life, and they finally made their way to the mouth of the cave where they saw that the mother wolf and her babies were gone.

There was a plain, well traveled trail in the sand leading from the cave, showing that she had grown suspicious and moved her offspring. As the pups were too young to travel, she had been forced to carry them in her mouth, one by one, and from the number of tracks back and forth the men estimated she must have a large litter. They soon traced her to the new cave, about half a mile distant. Shielded by brush, they waited. An hour later the she-wolf was seen slipping cautiously along the ledge toward her new home. The wind was in the hunters' favor, and both slipped their rifles into position. As she reached the cliff from which the cave led, the animal stopped for a moment to look about her. Both rifles rang out at the same moment and—yes, they were good shots.

Since the cave was too small to admit the body of a man they were forced to use strategy to get the pups out alive. They carried the body of the mother back to the ledge and laid it down in front of the opening, inside of which they could hear the little fellows whining for their dinner. The ruse worked, and ultimately twelve pups were caught. Two, a male and female, were saved and taken to the ranch. They were raised on a bottle and in time became great pets, although they were always shy and surly with strangers.

The next day the men found the body of the male wolf within fifty yards of the dead burro. He had dodged the cleverly located traps, but the attraction of the bait proved too great for him and one of the pieces of meat with the thread and packet of rice paper had been his undoing.

The orphaned burro survived his experience, and he too was raised on a bottle.

The wolf is the most dangerous enemy of the cattleman. Like wildcats, they seem to destroy for the pleasure of the kill. They are the most difficult of animals to trap or poison. Their ingenuity in evading traps, no matter how skillfully concealed, or detecting the hated "man smell" on poisoned bait is wonderful and almost beyond belief. Wolves will travel over the roughest parts of the country in order to leave no trail or sign.

Fortunately, the wolf, unlike the coyote, does not thrive with civilization. With the settling up of the country the wolves gradually decline in numbers. In such circumstances they are unusually keen from being hunted so hard. They travel in pairs, and many instances are known where a pair of wolves have traveled twenty or twenty-five miles and back in a night, making their kill and returning to their dens before daylight.

Mountain lions confine their raids mostly to horses, and in some sections of the West, such as the Tonto Basin country in Arizona, kill off so many colts every year that the raising of horses is almost out of the question.

The wildcat and the lynx kill sheep almost exclusively, often for the mere lust of bloodletting. As for bears, there is a wide difference of opinion concerning their depredations. Cattlemen do not charge the little brown and black bears with being generally undesirable citizens, and most of them are willing that these bears should be classed as game animals and treated as such.

In southern Utah several years ago the destruction by one grizzly earned him a reputation which will not soon be forgotten. A hundred dollars' bounty was offered for his scalp, but he dodged traps, poison, and bullets for three years or more. In that time various estimates placed the value of the live stock killed by him as high as two thousand dollars; pigs, sheep, goats, cows, and calves all looked good to him, and he seemed to select the choicest of the bunch. The whole country celebrated his capture and death.

Occasionally the brown and black bears kill sheep, and when one of them gets a taste for mutton he becomes a veritable glutton and is never satisfied. As a rule, however, the losses from these bears are due more to their frightening the herds, causing them to stampede and smother.

The settling up of a country generally leads to the rapid extinction of almost all the wild animals unless they are carefully guarded by law. The coyote, on the contrary, rather enjoys the coming of the settler, makes himself very much at home with him, raises his young right under the nose of the stockman, and in spite of bounties and efforts at extermination, manages to increase. In the spring the coyote follows the sheepmen's herds up into the mountains, there to prey on the little lambs, or even the older ewes. In the fall he comes down with them and winters close to the farmer's feed lot and chicken coops, or moves along to the winter ranges of the sheep.

The coyote takes an occasional meal at the cattleman's expense, too, when he finds a small calf lying under the shelter of some bush where it has been left by its mother while she grazes or goes to water. But the sheepman's lambs and the farmer's poultry are the coyote's chief sources of food. He is a good feeder, and when other provender is not to be had will hunt jack rabbits or prairie dogs.

Some years ago California paid a bounty of $5 a head on coyotes, with the result that more than seventy-five thousand scalps were turned in to the state authorities within the first year. In a year or two California farmers began to complain of the increasing numbers and depredations of the jack rabbits. Careful investigation proved beyond doubt that the increase of rabbits was largely due to the decrease of their greatest enemy, the coyote. Thus nature seems to maintain a balance between the species. The law was then repealed by a unanimous vote.

2

It is generally assumed that animals such as cattle, horses, and sheep are endowed with a so-called sixth sense which enables them to determine for themselves with unerring certainty what plants are dangerous to them and what are not.

This is a mistake. If forage is palatable to them they eat it, no matter how deadly. To a hungry cow larkspur is quite as sweet and desirable as clover or alfalfa. Apparently she recognizes no difference. No sheep can distinguish between good grass and the fatal death camas of the Northwest. It is all food to him.

A large percentage of losses from poisonous plants is due to hunger. Cattle or sheep driven for miles through narrow lanes or over driveways on which little or no feed may be found naturally devour with avidity any plants they can reach whenever the opportunity offers. Ordinarily sheep will nibble a little at the leaves of the chokecherry (*Prunus demissa*) without harm, but drive a band through a cherry thicket after a long day's travel over a highway with no feed, and they will gorge themselves on the cherry leaves and die by hundreds in a few hours.

Cattle are very fond of water hemlock (*Cicuta*), which grows along the banks of streams and irrigation ditches. They will go to a great deal of trouble to reach this plant, wading far out into the stream or actually kneeling down on the banks to reach it below them. Unfortunately it is very deadly. Within a few hours the animals are rigid. Stockmen call the plant "wild parsnip." It is said to be the one from which Socrates brewed his fatal draft.

Some plants are dangerous to cattle and not to sheep. Loco (a Spanish word meaning crazy) is an example of this. Although sheep are poisoned by it, they are under the care of a herder and can be kept away from those parts of the range where it grows in large quantities. To become locoed an animal must eat a large amount of the weed and keep it up for some time, the effect of the poison being cumulative.

Of all animals, horses are the most easily affected by the plant. As far as the open range industry goes, horse production is now a very small item. Here and there wild horses are still to be found. They are fast disappearing, however, and will eventually be a thing of the past—another bit of range romance gone into history. But in the days when every rider had at least fifteen horses in his string, and every cattleman ran a small herd of range mares from which to raise his own saddle animals, the losses from loco were serious.

Loco is found generally throughout the entire Rocky Mountain region but is unusually prevalent in the country south of Denver, covering southern Colorado, Arizona, New Mexico, western Oklahoma, and western Texas. Over the open prairies one may often see great bodies of it. In full bloom, with lovely purple flowers, it might well be taken for a field of alfalfa.

Not every year is a loco year. It seems to come along about every seventh or eighth spring. Let the winter be a wet one, with early and heavy rains, and the Southwestern range men will shake their heads and prophesy a bad loco year. On such occasions the lovely green bunches seem to come up on the barren ranges almost overnight. By the middle of April in the Southwest, when all other vegetation is still dead and brown, the loco plants show up green and enticing everywhere. Naturally the range stock eat it hungrily, for if appearance means anything it is a dainty food.

The effect of loco on horses is singular. They seem to lose all sense of proportion. Their eyesight is apparently affected, and they have some brain trouble that makes them stagger around like drunks. A locoed cowpony will shy at a small stick and will not step over a rope lying on the ground. While being ridden on the range he will sometimes jump three feet into the air to avoid a shallow crack in the ground that looks dangerous to him.

That lovely old-fashioned flower of our grandmothers, larkspur (*Delphinium*), with its glorious purple and blue blooms, is probably the worst enemy of the Western range cattleman. There are two kinds, tall or giant, and dwarf larkspur, equally deadly to cattle. Sheep they do not affect. In fact, sheep have been used by the Forest Service in an attempt to kill out the plant by heavy grazing of the larkspur areas. On many ranges cattle cannot be grazed safely until August, after the larkspur has bloomed. On such ranges as high as 10 per cent. of the cattle may die.

The only remedy so far discovered is to grub out the plants by hand. Larkspur is gregarious and grows in great bunches, often several acres in extent. Under such circumstances the forest rangers have grubbed it out clean and reduced the losses to almost nothing.

It is estimated that larkspur losses cost Western cattlemen many million dollars each year. The total annual losses among all range live stock from poisonous plants are placed at more than twenty million dollars.

INDEX

INDEX

Abilene, Kansas:
  first cattle shipment from,
    73.
  first herds to reach, 86.
  number of cattle shipped
    from, 109.
  solicits cattle trade, 74.
  troubles of the marshal,
    101.
  vicious element in control,
    104.
  wide-open town, a, 99–
    109.
Absentee Ranch ownership,
  evils of, 239.
Adobe Walls:
  fight at, 123, 125.
  Kit Carson in fight at, 123.
  only woman at fight, 127.
Alamo, story of the, 14.
Alvord, Burt, Arizona cowboy
  and bad man, 213.
America:
  first cattle in, 53.
  first horses in, 53.
Arapahoe Brown, commands
  Johnson County Wyoming
  forces, 278.
Arbuckles' coffee, the cowboy's
  beverage, 295.
Arizona:
  bad men driven to, 202.
  bookkeeping very poor,
    215.

Arizona—*Continued.*
  establishes a Ranger force,
    212.
  large cattle outfits in, 211.
  Pleasant Valley War, 258.
  Rangers, Captain of, 212.
  southeastern, fine cattle
    country, 201.
Austin, Stephen F., the Father
  of Texas, 11, 12, 13, 22.
Averill, James, hanging of, 271
Aztec Land & Cattle Company
  of Arizona, 211.

Bad season for trail herds, 110.
Banner year for trail herds,
  152.
Bar W Ranch, in New Mexico,
  211.
Barbed wire:
  changes conditions on
    ranges, 268.
  early use of, 9.
Barber, Gov. A. W., of Wyom-
  ing, appeals for help in
  Powder River Invasion, 278.
"Barnyard Cattle," heavy
  losses in, 238.
Barton, Jerry, constable at
  Charleston, Arizona, 206.
Baxter Springs, Kansas, 68,
  69, 70.
Bears, losses from, among
  stock, 321.

Berry-Boice Ranch in North Dakota, 216.

Big versus little cattlemen, 187, 240.

Billy the Kid:
  arrested by Pat Garrett, 169.
  boy of eighteen, a, 163.
  escapes from Lincoln (N. Mex.) jail, 169.
  kills Ollinger at Lincoln, 169.

Blizzards, play havoc with range stock, 247.

Blocker, John, drives cattle north, 238.

Blue Mountain, Oregon, sheep war, 261.

Boice, Henry S.:
  buys many Southern cattle, 216, 217.
  expert judge of steers, 217.

Bois d'Arc:
  meaning of, 63.
  wagon and timber, 63.

Bonney, Wm. H., alias Billy the Kid, 163.

"Books won't freeze," 232.

Boom in cattle prices, 232.

Boot Hill, Tascosa's burial ground, 175.

Boyce, Colonel A. C., of Texas, defies stock thieves, 183.

Bozeman Trail, 70.

Branding, hair, 181.

Brands:
  burning of, 158.
  examples of, 184.
  Mexican, 185, 186.

Brazos, pioneer life on the, 16.

Breakenridge, Colonel Wm. E. Arizona peace officer, 103, 205, 208, 212, 216.

Breakfast on the round-up, 299.

British diplomatic warning to Texas, 13.

Bronco busting, a lost art, 283.

Brush country of Texas, in the, 35.

Buckaroos, 290.

Bucket of Blood saloon, at Holbrook, 216.

"Buckshot" Roberts, death of, 166.

Buckskin, heroic figures in, 1.

Buffalo Bill's buffalo-killing contest with Comstock, 120.

Buffalo:
  bones, shipments of, 119.
  country, the conflict over, 115.
  hunted by Indians, 119.
  hunters, a hard-looking lot, 122.
  hunters, busy, 228.
  meat, shipments of, 121.
  methods of hunting, 120.
  number of, 118.
  or the cow, 113.
  passing of, mentioned by English writer in 1846, 117.

Bulls:
  shoeing on range, 200.
  Texas, prohibited on most ranges, 242.

Burleson, Jim, of Texas, 65.

Burnett, Judge, an Arizona law enforcer, 208.

Burnham, Major Frederick R., mixes in Pleasant Valley War, 257.

Burning brands, 158.

Burro, bait for wolves, 319.

Busting broncs, a lost industry 283.

Buttermilk Ranch, near Dodge City, 135.

Buying water for cattle, 197.

California cattle:
losses from drought in, 225.
valuable only for tallow and hides, 221.

California land:
cheap in early days, 219.
grants, 218.

California:
Texas trail herds to, 201.
vaqueros, 290.

Californians, expert ropers and riders, 220, 290.

Capital Syndicate:
builds Texas statehouse in exchange for land, 179.
operations of, 180.

Carson, Kit, at Adobe Walls, 123.

Cattle:
early shipments from England, 55.
first in America, 53.
follow soldiers into West, 228.
in California in early days, 218.

Cattle—*Continued.*
inspectors hired, 243.
killed by railroads, 215.
low prices for, 153, 227.
market depressed, 153, 227.
not indigenous to American continent, 52.
ranching in slump, 246.
rise in price of, 231.
rustlers appear, 157.
rustling in Wyoming, 270.
syndicates out of business, 287.
thieves, "Sug" Robertson fights them, 182.

Cattle Bubble bursts, 226.

Cattle Kate, hung in Wyoming, 271.

Cattleland:
buzzes with activity, 60.
definition of, 10.

Cattlemen become desperate, 244.

Cattle Raisers' Association of Texas, 243.

Center fire saddles, 290.

Chacon, Augustine:
bad man from Mexico, 212, 213.
capture of, 214.

Chaffin, Nick, early trail driver 91.

Champion, Nate:
attacked in cabin, 272.
description of his death at K C Ranch, 275, 276.
his diary, 276.

Charleston, Arizona, a wild cow town, 203, 205.

Cherry Cow Outfit, *see* Chiricahua Cattle Company.

Cheyenne:
 capital of the Northern range country, 236.
 Cattlemen's Club, 236.
 Leader, Cheyenne, extracts from article in, 279.

Chiricahua Cattle Company of Arizona, 211, 218.

Chisholm, Jesse:
 death of, 95.
 history of, 93.
 trail named for, 96.

Chisholm Trail, the, 128.
 deaths from cholera on, 94.
 length of, 95.
 origin of, 93.
 songs of the, 96.

Chisum, John S.:
 and the Lincoln County War, 162.
 description of his ranch and brand, 161.
 drives herd to New Mexico, 159.
 his outlawed notes, 178.

Choctaws, charge for driving cattle across reservation, 67.

Chokecherry, deadly to sheep, 323.

Cholera:
 82.
 epidemic on the plains, 82, 93.
 deaths from, on the plains,

Chuck wagon:
 crossing deep streams with, 87.
 the first up the trail, 63.

Cimarron River, crossing of, 86.

Circle riders on round-up, 300.

Claibourne, Billy, saves John Slaughter's life, 212.

Clanton, Billy, 210.
 ranch in Arizona, the, 203.

Clarendon, Texas, a respectable home town, 177.

Clay, John:
 defends cattlemen, 245.
 describes early day range grasses, 156.
 quoted, 235.
 tells a good story, 232.

Clothing, of early Texas cattlemen, 17.

Clover, Sam T., correspondent Chicago *Herald* with Powder River Invasion, 274.

Coble, John, shoots hole through famous painting in Cheyenne, 236.

Cochise County, Arizona, a rustlers' paradise, 202.

Cochran, Al, noted cattle rustler, 241.

Coffeyville (Kansas) boots, 288.

Colbert's Ferry, 67

Colorado:
 sheep troubles in, 262.
 Stock Growers' Association, organization of, 242.

Confederate Army, Texans in, 29.

Conflicts, *see* Sheep and Cattle Conflicts.

Cook, the round-up:
an uncrowned king, 293, 297, 298.
decorates kitchen with signs, 297.
"Old Dad," 298.

Coronado's expedition to the plains region, 53.

Cortez, brings first horses to America, 53.

Cow hunts, early, 31.

Cow, mother of the West, 5.

Cow ponies, demand for, 136.

Cowboys:
character of, 77.
costume, 32.
dress in early days, 288.
educated, a myth, 287.
equipment, 98.
health of, 296.
loyalty to employer, 239.
poetry, 80.
who owned cattle not hired, 25.

Coyotes:
bounties on, 322.
take heavy toll from sheep men, 322.

Crash in cattle prices of 1885, 246.

Crazy Woman Creek in Wyoming, 278.

Cross Timbers (Texas), description of, 92.

Crosscurrent, The, 1.

Crossing the Longhorn with locomotives, 215.

Curly Bill, bad man, 204.

Daugherty, J. M., drives a herd north, 68.

Dawn in Texas, 11.

Dawson, Si, of New Mexico, 290.

Dead lines drawn against sheep, 251, 259, 262.

Dead men tell no tales, 260.

Diamond A outfit of New Mexico, 211, 216.

Dixon, Billy, describes Adobe Walls fight, 126.

Doan's Crossing on Red River, 97.

Dobbins, John, killed by Kansas outlaws, 68.

Dobie, J. Frank, quoted, 40–49.

Dodge City, Kansas:
a picture of, 130, 140.
marshals of, 133.

Double-rigged saddles, 291.

Dunn, Sam, expert cattle inspector, 243.

Dunphy, William, pioneer cattleman, 224.

Drovers' Cottage, at Abilene, the, 99.

Earp Brothers of Arizona, Wyatt, Virgil, Morgan, 208, 210.

Eastern farm cattle shipped west to ranges, 228.

Educated cowboy, largely a myth, 287.

Empire Ranch, of Arizona, the 211.

Enemies of range cattle, 316.

Englishmen:
  as ranchers, 235.
  invest heavily in range cattle, 233.

Everybody loses money in cattle, 154.

Farmers:
  crowd onto Western ranges, 150, 227.
  fields in Kansas destroyed by trail cattle, 73.

Fence cutting on the ranges, 195.

Fencing the ranges, 268.

Fencing versus free grass, 194.

Fisher, King:
  his sign on road, 44.
  killing of, 44, 45.

Flagg, Jack, escapes from Wyoming army, 277.

Foreign capital flows into range country, 233.

Forest Rangers, generally local men in early days, 309.

Forest Reserves:
  creation of, 306.
  stockmen object to, 306.

Fort Griffin, Texas, headquarters for hide hunters, 121.

Fort Lupton, Colorado, origin of name, 146.

Fourth of July roping matches forbidden, 284.

Free grass, end of, 267.

Galeyville, Arizona, a wild and woolly town, 203.

Garrett, Pat:
  elected sheriff of Lincoln County (New Mexico), 168.
  kills Billy the Kid, 170.

Gillette, James B., Indian fighter and law officer, 49.

"Going over their withers," 285.

Goodnight, Chas.:
  first man to put cattle in Palo Duro Canyon, 171.
  forms partnership with Adair, 174.
  keeps gamblers out of Clarendon, 178.
  locates Palo Duro Canyon, 66.
  quoted, 116.
  stocks Colorado ranges, 151.
  takes cows to Colorado, 145.
  see also 62–64–66–96.

Goodnight Trail, the, 66.

Gore, Mrs. Lou, runs Drovers' hotel at Abilene, 72.

Gosling, Marshal, killing of on the train, 43.

Government lands, fencing of, prohibited, 269.

Grahams, last of the, 257.

Grasses of the Great Plains region, 156.

Great American Desert, passing of, 5, 9.

Greene, William C., famous Arizona cattleman, 208, 211.

Gregorio Villalobos, brings first cattle to America, 53.

Gunnison National Forest in Colorado, sheep killed in, 263.

Hackamore, 313.
Hair branding, 181.
Hair ropes, making of, 313.
Hardin, John Wesley:
adventures of, 107.
death of, 108.
Hart, John A., rescues girls from Indians, 18, 23.
Hartsel, Samuel, brings registered bulls to Colorado, 148.
Hell Roaring Creek, blizzard near, 91.
Herald, Chicago, messages to, from Powder River Invasion, 276.
Hickok, Wild Bill:
death of, 106.
description of, 105.
Marshal of Abilene, 103.
"Hog-leg" (cowboy for six-shooter), 286.
Holliday, Doc, robs the Tombstone stage, 209, 210.
Hondo, Spanish for loop or sling, description of, 312.
Hoosgow, *see* Jusgado.
Horace Greeley's epigram, 4.
Horn, Tom:
description of, 281.
hanging of, 281.
"Horned jackrabbits," longhorns so called, 32.
Horrell-Higgins Feud in Texas, 50.
Horsehead Crossing (New Mexico), 64.

Horses:
first in America, 53.
not indigenous to American continent, 53.
Pike's account of wild horses, 56.
wild on plains, 56, 57.
Hospitality of Texans, 17.
Hostility of settlers to trail herds, 230.
Houston, Sam, his life and character, 12.
Hunt, Zwing, killed in fight in Arizona, 208.
Hunter and Evans seize Chisum's cattle in New Mexico, 178.
Hunter, H. D., ships many steers to Omaha, 73.

Iliff, John W., Colorado cattle king, 66, 148.
Indian Department of U. S. Government, its failures, 15.
Indian problem, the, 113.
Indian Territory, cattle ordered out of, 196.
Indian tribes, meeting of, at Medicine Lodge, 115.
Inland sheep shooters of Oregon, 259.

Jack Harris's Variety Theatre in San Antonio, 43.
James, W. S., quoted, 38.
Jay Cooke's failure paralyzes the cattle business, 154.
Jingle Bob brand, the, 95.
"John Chinaman" for supper, 294, 295.

Johnson County (Wyoming) War, 269.

Joseph's advice to his brethren who own sheep, 249.

"Jusgado," the prisoners' dock in a Mexican court, 289.

K. C. Ranch in Wyoming, attack on, 275.

Kansas-Pacific Railroad, builders of, 31.

Kendrick, Senator John B., drives trail herd to Wyoming, 227.

Keyes, Ben, cattle buyer, 68.

Kiamichi Valley, in Indian territory, 67.

King, Captain Richard, history of his Texas ranch, 20.

Kipling, verses quoted, 15.

Kitchen, Pete:
    Arizona pioneer, 201.
    has a happy thought, 207.

Kreutzer, Wm. E., Forest Supervisor, protects sheepmen from raiders, 263.

Land grants in California, 218.

Large outfits in the North become bankrupt, 235.

Lasso (lazo), a slip knot or loop, the proper word for reata, 313.

Las Vegas, New Mexico, a trading point, 116.

"Levi's" (after old Levi Straus of San Francisco), cowboy slang for overalls, 283.

Lightning, cattle killed by, 83.

Lincoln County (New Mexico) War, 162.

Littlefield, Monroe, wounded by Comanches, 24.

Livery stables go out of business, 283.

Llano Estacado (Staked Plains), 89.

Loco:
    effect of, on horses, 324.
    eradication of, 324.
    losses from, 323.

Longhorn cattle:
    description of, 8, 33.
    march boldly on, the, 75.

Longhorns:
    pour into Arizona, 211.
    where they came from, 52.

Losses on winter ranges, 85, 238.

Love, Harry, captures Murieta, 224.

Loving, "Long Joe," wounded by Indians, 64.

Loving, Oliver, Sr., drives first trail herd north, 62.

Lytle, Captain John T., sends huge numbers of cattle north, 238.

McCoy, J. G.:
    locates at Abilene, 71.
    quotation from, 21, 36, 84, 111, 154.

Mackenzie, Murdo, noted range cattleman, 235.

McKinney, Fort, Powder River prisoners taken to, 279.

McNelly, Captain, captures stolen stock, 50.

Making a watering place on the range, 200.

Man on horseback, the, 1.

Marlowe brothers, adventures and death of, 188.

Mary's little lamb comes to the ranges, 249.

Masterson, Bat, at Adobe Walls, 44, 124.

Matador Cattle Company of Texas, 233.

Maverick law, 62.
 origin of name, 37.

Mavericks, bonus for branding, 239.

Maxwell, Billy, is killed by outlaws, 214.

Mecate, a hair rope, 313.

Medicine Lodge Meeting, Indian tribes present at, 115.

Men hired as killers, 272.

Mesquite beans for cattle, 27.

Mexican iron (rawhide), 310.

"Mexicans not counted," 207.

Mexico, livestock in, 53.

Miller and Lux, California cattlemen, 224.

Mobeetie, Texas, headquarters for twenty-six counties, 173.

Modern Moses, a, 199.

Mohle, G. H., quoted, 88.

Mossman, Burton C., Captain of Arizona Rangers, 212.

Mountain lions, losses from, among stock, 321.

Moving day for Texas, 59.

Murieta, Joaquin, California outlaw, 222.

Mustanging, 57.

Mustangs:
 first importation of, 52.
 habits of, 57.

Myers, A. C., builds station at Adobe Walls, 124.

National Livestock Trail, establishment of, asked, 229.

Navajo Indian ponies, 82.

Nesters, killing cattle, 240.

New Year's Day in Oregon, 260.

Northwest Ranges, stocking of, 226.

Nuney, Mary A., an early Texas schoolteacher, 19.

Old Dad, the cook, 298.

"Old Julia's Deadfall," 98.

Olds, Mrs. William, only woman at Adobe Walls, 127.

Old-time cowboy was picturesque, 287.

One-armed cowboy, 289.

One-legged cowboy, 289.

Oregon:
 Blue Mountain region of, 258.
 Inland sheep shooters, the, 259.
 New Years' Day in, 260.
 sheep killing in, 261.

Outside the law, 267.

Overstocking, evils of, 237.

Palo Duro Canyon, Goodnight locates in, 171.

Panhandle of Texas, description of, 174.

Parker, Quanah, Comanche chief at Adobe Walls, 126.

Pata Pala (Peg Leg), one-legged cowboy, 289.

Paul Potter's bull, painting in Cheyenne Club, 236.

Pemmican, manufacture of, 119.

Pickles in the keg, 295.

Pike, Captain, describes wild horses on plains, 56.

Pinchot, Gifford, heads Forest Service, 307.

Pioneer days in the Southwest, 22.

Plains country, a hunter's paradise, 117.

Plants poisonous to stock, 323.

Pleasant Valley War in Arizona, 256.

Poe, John W., of New Mexico, appointed inspector for Cattle Association, 168.

Pony Cattle Company, cattle stolen from, 241.

Powder River (Wyoming) Invasion, 269.

a failure, 280.

Prairie Land & Cattle Company of Colorado and Texas, 233.

Predatory animals, bounties on, 317.

Pryor, Ike T.:

sends herds north, 229, 238.

buys cheap cattle, 246.

Quanah Parker at Adobe Walls fight, 126.

Quirts, making of, 315.

Raiding sheep camps, 264, 266.

Railroad building, stops cattle drives, 229.

Range bookkeeping, deceiving, 234.

Range counts:

detectives hired, 243.

losses in winter of 1884–1885, 238.

men want no neighbors, 156.

taken by purchasers, 232.

watering places, buying water for cattle, 197.

Rangers, Texas, Lieutenant Reynolds, of, 51.

Ranges fenced and plowed everywhere, 229.

Raton Pass, New Mexico, 63.

Ray, Nick, killing of at K C ranch, 275.

Reata:

breaking in, 312.

cutting strands for, 310.

must be used with care, 313.

plaiting, 311.

rawhide, making of, 310.

See also Lasso.

Red River Cattle Company of New Mexico, 211.

Rhodes, Eugene Manlove, quotations from, 83.

Rhodes, John, trial of at Tempe, Arizona, 258.

Richardson, A. D., describes farming in Colorado, 148.

Riders who owned cattle refused employment, 240.

Riding the chuck line, 159.
"Rim-fire" saddles, 29.
Ringo, John, of Arizona:
    an educated man, 203.
    defies Tombstone outlaws,
      210.
Rivers, swimming cattle across
    87.
Robertson, "Sug," fights cat-
    tle thieves, 182.
Rock Bluff Ford, on Red
    River, 67.
Rollins, Philip Ashton, quoted,
    98.
Roosevelt's estimate of the
    cowboy, 85.
Rope:
    hair, 292.
    rawhide, 290.
    sisal or grass, 291.
Roping:
    cattle, 285, 291.
    exhibitions forbidden by
      law, 284, 285.
    lost art, a, 284, 285.
Rough Rider regiment, Ari-
    zonians in, 212.
Round-up:
    branding calves, 301.
    breakfast on, 299.
    cooks, their ways, 298.
    cutting strays, 302.
    driving cattle to, 301.
    hobbling out, 302.
    riders "on Circle," 300.
Rustling, increases on ranges,
    240.
Ruxton, Geo. F., mentions the
    passing of the buffalo in
    1846, 117.

Saddle, the Cowboy's, 98.
Sam Bass:
    his doings, 137.
    his epitaph, 139.
San Antonio, in early days, 42.
Sandy Bob stage held up, 209.
Santa Fe, city of, 5.
Santa Gertrudis Ranch, of
    Texas, 20.
Saunders, Geo. W., quoted,
    229, 238.
"Sea lions," slang for long-
    horns, 201.
Settlement, westbound flux of,
    6.
"Shanghai" Pierce of Texas,
    30–61.
Sheep and cattle conflicts all
    over range region, 251.
Sheep and cattle graze ranges
    without injury to them un-
    der Forest Service, 251.
Sheep and cattle owners, con-
    flicts between, 250, 251, 264,
    266.
Sheep camps raided, 264, 266.
Sheep conflicts:
    in Arizona, 251, 252, 254.
    in Colorado, 26?
    in Oregon, 261.
    in Wyoming, 264.
Sheep, destructive to range,
    reasons why, 250.
Shepherd, an abomination to
    Egyptians, 249.
Sheridan, General, his ideas
    about the buffalo, 25.
Single-rigged saddles, 291.
Siringo, Chas., activities of,
    181.

hooter, day of, 46.
...eton Canyon, Arizona, massacre in, 204.
...eleton Creek, Kansas, origin of name, 94.
Skinning war in Texas, the, 30.
Slaughter, John, sheriff of Cochise County, Arizona, 205, 212.
Small versus large owners, hostility between, 240.
Smallpox, among plains Indians, 94.
Smith, Tom:
  killing of, at Abilene, 103.
  Marshal of Abilene, 101.
Southern cattle, not welcome in North, 71.
Spanish, or Texas, fever breaks out, 74, 236.
Spanish settlements, development of, 54.
Staked Plains, water scarce on, 89.
Stampedes, 89, 91.
Steers, prices of, rise, 110.
Steinel, quotation from *History of Agriculture in Colorado*, 86.
Stewart, Mac, saved from drowning, 88.
Stiles, Billy, noted train robber and cowboy, 213.
Stilwell, Frank, killed by the Earps in Arizona, 211.
Stock growers' associations, danger from, 239.
Stock stealing, 31, 270.
Stock thieves hung, 244.

Stocking the Northern plains, 152.
Stolen horses and cattle, trade in, 116.
Sulphur Spring Valley of Arizona, 203.
Sutherland, David M., solicits trail herds for Abilene, 74.
Swan Land & Cattle Company of Cheyenne, their vast holdings, 233.
Swimming a trail herd, 87.

Tascosa, Texas:
  favorite trading point for stolen stock, 116.
  life in, 174.
Tewksbury Brothers, in Pleasant Valley War, 256.
Texans, first, 13.
Texas:
  cattle drives, men in, 7, 8.
  cattle,
    improvement in breeding of, 193.
    not welcome in Colorado, 150.
  fever among cattle, 74, 236.
  hospitality, 17.
  rangers, work of, 46, 47.
  roping methods, 291.
  shows Cattleland some new wrinkles, 293.
  steer, a product of environment, 193.
  war veterans, 2.
Thompson, Ben, a brave man, 44.

Tide of cattle sweeps the high plains, 149.

Tisdale, J. A., killed by ambushed men in Wyoming, 272.

Tombstone, Arizona, rush of settlers to, 201.

Tomson, Robert, describes live stock in Mexico, 53.

Tongue River, Texas, origin of name, 117.

Tonto Basin War in Arizona, 255, 256.

Tonto National Forest in Arizona, 258.

Trail herds:
bad season for, 110.
banner year for, 152.
mixed in a storm, 91.

Trail, public stock, asked for, 229.

Trap corrals, 23, 33.

Valenzuela, Joaquin, of California, 222.

Vallejo, Don Mariano, of California, 220.

Van Dyke, John C., writes of the cowboy, 84.

Van Horn, Colonel J. J., commands U. S. troops in Wyoming, 279.

"Vaquero of the Brush Country," quoted from, 40.

Waggoner, Tom, hanged in Wyoming, 271.

Wallace, General Lew:
and Billy the Kid, 168.

Wallace, General—*Continued.*
tries to stop Lincoln County (New Mexico) war, 168.

Water: and the range, 149.
for herds, often scarce, 89.
hemlock, 323.

Weedy ranges for sheep, 263.

White and Red man, no compromise between, 113.

Wichita, Kansas:
Chisholm Trail starts from, 93.
Jesse Chisholm lived near, 93.
Santa Fe Railroad reaches, 111.

Wild cattle capturing in trap corrals, 33.

Wild Horses, Pike's description of, 56.

Wild parsnip, deadly to cattle, 323.

Williams, Mrs., adventures in Texas, 18.

Winter losses all over range country, 85, 238, 246.

Wolves:
cattle killed by, 317.
do not thrive with civilization, 321.
poisoning of, 319.

Wootten, Dick, pioneer of New Mexico, 63.

"Wreck pan," the, 296.

Wyoming:
cattlemen's army, the, 272
cattle rustling in, 270.

Wyoming—*Continued.*
early Texas herds to, 227.
Green River sheep war,
the, 264.
Johnson County War, 269
mysterious expedition,
272.
Powder River Invasion,
269.

Wyoming—*Continued.*
sheep camp raided, **266.**
Stock Grazers' Associa-
tion, organization of,
242.

X I T Co. of Texas,
See also Capital Syndicate,
233

Wyoming—Continued.
cattle Texas herds to, 237.
Great River sheep war,
the, 281.
Johnson County War, 286.
expenditure expedition,
274.
Powder River invasion,
206.

Wyoming—Continued.
sheep camp raided, 286.
Stock Grower's Associa-
tion, organization of,
235.

X I T Co. of Texas.
See also Capital Syndicate,
236.